A ZBC OF EZRA POUND

A
ZBC
of Ezra Pound

CHRISTINE BROOKE-ROSE

Faber and Faber
London

First edition 1971

Published by
Faber and Faber Limited
3 Queen Square London WC1

ISBN 0 571 091350

Printed in Great Britain
by R. MacLehose and Company Limited
The University Press Glasgow W3

For the child in her basilica

CONTENTS

———————————⟫✦⟪———————————

CONTENTS

ACKNOWLEDGEMENTS

I want to express my particular gratitude to Eva Hesse and Michael O'Donnell for reading the typescript so carefully, making innumerable helpful suggestions and answering many questions of fact; to Peter du Sautoy for checking all Greek quotations and correcting errors of same when they occur in *The Cantos*; to Hugh Gordon Porteus for checking all Chinese idiograms, for help on specific points, and for the careful calligraphy used in this book.

I am also grateful to Ezra and Dorothy Pound, and to Faber & Faber and New Directions, the publishers concerned, for permission to quote extensively from the works of Ezra Pound.

Again I reiterate that if my respected pubrs. expect of me, in accord with contract, a chronological exposition, they will have to wait for tables and an appendix, I have no intention of writing one HERE.

Ezra Pound—Guide to Kulchur.

CHAPTER ONE

'Why Books? This simple first question was never asked' [1]

———————◦◦◦◦◦◦◦◦◦———————

And, moreover, why ANOTHER book on Pound? Why contribute further to what he himself has called, somewhat bitterly, the Pound Industry? Well, my respected publishers—who happen also to be Pound's English publishers—wanted a book for students. So it is the students and newcomers that I shall be addressing, rather than expert Poundians who sometimes seem to write solely for other Poundians, echo-chambers of allusions, cross-references and ideogrammic short cuts, even though I am just such an echo-chamber myself, pounded, impounded and compounded. On the other hand, I do not know my Pound in an orderly manner, as will presently appear. Nor, I suppose, does Pound. And I must therefore also make it clear that for this very reason, I have no intention of writing the kind of quick guide, in chronological order, to the Life and Works, which some students often expect—hence the slightly defiant quotation by way of epigraph—although I shall append a chronological list and an index to themes discussed, so that the reader can easily find his way. Pound cannot be approached in this manner and fully appreciated, and perhaps the various adverse judgments of his poetry are due to such traditional approaches. Mine is bound in the end to be very personal, though I shall use and discuss the work of other critics. For I find *The Cantos* funny, soothing, exhilarating, infuriating, tender beyond endurance, dogmatic beyond belief,

[1] *How to Read* (New York Herald 1928, reprinted in *The Literary Essays of Ezra Pound* (London 1954, Faber Paper Covered Editions 1960).

1

bawled out, murmured, whispered, sung, true, erroneous, beautiful, ugly, craftsmanly, confident, contradictory, collapsing —in short, totally human, alive, and relevant.

> But the salt works . . .
> Patience, ich bin am Zuge . . .
>
> C.98

And why not plunge *in medias res*, or rather in the middle of the end, the most difficult, and quote in full, just for a bit of flavour at this point:

> And that Leucothoe rose as an incense bush
> —Orchamus, Babylon—
> resisting Apollo.
> Patience, I will come to the Commissioner of the Salt Works
> in due course.
> Est deus in nobis.   and
> They still offer sacrifice to that sea-gull
> est deus in nobis
> Χρήδεμνον
> She being of Cadmus line,
> the snow's lace is spread there like sea foam
> But the lot of 'em, Yeats, Possum and Wyndham
> had no ground beneath 'em.

[pu : none, pictogram for bird in flight]

> Orage had.
> Per ragione vale
> Black shawls for Demeter.
> 'Eleven literates' wrote Senator Cutting,
> 'and, I suppose, Dwight L. Morrow.'
> Black shawls for Demeter.
> The cat talks—μάω—with a greek inflection,
> Mohammed in sympathy : 'is part of religion'
> Sister to Phoebus;
> And some with the tone of bird talk

'Noi altri borghesi
    could not speak efficiently to the crowd
    in piazza,'
said the Consiglieri, 'we thought we could control Mussolini.'

Uncle William two months on ten lines of Ronsard
    But the salt works . . .
    ψεῦδος δ'οὐκ ἐρέει
    . . . γὰρ πεπνυμένος[1]
Patience, ich bin am Zuge . . .
    ἀρχή
    an awareness
Until in Shensi, Ouang, the Commissioner Iu-p'uh

volgar' eloquio      [ideogram for Iu-p'uh]

The King's job, vast as the swan-flight:
thought built on Sagetrieb

                                 C.98 (*Thrones*, 1960)[2]

Yes, yes, it can be explicated. Most things in *The Cantos* can
be are being will be explicated. I shall myself explicate this
here and there as I go along, so that if you read this book with
reasonable attention you will find that you can come back to the
above passage and understand it straight off. For the moment,
let it just roll over you, with perhaps only a gloss or two
(Possum is T. S. Eliot, Wyndham is Wyndham Lewis, Orage
was the editor of *The New Age*, 1908–1922, Uncle William is
Yeats), and with one item of source-hunting to help: namely
that Pound has in front of him (and tells us so four pages later:
'And our debt here is to Baller'), but keeps interrupting himself

[1] He won't tell lies; he is much too clever (of Nestor. Od. Bk. III/20).
Cp. 'Nestor "too intelligent to prevaricate" ' (C.99).
[2] *Thrones* contains Cantos 96–109. The title is an allusion to the
penultimate rank of Dante's Paradiso: 'That it is of thrones, / and above
them Justice' (C.94). *Rock-Drill* (Cantos 85–95, 1957, named after the
Epstein sculpture) can be regarded as drilling through to the light. I
shall in future refer only to Canto numbers.

from, the Victorian F. W. Baller's edition and translation of *The Sacred Edict* of K'ang Hsi, originally published in 1670 in the highest literary style, then redone in enlarged and simplified form by K'ang Hsi's son Iong Cheng (of Canto 61). But a high official called Uang-iu-p'uh, who was Salt Commissioner in Shensi, felt that it was still too difficult for simple people and translated it into more colloquial Chinese (just as Dante wrote *De Vulgari Eloquentia*[1] on the common Tuscan vernacular as opposed to Latin and then, in that tongue, the *Divina Commedia*).

But the students . . .

Right then, hear him on your own ground, circa 1928:

'Literary instruction in our "institutions of learning"[2] was, at the beginning of this century, cumbrous and inefficient. I dare say it still is. Certain more or less mildly exceptional professors were affected by the "beauties" of various authors (usually deceased) but the system, as a whole, lacked sense and co-ordination. I dare say it still does. When studying physics we are not asked to investigate the biographies of all the disciples of Newton who showed interest in science, but who failed to make any discovery. Neither are their unrewarded gropings, hopes, passions, laundry bills, or erotic experiences thrust on the harried student or considered germane to the subject . . .' *How to Read*, 1928 (*Lit. Essays*, 1954).

Or later, on the shortcomings of education and the professor:

'The first symptom he finds will, in all probability, be mental LAZINESS, lack of curiosity, desire to be undisturbed. This is not in the least incompatible with the habit of being very BUSY along habitual lines.' *The Teacher's Mission* (*Engl. Journal*, 1934) (*Lit. Essays*, 1954).

Or earlier:

'We await, *vei jauzen lo jorn*, the time when the student will be encouraged to say which poems bore him to tears, and which he thinks rubbish, and whether there is any beauty in "Maecenas

[1] Pound always refers to it as *De Vulgari Eloquio*.
[2] In the *Literary Essays* Pound adds: 'Footnote a few decades later: The proper definition would be "Institutions for the obstruction of learning" E.P.'

4

sprung from a line of kings". It is bad enough that so much of the finest poetry in the world should be distributed almost wholly through class-rooms, but if the first question to be asked were : "Gentlemen, are these verses worth reading?" instead of "What is the mood of 'manet', if, in short, the professor were put on his mettle to find poems worth reading . . . he might more dig out the vital spots in his authors and meet from his class a less persistent undercurrent of conviction that all Latin authors are a trial.' *Notes on Elizabethan Classicists* (*The Egoist*, Sep.–Dec. 1917, Jan. 1918, *Lit. Essays*, 1954).

'Gentlemen, are these verses worth reading?' This is the question Pound has always asked, and answered, in his own highly personal fashion, by being first and foremost concerned to 'dig out the vital spots'. This pedagogic aspect of Pound, Pound as Teacher or 'one-man university' is inextricably linked with Pound as a poet, not only in the sense that Eliot meant when he wrote :

'. . . And of no other poet can it be more important to say, that his criticism and his poetry, his precept and his practice, compose a single *œuvre*. It is necessary to read Pound's poetry to understand his criticism, and to read his criticism to understand his poetry . . .' (*Introduction to Lit. Essays*, 1954)

not only in the sense that Pound himself learnt so much from the poets he admired, imitated, translated or even later rejected;

but in the much more important sense that *The Cantos* themselves, and all of Pound's poetry, are a digging out of 'the vital spots'.

Now of course he may be totally, or partially, or for the time being, wrong as to what these vital spots are. Hence the fury, bafflement, veneration etc. of the innumerable commentators. Or as Pound himself has commented :

'At last a reviewer in a popular paper . . . has had the decency to admit that I occasionally cause the reader "suddenly to see" or that I snap out a remark . . . "that reveals the whole subject from a new angle".

'That being the point of writing. That being the reason for presenting first one facet and then another. . . . The ideogrammic method consists of presenting one facet and then another until at some point one gets off the dead and desensitized surface of the reader's mind, onto a part that will register.

'The "new" angle being new to the reader who cannot always be the same reader. The newness of the angle being relative and the writer's aim, at least this writer's aim being revelation, a just revelation irrespective of newness or oldness.' *Guide to Kulchur*, 1938 (p. 51).

And a little later he quotes Frobenius in an interview : 'It is not what a man says, but the part of it which his auditor considers important, that measures the quantity of his communication.'

I was determined, in this first chapter, not to get onto the subjects of (*a*) the 'rightness' or 'wrongness' of 'what a poet says' as opposed to 'the way he says it' etc., i.e. that old chestnut, Form and Content; (*b*) the ideogrammic method, and (*c*) communication. Inevitably, I have touched on all three. As regards (*a*) rightness or wrongness, I had also hoped not to plunge the new student into footnotes to *The Cantos* at this stage, but Frobenius happens to be apposite as one of the many cultural 'vital spots', about which Pound feels that there has been a conspiracy of silence. Leo Frobenius was Spengler's German teacher, and also influenced Jung. He was the first anthropologist to treat a plurality of cultures as equally valid and contemporaneous.[1] 'Frazer worked largely from documents. Frob. went to *things*, memories still in the spoken tradition, etc.'[2] Author of the seven volume study, *Erlebte Erdteil*, he provided Pound with one of his favourite words, *paideuma* : 'the tangle or complex of the inrooted ideas of any period. . . . The Paideuma is not the Zeitgeist. . . . At any rate for my own use. . . . I shall use Paideuma for the gristly roots of ideas that are in action'.[3] Frobenius also stands as Pound's ideal of historical method : 'to see through the debris of a

[1] The concept, however, goes back to Johann Gottfried Herder (1744–1803).

[2] Letter to T. S. Eliot, Feb. 1940 (*The Letters of Ezra Pound 1907–1941*, ed. D. D. Paige, New York 1950).

[3] *Guide to Kulchur*, London 1938, p. 58.

civilization its paideumic structure which is somehow never lost and which is ripe for rejuvenation and influence from the best of other cultures, provided the nature of error which ruined it can be known and removed.'[1] Apart from method, Frobenius is important for certain passages in *The Cantos*, notably as 'The white man who made the tempest in Baluba / Der im Baluba das Gewitter gemacht hat' (C.38; 53, 74, 77—Ba-luba being the name of a Congo tribe); but more important, for the city of Wagadu, or spiritual strength among the Faasa (legendary heroes), a city four times destroyed and rebuilt, according to the legend of Gassire's lute :[2]

> 4 times was the city rebuilded, Hooo [hail] Fasa
> Gassir, Hooo Fasa dell' Italia tradita
> now in the mind indestructible, Gassir, Hoooo Fasa,
> With the four giants at the four corners
> and four gates mid-wall Hooo Fasa
> and a terrace the colour of stars

C.74

Wagadu, often linked in *The Cantos* with Ecbatana, the city of Dioce (Deioces, king of the Medes, sixth century B.C.), which according to Herodotus was surrounded by seven circular walls, each a different colour, represents 'the paideumic structure which is somehow never lost', or, if you prefer, the 'vital spots' of any culture :

'But the one thing you shd. not do is to suppose that when something is wrong with the arts, it is wrong with the arts ONLY.

'When a given hormone defects, it will defect throughout the whole system.

'Hence the yarn that Frobenius looked at two African pots and, observing their shapes and proportions, said : if you will go to a certain place and there digge, you will find traces of a civilization with such and such characteristics.

[1] Guy Davenport, *Pound and Frobenius* (in *Motive and Method in The Cantos of Ezra Pound*, ed. Lewis Leary, Col. U.P. 1954, p. 39).
[2] *Erlebte Erdteil*, VI, 42. Guy Davenport, *op. cit.*

B   7   B.-R.E.P.

'As was the case. In the event proved.' *Guide to Kulchur*, 1938 (pp. 60–1).

Well, it's a good story. In fact Frobenius could be and was sometimes wrong and amateurish, but, and here is the point :

'The value of Leo Frobenius to civilization is not for the rightness or wrongness of this opinion or that opinion but for the kind of thinking he does (whereof more later) . . .

'. . . The question whether I believe Frobenius right or wrong in any given point seems to me frivolous. He cd. be wrong in 40 points and still bear gifts above price.' (*op. cit.* p. 57, pp. 243–4).

So Pound, right or wrong? Whereof more (much more) later.

As to (*b*), the ideogrammic method, I imagine that anyone who is remotely interested in Pound will by now have heard about that, since it is one of those critical terms like 'monologue intérieur' in the novel, which are constantly being bandied about and more often than not misused. Its basic principles have been repeated in every book on Pound.[1] Still, it's as well to have got in one of Pound's own descriptions of it (pp. 5–6). For the ideogrammic method has produced his most perceptive and startling insights and some of the best poetry of this century; it has also engendered some disastrous lapses of tone and serious errors of judgment for which he has paid, personally, a tragically heavy price.

So I suppose I can't avoid it even now, but will be brief. At its simplest it is juxtaposition of disparate but particular elements, as in (supposedly) the Chinese ideogram. In fact I shall be so brief as to leave it at that for the moment, so as not to complicate things at this stage, since Pound's interest in Chinese poetry and his work on the Fenollosa papers[2] are both

[1] The most stimulating, though complex, presentation of Pound's method is still that of Hugh Kenner's pioneer work, *The Poetry of Ezra Pound* (London, Faber & Faber, Norfolk, Conn., New Directions, 1951).

[2] Ernest Fenollosa, *The Chinese Character as a Medium for Poetry*, ed. Ezra Pound (London 1936), first appeared in *The Little Review*, Sep.–Dec. 1919. Reprinted in *Instigations*, Washington D.C., 1951.

intimately connected with Imagisme (direct treatment of the 'thing' whether subjective or objective) as well as with the scholastic principle 'Nothing is in the intellect that is not first in the senses.' Whereof more later.

What I want to emphasize now is that Pound, long before the present fashion for the 'two cultures', insisted that this ideogrammic way of seeing, or proceeding, was the way not only of art but of science, which he liked to bring together, but together against 'logic':

'Ernest Fenollosa attacked, quite rightly, a great weakness in Western ratiocination. He pointed out that the material sciences, biology, chemistry, examined collections of fact, phenomena, specimens, and gathered general equations of real knowledge from them, even though the observed data had no syllogistic connection with one another.' *Guide to Kulchur*, 1938 (p. 27).

'You don't necessarily expect the bacilli in one test tube to "lead to" those of another by a mere logical or syllogistic line. The good scientist now and then discovers similarities, he discovers family groups, similar behaviour in presence of like reagents, etc. . . . I see no reason why a similar seriousness should be alien to the critic of letters.' *Date Line* (*Make It New*, 1934) (*Lit. Essays*, 1954).

One can see the attraction, intoxicating for poetry but dangerous, precisely, in the fact-finding disciplines which do more than 'gather general equations of real knowledge' (whatever that means, since an equation is not 'gathered' but worked out by a series of complex quasi-syllogistic means). But Pound distrusts logic. He can praise Stoicism, for instance, as 'a system of ethics with logic and cosmology as periphery':

'They, the Stoics, did have some respect for terminology or "representation" which gathered or seized the object with clarity.

'WITH emphasis on the individual object, "reality existed only in the particular", "universals were to them subjective concepts formed by abstraction."

'The syllogism was counted as "merely a grammatical form".

It didn't pull any weight. Was merely useful for hypothesis and dissociation. Didn't PROVE anything. In that position lies the intellectual greatness of the school of the Porch. That the syllogism was not apodictic but anapodictic. After all the greek blather. Here they got their teeth into something.' *Sophists*, *Guide to Kulchur*, 1938, (pp. 122–3).

Pound rarely argues or 'proves' anything, he wants us to make up our own minds, and simply puts down facts, or what he supposes to be facts, 'a sufficient phalanx of particulars' (C.74— *The Pisan Cantos*, 1947), in as vivid and exact a way as possible, 'one facet and then another'—often totally apart in time or place : as when (to stick to Frobenius and choosing an example which some would count against him), he takes the name Wanjina and immediately changes it into Ouan Jin. Wanjina was an Australian rain-god from a Frobenius legend : the wondjina or mouthless rain icons in Kimberley, Australia, were discovered in 1837 and studied by an expedition of Frobenius' pupils in 1938; Ouan Jin, however, is the French transliteration of the Chinese Wen jen or 'literary gent', or (in a better sense) 'man with an education'. This change of Wanjina into Ouan Jin is itself juxtaposed with the journey which W. H. D. Rouse, a translator of Homer, made along the Odyssean route, when he discovered that in certain Greek islands they were still telling tales of Odysseus, in some versions confused with Elias. I find the fusion of Wanjina (whose mouth was removed for talking too much) with the 'literary gent' and with Odysseus ($OYTI\Sigma$ or no man, the pun on his name which Odysseus gave to the Cyclops), as well as with the 'oral tradition', very funny and revealing, ending as it does with the light of the paraclete, itself identified (by a colon), with 'sincerity' or the Neo-Confucian 'light which comes from looking straight into the heart', sincerity being also the first quality of the wen jen or 'man who knows good' :[1]

> and Rouse found they spoke of Elias
> in telling the tales of Odysseus $OYTI\Sigma$

[1] Guy Davenport, *op. cit.*

WHY BOOKS?
ΟΥΤΙΣ

'I am noman, my name is noman'
but Wanjina is, shall we say, Ouan Jin
or the man with an education
and whose mouth was removed by his father
              because he made too many *things*
whereby cluttered the bushman's baggage
vide the expedition of Frobenius' pupils about 1938
              to Auss'ralia
Ouan Jin spoke and thereby created the named
              thereby making clutter
the bane of men moving
and so his mouth was removed
as you will find it removed in his pictures
              in principio verbum
         paraclete or the verbum perfectum : sinceritas
                        C.74

Actually it does not 'end' with sinceritas (which is why it is always so difficult to quote from *The Cantos*, there is always a new juxtaposition), but jolts us suddenly back to Pound's appalling personal predicament in the concentration camp at Pisa when arrested for treason in 1945 (for, in a way 'talking too much'), the effect of this experience being, twenty years later, silence, or having his mouth removed.[1] But this without a trace of self-pity, no dwelling on it, we are at once lifted out again to objective outside images, or rather, a bringing of a Chinese sacred mountain (T'ai Shan) to Pisa, here and now, and a bringing of a Japanese sacred mountain to Gardone on Lake Garda, in memory (which recurs in C.76)

                      . . . sinceritas
from the death cells in sight of Mt Taishan @ Pisa
as Fujiyama at Gardone
when the cat walked the top bar of the railing
and the water was still on the West side . . .
                        C.74

[1] See my last chapter.

11

Talking of cats, and while we are on the playful, multi-lingual punning aspect of Pound (wen jin), you may have noticed another example in the earlier quotation from C.98 on p. 2 :

The cat talks—μάω—with a Greek inflection

Baller's vocabulary to his edition of *The Sacred Edict* gives 'mao : a cat'. A cat is also 'mao' in Italian. And the line is in fact repeated with mao in brackets in C.102. All right, there is no further significance and no 'pregnant juxtaposition'—to use a term of Donald Davie, on *Guide to Kulchur* as an 'incomparable book', 'a genuine educational experiment', but improvised : . . . 'no one can be deceived for more than a moment by Pound's pre-tense that the abruptness of his transitions is really a matter of pregnant juxtapositions, contrived according to the so-called "ideogrammic method" as recommended by Fenollosa. On the contrary, the appeal of *Guide to Kulchur*, and its uniqueness, are in its being so desperate and so harried, in Pound's vulnerability which, in consequence, he exposes consciously as well as unconsciously.'[1]

Donald Davie's description of *Guide to Kulchur* is very just, but does raise the question, so important for reading *The Cantos* : when is a juxtaposition pregnant and when is it not pregnant? Does the answer lie in the intention of the conceiver or in the mind of the public who sees the result, 'the reader who cannot always be the same reader' ?

Personally I think of T. S. Eliot whenever Pound mentions a cat, no doubt because of Eliot's *Old Possum's Book of Practical Cats* and Pound's many affectionate references to him as the Possum (see quotation on p. 2, or : 'yet say this to the Possum : a bang, not a whimper'—C.74); also because of Pound's ambiguous respect and admiration for Eliot as a cautious pussy-cat, e.g. *Guide to Kulchur*, *Maxims of Prudence* : 'Has Eliot or have I wasted the greater number of hours, he by attending to fools and/or humouring them, and I by alienating imbeciles suddenly ?'

[1] *Ezra Pound: Poet as Sculptor*, London 1965, p. 150.

Consequently, lines like 'the cat talks . . . etc', especially
with the Possum so nearby, make me laugh, as does also:
'Prowling night-puss leave my hard squares alone / They are
in no case cat food' (C.80, a real cat, no doubt, near Pound's
open-air cage in Pisa, but occurring soon after: 'Curious, is it
not, that Mr Eliot / has not given more time to Mr Beddoes /
(T.L.) prince of morticians / where none can speak his
language . . .').

Now Professor Davie is a most sensitive and perceptive
critic of Pound, and anyone further interested should read his
book, among others. But does that mild joke about a cat deserve
such pompous (and cruel) treatment as this:

'In fact, one cannot read *Thrones* without remembering that
the author had spent twelve years in a hospital for the insane.
The best one can do is to remember Christopher Smart's *Rejoice
in the Lamb*, with which *Thrones* has some things pathetically in
common, as when a cat, because it says miaow, is said to "talk . . .
with a Greek inflection" (C.98). *Rejoice in the Lamb*, though
plainly the product of a mind unhinged, is none the less a work
of genius and somehow a great poem.' (*op. cit.* p. 240).

Oh dear, here we touch on Form and Content again. The
thing said is barmy therefore no good however well etc. (some
critics), or, as here, the thing said is barmy yet 'somehow'
great. Let us leave THAT for a later chapter.

And as for (*c*) communication, the less said about it the better.
Or: 'In the gloom, the gold gathers the light against it' (C.11,
C.17). Or leave blanks in your mind for what you don't yet
know: 'And Kung said . . . / And even I can remember / A day
when the historians left blanks in their writings, / I mean for
things they didn't know, / But that time seems to be passing . . .'
(C.13—Kung is Kung Fu-tzu or Confucius). But I do not myself
believe that this present generation, of the McLuhan age, which
takes for granted television and modern films with their quick
cuts and unexpected juxtapositions (pregnant or otherwise),
can possibly find the ideogrammic method difficult as such, apart
from Pound's specific field of reference. Any method which
causes the reader 'suddenly to see' is a swift, live thing:

WHY BOOKS?

' "By Hilaritas," said Gemisto, "by hilaritas : gods,
        and by speed in communication.'
    Anselm cut some of the cackle, and relapsed for the sake of
                                                    tranquillity.
                                                            C.98

Which brings us back to the professors and Pound as a digger
out of vital spots. Or :

As the sea-gull Κάδμου θυγάτηρ said to Odysseus
KADMOU THUGATER
                            'get rid of paraphernalia'
                                                            C.91

14

CHAPTER TWO

'Knowledge is NOT culture. The domain of culture
begins when one HAS "forgotten-what-book" '[1]

O r, to gloss the quotation which ended the last chapter
at once, before the reader loses his curiosity:
KADMOU THUGATER (Κάδμου θυγάτηρ or
daughter of Cadmus) is the sea-nymph Leucothea, white sea-
goddess, who appeared as a bird (sea-gull, says Pound) on
Odysseus' raft when it was being overwhelmed by the waves
(Od. V. 333) and told him to swim for it, giving him her magic
veil to put under his chest ('My bikini is worth your raft'. Said
Leucothea[2]) and enabled him to reach Phaeacia. The fact that
she is daughter of Cadmus—inventor of the alphabet and builder
of Thebes out of dragon's teeth left after a fratricidal struggle—
makes her one of the most apt of the many figures-from-flux
which recur in *The Cantos* (the chief of which is Aphrodite), to
help Odysseus at this point. Leucothea also tells Odysseus to
cast off the clothes which Calypso had given him, or, as Pound
crisply 'translates' : 'Get rid of paraphernalia'.[3]

'All is paraphernalia that does not at length float easily in the
mind', says Hugh Kenner in *Leucothea's Bikini*, having pointed

[1] *Guide to Kulchur*, 1938, p. 134.

[2] C.95. Pound has 'Leucothoe' here, clearly a typographic error,
Leucothoe being a different figure altogether, who 'rose as an incense
bush / resisting Apollo' (C.98, quoted p. 2. See my discussion of whole
Leucothea complex in ch. 8, pp. 138–155 ff).

[3] See Hugh Kenner, *Under the larches of paradise* (review of *Rock-Drill*
or Sections 85–95 of Cantos), *Hudson Review* IX/3, autumn 1956. Leucothea has clearly fascinated Professor Kenner for he comes back to her, and
brilliantly, in *Leucothea's Bikini: Mimetic Homage* (in *Ezra Pound:
Perspectives*, ed. Noel Stock, Chicago 1965).

out that the KADMOU THUGATER lines are immediately
followed by a story from Philostratus' *Life of Apollonius* [of
Tyana], long proscribed by the Christians and one of the
many neglected books to which Pound has drawn our attention,
quoted extensively in C.94. Apollonius travelled to Egypt and
India and talked peaceably with many wise men. He taught that
'the universe was alive', and when he left, his Indian host he said
'You have presented me with the sea, farewell'. His journey
echoes that of Odysseus, as well as the Carthaginian Hanno's
pioneer journey down the West coast of Africa (500 B.C.) in
C.40, and, naturally, Pound's own journey through the 'flux'
of civilizations. The particular story here (from Book VIII/iii)
is that of Apollonius going on trial before Domitian, when he is
told that he must enter the court with nothing on him, that is, no
books or papers (much as Pound was deprived of books in the
open-air cage at Pisa). Pound folds Apollonius' delicious reply
around a line from Odyssey V. 332 (i.e. just before the Leucothea
incident), a line about the winds (Eurus and Zephyr: has the
East wind abandoned him to the stormy West wind to play with):

> . . . 'get rid of paraphernalia'
> TLEMOUSUNE   [adversity; or
> And that even in the time of Domitian   patience in
>   one young man declined to be buggar'd.   adversity]
> 'Is this a bath-house?'
> ἄλλοτε δ'αὖτ' Εὖρος Ζεφύρῳ εἴξασκε διώκειν
>   'Or a Court House?'[1]
> Asked Apollonius
>   who spoke to the lion
>   charitas insuperabilis . . .
>
>   C.91

Apollonius, like Adonis at the end of C.47 (whereof more
later) had 'the power over wild beasts'.
    I realize that I am here plunging you in at the deep end. But I

---

[1] Philostratus VIII/iii, Conybeare's translation (Harvard 1960):
' "Are we to take a bath", said Apollonius, "or to plead?" '

16

really can't do it any other way and isn't that how one is supposed to learn to swim? Rather as when one comes up to Chaucer from behind (or rather, from before), after several centuries of Anglo-Saxon, and then twelfth, thirteenth and early fourteenth century English, as I did, then he seems so delightfully easy and above all modern, not 'quaint' or 'difficult' at all. The analogy is perhaps unfortunate, since Pound's early verse will in fact seem 'quaint' by the time I get to it this way round, but that is the idea, and the analogy is meant to go no further than to show how easy everything can be if you do the difficult first. Because that is the point I am coming to, see chapter-title or, from elsewhere in the same book:

'Culture: what is left after a man has forgotten all he set out to learn?' *Guide to Kulchur*, 1938, (p. 195).

Soon apparently contradicted but in fact not:

'Culture is not due to forgetfulness. Culture starts when you can DO the thing without strain. The violinist, agonizing over the tone, has not arrived. The violinist lost in the melodic line or rather concentrated effortlessly on reproduction of it has arrived.' *op. cit.* p. 209.

Or, put much more clearly already quite early in the book:

'Knowledge is or may be necessary to understanding, but it weighs as nothing against understanding, and there is not the least use or need of retaining it in the form of dead catalogues once you understand the process.

'Yet, once the process is understood it is quite likely that the knowledge will stay by a man, weightless, held without effort.' p. 53.

A string of quotations. This was often Pound's own procedure in criticism, of which he says there are four categories (I paraphrase): criticism by discussion, criticism by translation, criticism by exercise in the style of a given period, criticism via music (i.e. setting somebody's words—which Pound has also done). This last is the most intense form except for a fifth, which is criticism by new composition (e.g. the criticism of Seneca in Eliot's *Agon* is more alive than in his essay on Seneca).[1]

[1] *Date Line* (*Make It New*, 1934, *Lit. Essays*, 1954).

All of which is leading me to three extremely important aspects of this getting-rid-of-paraphernalia business :

(1) the 'excernment'
(2) the polyglottism
(3) the personae

(1) *the excernment*

This is Pound's own term (*Date Line, op. cit.*) for one of the functions of criticism (the other being to forerun composition, to serve as 'gunsight'). Both, as you can see, give the poet's rather than the reader's point of view, though Pound has expressed himself elsewhere on that.[1]

Excernment is : 'The general ordering and weeding out of what has actually been performed. The elimination of repetitions. . . . The ordering of knowledge so that the next man (or generation) can most readily find the live part of it, and waste the least possible time among obsolete tissues' (*Date Line*). He also says modestly that this work is analogous to that performed by a good hanging committee or curator.

Now I am not interested so much in whether or not this *is* a function of criticism or in who should do it, as in the way Pound himself has done it. For his views on what is worth excerning from the past are very individual, to say the least.

'To tranquillize the low-brow reader, let me say at once that I do not wish to muddle him by making him read more books, but to allow him to read fewer with greater result.' *How to Read*, 1928 (*Lit. Essays*, 1954).

In other words, we are back at encouraging the student to say which poems bore him to tears, and to ask 'are these verses worth reading?' *Notes on Elizabethan Classicists, 1917–18* (*Lit. Essays*, 1954).

[1] e.g. 'It is the critic's BUSINESS *adescare* to lure the reader. . . . He is not there to satiate. A desire on his part to point out his own superiority over Homer, Dante, Catullus and Velasquez, is simple proof that he has missed his vocation. Any ass knows that Dante was not a better racing driver than Barney Oldfield, and that he knew less of gramophones than the late Mr Edison.' (*Guide to Kulchur*, 1938, p. 161).

Pound has 'excerned' for us, in the sense of making us see from a new angle, making alive, making new (by translation, by criticism, or both) : the Anglo-Saxon *Seafarer*, the *Grettirsaga* and *Burnt Njál*, Chaucer, Gavin Douglas, Arthur Golding and Marlowe as translators; the best of Provençal poetry, the Tuscan poets, especially Cavalcanti and Dante; Villon; and before that Propertius, Catullus, Horace, Martial, Ovid, Bion, Homer, Hesiod, Sappho (because there is so little left one may as well read it). Above all Homer. And in more modern times Gautier, Laforgue, Corbière; Stendhal, Flaubert, de Gourmont; Landor, James, Wyndham Lewis, Joyce, Yeats, Eliot, Frost, Carlos Williams. This is a short list but basic.[1]

On the other hand he more or less dismisses Virgil, almost the whole of the Renaissance from ornamental Petrarch onwards; and by the same token all seventeenth-century Baroque including most of the Metaphysicals; Milton (his pet abomination); but not the song-writers Campion, Herrick, Waller, Dorset, nor the satirist Rochester; most of the eighteenth century ('a cliché'), except for some Pope, some Crabbe, some Goethe, Heine, Fielding's *Tom Jones*, Sterne's *Tristram Shandy* and *A Sentimental Journey*, Voltaire; he also cuts out the whole of the nineteenth century except for those mentioned in the above paragraph, and those whose influence he underwent at first and then rejected (Browning, Morris, Pater, Rossetti, Swinburne, Dowson, Symons, early Yeats).

He has been blamed for this exclusivity. Eliot reproaches him for not liking Mallarmé and for not, as he himself did, recanting on Milton (*Introd. to Lit. Essays*). A. Alvarez cannot forgive him for his blind spot on the Metaphysicals and especially Donne.[2] The passage Alvarez cannot forgive is in *How to Read* (1928), where Pound places Donne in class (*d*), below *The diluters*, i.e. among the men who do more or less good work in

---

[1] Cp. *How to Read* (1928) and *The Renaissance* (*Poetry*, Chicago 1914). —In *Lit. Essays*, 1954.

[2] *Craft and Morals*, in *Ezra Pound: Perspectives*, ed. Noel Stock, Chicago 1965. Reprinted from *Stewards of Excellence*, by A. Alvarez, New York & London 1958.

the more or less good style of a period: 'choice among them is a matter of taste, for you prefer Wyatt to Donne, Donne to Herrick, Drummond of Hawthornden to Browne, in response to some slight personal flavour. . . .' As with Eliot, it is his own special interest which Alvarez cannot understand Pound not sharing. In the *ABC of Reading*, however, Pound devoted four and a half pages to Donne, called him 'the one English metaphysical poet who towers above all the rest', and included him in the short list of authors 'through whom the metamorphosis of English verse-writing may be traced' (*ABC*, 1934, pp. 137–141, 173); he also called *The Ecstasy* 'the only English poem that can be set against Cavalcanti's *Donna mi prega*' (*ibid.*, p. 60). In *Date Line* (*Make It New*, 1934) he returned to this and said with reference to Donne 'that it is perfectly ascertainable that a number of men in succeeding epochs have managed to be intelligible to each other concerning a gamut of perceptions which other bodies of men wholly deny.' And in *Mr Housman at Little Bethel* (*Criterion*, Jan. 1934, *Lit. Essays*, 1954) he wrote about intellect in poetry: 'As the text stands we are invited to suppose that "the intelligence (they are discussing the eighteenth century) involved 'some repressing and silencing of poetry'. [New para] The intelligence never did anything of the sort. (Ref. Donne's 'Ecstasy', 'Voi ch'avete intelletto d'amore', Voi ch'intendendo il terzo ciel movete", or the pawky comments of Homer!).'[1] It seems that around 1934 something or someone (Eliot?) made Pound change his mind about Donne. That is part of Pound's charm: with all his apparent arrogance his mind was always open, at least in matters of poetry.

We must remember also that Pound's anathemas are not intended, like those of F. R. Leavis (and *pace* Donald Davie who brackets him with Leavis in this respect), to close the student's mind: 'I can not make it too clear that this is not a destructive article. Let anyone drink any sort of liqueur that suits him. Let

[1] On intellect he says later in the same essay: 'Saxpence reward for any authenticated case of intellect having stopped a chap's writing poesy! You might as well claim that railway tracks stop the engine. No one ever claimed that they would make it go.'

20

him enjoy the aroma as a unity, let him forget all that he has heard of technic, but let him not confuse enjoyment with criticism, constructive criticism, or preparation for writing. There is nothing like futurist abolition of past glories in this brief article. It does not preclude the enjoyment of Charles d'Orléans or Mark Alexander Boyd. "Fra bank to bank, fra wood to wood I rin." '[1]

'Preparation for writing'. That is really always the point with Pound. He has 'excerned' what seemed to him important for the craft of poetry as he saw it and worked at it. He was looking for particular qualities (which we shall examine later): visual clarity, precision of language, 'hardness', rhythmic tension, melodic invention (melopœia) or musicality (by which he means the one-ness of words and music, which was 'lost' with the 'fioritura' or adornment of the Renaissance so that poetry split away and became latinate, rhetorical, argumentative; or descriptive, decorative, sentimental etc.). And of course, he sought the 'mythopœic' quality in the ancients, Homer and Ovid especially. The passion of his search was all the more intense because he had himself undergone what he later came to regard as the mush, 'fools or flapdoodles or Tennysons . . . Keats, out of Elizabethans, Swinburne out of a larger set of Elizabethans and a mixed bag (Greeks, *und so weiter*), Rossetti out of Sheets, Kelly & Co. plus early Italians (written and painted); and so forth, including *King Wenceslas*, ballads and carols.' [2]

Or, put in another way:

'One is a fool, of course, if one forego the pleasure of Gautier, and Corbière and the Pléïade, but whether reading them will more discontent you with bad writing than would the reading of Mérimée, I do not know.

'A sound poetic training is nothing more than the science of being discontented. . . .

'. . . Milton and Virgil are concerned with decorations and

---

[1] *The Renaissance* (1914).—In *Lit. Essays*, 1954. The Boyd poem—a very fine one—is in *The Oxford Book of English Verse*, and in Pound's little anthology at the end of *ABC of Reading*.
[2] *Cavalcanti*, in *Make It New*, 1934, *Lit. Essays*, 1954.

trappings, and they muck about with a moral. Dante is concerned with a *senso morale*, which is a totally different matter.
He breeds discontentments. Milton does not breed discontentments, he only sets the neophyte trying to pile up noise and
adjectives, as in these lines :

> Thus th'ichthyosaurus was dubbed combative . . .
> Captive he led with him Geography . . .
> Whom to encompass in th'exiguous bonds . . .

There is no end to this leonine ramping.'[1] *The Renaissance*,
1914 (*Lit. Essays*, 1954).

More than for the science of being discontented, Pound's
exclusions have an artistic purpose (or result), whether they
are rejected after he has 'gone through' the influence, or whether
(and this is perhaps more important, especially with reference to
Shakespeare as well as Milton) he never did go through the
influence. A. Alvarez has observed acutely :

'He is the only poet in the last three hundred years to write
English as though he had never read Shakespeare. For with
Shakespeare the English language crystallized out. The imaginative fullness, the power and flexibility of Shakespeare's verse
have been the abiding fact for every subsequent major poet. His
[the poet's] originality and strength are what is left to him after
he has fought it out with Shakespeare. But Pound has had no
part in that fight. When I suggested this to him, he replied that
his literary ancestor was Dante. He has, in fact, struggled with
translation and with the business of writing verse to foreign

[1] Cp. also *Notes on Elizabethan Classicists* (*The Egoist*, Sep. 1917–
Jan. 1918, *Lit. Essays*, 1954) : 'The sin or error of Milton—let me leave
off vague expressions of a personal active dislike, and make my yearlong
diatribes more coherent. Honour where it is due! Milton undoubtedly
built up the sonority of the blank verse paragraph in our language. But
he did this at the cost of his idiom. He tried to turn English into Latin; to
use an uninflected language as if it were an inflected one, neglecting the
genius of English, distorting its fibrous manner, making schoolboy
translations of Latin phrases : "Him who disobeys me disobeys".' See
however Frank Kermode, *Adam Unparadised* (in *The Living Milton*, ed.
Kermode, London 1960), for examples of Greek syntax put to good use
in English.

plans. Yet it has left him with a language that is curiously his own, curiously undisturbed by the English tradition that preceded it. It is for this that I have called him the first really American poet.'[1]

So that if we are not attuned to all this, it comes as a slight shock, when we read the famous opening of Canto 7, which is a sort of counterpart to *The Waste Land*, to find that the first 18 lines are a peculiarly Poundian homage or 'mimetic homage'— to use Kenner's phrase—from Homer to Flaubert:

> Eleanor (she spoiled in a British climate)
> "Ἑλανδρος and 'Ἑλέπτολις, and
> > poor old Homer blind,
> > blind as a bat,
> Ear, ear for the sea-surge;
> > rattle of old men's voices.
> And then the phantom of Rome,
> > marble narrow for seats
> 'Si pulvis nullus', said Ovid
> 'Erit, nullum tamen excute.'
> To file and candles, e li mestiers ecoutes;[2]
> Scene for the battle only, but still scene,
> Pennons and standards y cavals armatz
> Not mere succession of strokes, sightless narration,
> To Dante's 'ciocco', brand struck in the game.
>
> Un peu moisi, plancher plus bas que le jardin.
>
> 'Contre le lambris, fauteuil de paille,
> 'Un vieux piano, et sous le baromètre . . .'
>
> > > > > > > > > C.7

This has been so well commented I will just gloss it quickly

---

[1] *Craft and Morals*, in *Ezra Pound: Perspectives*, ed. Noel Stock, Chicago 1965.

[2] The Old French must be an error or a misquotation as it makes no sense; *li mestiers* (trade, calling) is in the nominative and doesn't go with the verb (to listen or to spy, 2nd person sing., present indicative or imperative. The verb anyway cannot occur at this stage without preconsonantal *s* (*escoutes*).

for the newcomer: Eleanor of Aquitaine married Henry II of
England; already in C.2 fused with Helen of Troy as *elenaus* and
eleptolis (Aeschylus' punning description, destroyer of ships,
destroyer of cities; Pound here adds *elandros*, destroyer of men);
Homer was blind as a bat but had a radar 'ear' or eye for the
sound of the sea and 'saw' Helen's beauty through the echo of
terror in the voices of the old counsellors who want to send
Helen back (here condensed from C.2 as 'rattle of old men's
voices');[1] Ovid's *Ars Amatorum* about narrow seats in amphi-
theatre helping flirtations; medieval romances, battle scenes
vivid in *El Cid* (pennons and standards line)[2] as opposed to
'sightless narration' in Northern Old French (probably an
allusion to *La Chanson de Roland*); Dante's famous comparison
(Paradiso XVIII) of the souls of Christian warriors rising like
sparks flying when a burning log is struck for soothsaying—a
high visual point in European poetry, and already mentioned less
cryptically in C.5. We then leap to Flaubert (pastiche from *Un
cœur simple*): exact observation of decay and solidity. This then
leads straight on to a memory of Henry James (not quoted here)
and the 'Waste Land' modern atmosphere that followed him.[3]
Dekker sees C.7 chiefly as reminiscences of Eliot's *Prufrock*,
Portrait of a Lady and *La Figlia che Piange*, but mentions in the
next chapter that the Canto seems to be 'a sort of Poundian
"Waste Land"'. Certainly the empty husks of men, of houses,
even the cicada song, and 'the bus behind me gives a date for a
peg' (surely an allusion to Eliot's parody of Marvell's 'And at
my back I always hear / Time's winged chariot . . .'?) would
confirm this view.[4]

[1] For Pound's discussion of this passage in Homer see *Translators of
Greek: Early Translators of Homer* (*Instigations*, 1920, *Lit. Essays*, 1954).
The essay first appeared in *The Egoist*, August, Sep., Oct. 1918, Jan.,
Feb., March, April 1919.

[2] From a passage quoted in Pound's *The Spirit of Romance* (1910), p. 67.

[3] See George Dekker, *Sailing after Knowledge—The Cantos of Ezra
Pound* (London 1963), from which this rapid gloss is condensed.

[4] C.7 first appeared in *The Dial* in August 1921, *The Waste Land* in
1922. The correspondence between Pound and Eliot on *The Waste Land*
began in Dec. 1921 but as Eva Hesse has pointed out to me in a letter on
this, they were reading the same books, notably, at Pound's suggestion,

KNOWLEDGE IS NOT CULTURE

We get this same scornful leap much later, in C.81 (when in Pisa Pound was questioning himself and his craft in a wild despair), after a passage about the music of Lawes and Jenkyns, he quotes directly from Chaucer's *Merciless Beaute* :

> Your eyen two wol sleye me sodenly
> I may the beaute of hem nat susteyne

and adds, contemptuously :

> And for 180 years almost nothing

It seems to me that as poet and craftsman Pound has every right to 'excern' what he likes and reject what he does not like. He has, after all, gone through it all, written in almost every style, done his apprenticeship the hard way, he knows it from the inside. And he is not forbidding us to read even Milton, merely telling us that if we want to be good poets we should not.[1]

(2) *the polyglottism*

From the quotations I have already given, the reader will have realized, if he did not already know it by merely glancing at *The Cantos*, or even at Pound's earlier poems, that many languages are used.

This is certainly a great obstacle for the reader, probably the greatest. It is, on the one hand, an aspect of Pound's internationalism, and, on the other, an aspect of his creative attitude to language. The first relates chiefly to the reader, the second chiefly to the poet, although of course the result of the second also affects the reader.

Remy de Gourmont from whom 'thin husks I had known as men' is taken (cp. *The Prose Tradition in Verse*, Chicago 1914, *Lit. Essays*, 1954, p. 371 : 'most men think only husks and shells of the thoughts that have been already lived over by others.').

[1] Eliot, in his famous recantation over Milton, seems to agree with him on this point, at any rate for his generation of poets. (*Milton*, Annual Henrietta Hertz Trust lecture, Brit. Acad. 1947.) Milton is coming back into critical fashion now for other reasons (cyclical and vertical construction, cp. Isabel MacCaffrey, *Paradise Lost as 'Myth'*, Harvard University Press 1959; J. I. Cope, *The Metaphoric Structure of Paradise Lost*, Johns Hopkins Press, Baltimore 1962; and for his idiosyncratic use of the English language, cp. *The Living Milton*, ed. Frank Kermode, London 1960).

On the first, the internationalism, it may well be that this has genuinely happened, that the world has caught up or is catching up with him. Many more young people than before do in fact learn at least one language other than their own, and those interested in literature are more and more leaning towards comparative literature. Or is this one of my many illusions? Let Pound speak:

'The same crime [cult of mediocrity] is perpetrated in American schools by courses in "American literature". You might as well give courses in "American chemistry", neglecting all foreign discoveries. This is not patriotism.' *The Renaissance*, 1914 (*Lit. Essays*, 1954).

It is true that this seems to be what still happens in countries like Russia where every scientific discovery is treated as Russian, but at least the discovery has to be learnt. It is also true that science does have other languages besides language, whereas literature does not, and poetry in particular, depends on the few, very few 'creative' translations or is otherwise lost. Pound insists:

'In mentioning these translations, I don't in the least admit or imply that any man in our time can think with only one language. He may be able to invent a new carburettor, or even work effectively in a biological laboratory, but he probably won't even try to do the latter without study of at least one foreign tongue. Modern science has always been multilingual. A good scientist simply would not be bothered to limit himself to one language and be held up for news of discoveries. The writer or reader who is content with such ignorance simply admits that his particular mind is of less importance than his kidneys or his automobile. The French who know no English are as fragmentary as the Americans who know no French. One simply leaves half one's thought untouched in their company.' *How to Read*, 1928 (*Lit. Essays*, 1954).

This sounds hard, particularly since Pound uses many more languages than French and English—not to mention Chinese ideograms and a few Egyptian hieroglyphs. 'Arnaut spoke his own language, 26th Purgatorio', Pound says in C.97, referring to Arnaut Daniel, whom Dante meets and who addresses Dante

in Provençal (*Ieu sui Arnaut, que plor e vau cantan.* ... Purg.
XXVI. 140–147). Of course we cannot understand every
language, but Pound in the above essay goes on—and this
seems to me capital :

'Another point miscomprehended by people who are clumsy
at languages is that one does not need to learn a whole language
in order to understand some one or some dozen poems. It is
enough to understand thoroughly the poem, and every one of
the few dozen or few hundred words that compose it.

'This is what we start to do as small children when we
memorize some lyric of Goethe or Heine. Incidentally, this
process leaves us for life with a measuring rod (*a*) for a certain
type of lyric, (*b*) for the German language, so that, however
bored we may be by the *Grundriss von Groeber*, we never wholly
forget the feel of the language.' (*ibid.*)

This is certainly true for personal appreciation, though one
would not, presumably, venture into criticism of nuances without
a knowledge of the whole language. It is particularly true for a
personal appreciation of Pound : a great many of the snatches
from foreign literatures that are scattered through his works
are from poems that he has himself translated and/or written
about, so that if, as Eliot advises, one reads his total *œuvre*, one
cannot help but become familiar with and recognize (the pleasure
of recognition being partly self-flattering) phrases like *dove sta
memoria* or *Per ragione vale* (the latter in the first passage quoted,
p. 2), both from Cavalcanti's *Donna mi prega*. Moreover, the
phrase will have acquired certain very precise connotations and
therefore acts as a short cut. For instance *per ragione vale* occurs
in the passage where love is said to be not a 'virtute' itself, but
to come from the kind of perfection which is so called (*virtu*
being the full realization of a thing's essence, its intellectia, a
concept important in *The Cantos*, both in love and government) ;
love is thus a source of perfection; not from the reason but felt,
it is without regard for salvation, maintaining its strength of
judgment in the intention *being equal to reason* : 'Fuor di salute
giudichar mantene / E l'intenzione per ragione vale'. The word
intenzione is discussed by Pound in the Cavalcanti essay as a

27

mode of perception (Averroes, Albertus Magnus, see *Lit. Essays*, p. 178). In C.36 (a later version of *Donna mi prega*), he translates the line 'Deeming intention to be reason's peer and mate'.

Or again, *dove sta memoria* (also *memora* in some readings) is extremely important in Cavalcanti's notion of love as a 'forma' permanently dwelling in the memory but taking actuality by the 'accidente' (in the philosophic sense) of a particular person. This is in fact the scholastic distinction between 'in potentia' and 'in actu', the two perfections of love that Cavalcanti deals with. The 'forma' is not yet love in the proper sense, it becomes love in the next stage, 'un accidente'. Love is the process from 'in potentia' to 'in actu'. For Pound the 'forma' which has 'loco e dimoranza' in memory always includes a cultural connotation, 'the immortal concetto' (see ch. 10, p. 186). So that the famous lines in C.76 where this phrase is quoted (as it is, less famously, elsewhere) are given a new as well as old dimension :

> nothing matters but the quality
> of the affection—
> in the end—that has carved the trace in the mind
> dove sta memoria   C.76

These are simple and well-known examples of the pleasure of recognition, which we can get from studying the whole of Pound. This even applies to the more important of the Chinese ideograms, which are given in his version of the Confucian texts (*The Great Digest* and *The Unwobbling Pivot*, New Directions 1947), and/or translated nearby in the text of *The Cantos*, at least at first occurrence. It is even possible to learn to use a Chinese dictionary, especially Matthews, which Pound used and refers to. Or as he exclaims himself after quite a string of ideograms :

> And as Ford said : get a dictionary
> and learn the meaning of words.[1]

C.98

[1] Ford Madox Ford in an interview published in *Pavannes and Divisions* 1918, New Directions 1958, London 1960.

Which leads us to the remaining problem of the languages which are not part of present-day internationalism (*if* that is coming about) but dead.

This is of course much more serious. Pound may well protest: 'while Erigena put greek tags in his excellent verses' (C.83, echoed in C.85: 'Erigena with greek tags in his verses'; and in C.87). Or even: 'I shall have to learn a little greek to keep up with this / but so will you, drratt you' (C.105—a self-deprecatory remark pour encourager les autres, for actually Pound has a fair reading knowledge of Greek). But the classics are fast disappearing. Moreover, both the classics and mediaeval studies still seem bogged down in nineteenth-century philology —very necessary for the editing of texts, placing them in dialect and period, emending etc., but not, I should have thought, for 'obscuring the texts with philology' (C.15, one of the so-called 'hell' cantos, philologists being among Pound's damned); nor at the expense of the student's lively interest, which is putting the cart before the horse: first get him excited by the quality of the poetry, then turn him into an expert if he so wishes. 'Gentlemen are these verses worth reading?'

For alas, parallel with the new internationalism (yes, perhaps it was an illusion), there seems to have arisen—out of reaction no doubt—a new, or old refurbished, provincialism, with its necessary and healthy no-nonsense attitude to established cults, but also with a number of prejudices which could prove as fatal to literature as an excess of the cults it mocks. One of these prejudices, perhaps also due to the supposed 'more-but-less-good' spread in higher education (including the loss of Latin as a minimum qualification) is the firm belief that the English-speaking world is the only one that counts. The French appear to have the same delusion about French. Hence the comforting notion in some of the new English universities that American literature is a 'foreign' literature, though fortunately written in English, and can therefore replace French, German, Spanish, etc. as a 'subject'. Xenophobia is rife. Or Pound:

'AT ABOUT THIS POINT [he has just talked about Bion's *Adonis*] the weak-hearted reader usually sits down in the road, removes his shoes and weeps that he "is a bad linguist" or that he or she can't possibly learn all those languages.

'One has to divide the readers who want to be experts from those who do not, and divide, as it were, those who want to see the world from those who merely want to know WHAT PART OF IT THEY LIVE IN.

'When it comes to the question of poetry, a great many people don't even want to know that their own country does not occupy ALL the available surface of the planet. The idea seems in some way to insult them.' *ABC of Reading*, 1934 (p. 42).

But there is another modern phobia, equally alarming and perhaps deeply connected with the other, and for which the same loss of linguistic adequacy might provide the explanation, namely the dislike of *early* literature, whether French, English, Latin or Greek. I call it originophobia. Some years ago one of our more famous writers in this 'no-nonsense' school, reviewing a new translation of *Beowulf* (admittedly not a very good one), dismissed not only the entire English heritage before Chaucer but the whole of *Troilus and Criseyde* as well, and, by implication, the entire French tradition which changed our language and literature from the twelfth century on. The dislike of one's own origins is all the more interesting because the preferred later traditions owe so much to the very older and foreign influences which are otherwise rejected.

> The thought of what America would be like
> If the Classics had a wide circulation
> Troubles my sleep,
> The thought of what America,
> The thought of what America,
> The thought of what America would be like
> If the Classics had a wide circulation
> Troubles my sleep.
> Nunc dimittis, now lettest thou thy servant,
> Now lettest thou thy servant
> Depart in peace.

KNOWLEDGE IS NOT CULTURE

The thought of what America
The thought of what America,
The thought of what America would be like
If the Classics had a wide circulation . . .
    Oh well!
    It troubles my sleep.
        Cantico del Sole, Instigations, 1920
        (*Coll. Shorter Poems,* 1962)

Which brings us back to Pound, who has also 'rejected' plenty, including his early influences or 'origins'. But this I have already touched on, and what interests me here is, on the contrary, the constant homage he pays to all the origins of the Western civilization of which he is part.

And this is the point, it is as a poet that he is doing it, for now I want to move away from the reader's viewpoint to that of the poet and his creative attitude to language. Even as a critic he demands more of himself than of his reader :

'When we know to what extent each sort of expression has been driven, in, say, half a dozen great literatures, we begin to be able to tell whether a given work has the excess of great art. We would not think of letting a man judge pictures if he knew only English pictures, or music if he knew only English music— or only French or German music for that matter.' *The Serious Artist,* 1913 (*Lit. Essays,* 1954).

But more important, he demands it of himself as a creative artist :

'Different languages—I mean the actual vocabularies, the idioms—have worked out certain mechanisms of communication and registration. No one language is complete. A master may be continually expanding his own tongue, rendering it fit to bear some charge hitherto borne only by some other alien tongue, but the process does not stop with any one man.' *How to Read,* 1928 (*Lit. Essays,* 1954).

We do certainly all recognize that something said in one language can sound much better than in another, more succinct or funnier, more true in the sense that the words mysteriously

31

seem 'closer' to what is being expressed, so that we feel ourselves back in a pre-Nominalist time when the word was believed
to be the thing, and not just an arbitrary symbol for it. Pound
himself plays with this in a perfectly ordinary sentence :

> 'Sono tutti eretici, Santo Padre,
> ma non sono cattivi'.
> It can't be all in one language.
> 'They are all prots YR HOLINESS,
> but not bad.'   C.86

Similarly when he quotes Mussolini :

> or 'Perché' said the Boss
> 'vuol mettere le sue idee in ordine ?'
> Pel mio poema.'   C.93

one can hear and visualize the scene : Pound meeting Mussolini
and saying 'I must put my ideas in order' and Mussolini in a
typically Italian way finding the idea very funny, why should
a poet have to put his ideas in order ? Or, more seriously, with a
strong sentence-stress on the *ché* : to what purpose ?[1]

Or again, certain things may sound sentimental in English
but not in Italian or French. Hence Pound's despair in *The Pisan
Cantos* is often expressed in French, either directly :

> J'ai eu pitié des autres
> probablement pas assez, and at moments that suited my own
> convenience
>   C.76

or in quotation, e.g. from Charles d'Orléans : 'Tout dit que
pas ne dure la fortune' (C.76); 'Que tous les mois avons
nouvelle lune' (C.80).

The real question however is whether the poet can do anything about this new feeling of insufficiency in any one language :
i.e. whether he should be content with trying his best in his
own, even 'putting the strengths of another language into

[1] This conversation took place at the end of the war, during the Salo
Republic, when Mussolini was at Gardone and was less occupied with
running the country than he had been before.

English' (as Alvarez has succinctly described Pound's achievement),[1] or go further, as Pound also does:

'The sum of human wisdom is not contained in any one language, and no single language is CAPABLE of expressing all forms and degrees of human comprehension.

'This is a very unpalatable and bitter doctrine. But I cannot omit it.' *ABC of Reading*, 1934 (p. 34).

Human comprehension. For that is the point. Not knowledge (which is NOT culture since culture begins when one HAS forgotten-what-book), but understanding: the process once understood, 'the knowledge will stay by a man, weightless, held without effort.'

For of course Pound wants us to go and read Cavalcanti and Dante and Arnaut Daniel and Confucius, if not in the original, then in his translations (indeed Confucius is pretty unreadable in any other, a plethora of stupefying platitudes, except, perhaps, to those who know how to read him).

But even if we don't, even if we get to know them only through his use of them, then this 'process' of human comprehension (however idiosyncratic the rendering) is what he is giving us, by ruthless 'excernment', by direct quotation, by creative translation, and above all by constant shifts of context through ideogrammic juxtaposition (whereof more later).

It may be, and has been, objected that (even supposing Pound's notions of human wisdom to be 'right'—which question I leave aside pro tem.), the way he sometimes gives it to us in snippets and nuggets interfolded with other snippets and nuggets, is hardly enlightening. If all we get to know, say, of Richard of St Victor is that he said UBI AMOR IBI OCULUS EST (end of C.90 and elsewhere), and that he divided mystical thought into three stages: ' "Cogitatio, meditatio, contemplatio."/ Wrote Richardus, and Dante read him' (C.87),[2] this is

---

[1] *Craft and Morals, op. cit.*, p. 22.

[2] Not in fact Richard's division but taken over by him from Hugh of St Victor. For anyone further interested in Richard there is a good selection of his writings, translated and introduced by Clare Kirchberger (Faber & Faber 1957).

not much better than learning history via phrases like 'let them eat cake' and 'a scrap of paper' etc. On the other hand, unless we become professional historians or continue to keep up our interest in an active way, this is precisely what does remain, floating 'easily in the mind', when we have forgotten what we learnt or have got rid of the paraphernalia. And I don't see what's wrong with that, it's part of our 'culture'. 'Real knowledge goes into natural man in titbits.' *Guide to Kulchur* (p. 99).

And Pound has at least added many such phrases to our store. Or as Donald Davie has said on this subject: 'His "gists and piths", as he calls them, are the mnemonics, the essential truths. The mnemonic for St Ambrose, for instance, . . . is "captans annonam" or "hoggers of harvest"; there is no intimation that we need to know more of St Ambrose than this single phrase in order to esteem him as highly as Pound does.'[1] This is fair criticism. But even Professor Davie, with a nice touch of Poundian humour, goes on to say: '. . . It is easy to laugh this out of court, indignantly; but it must be agreed that if the only "real" knowledge is that which stays in the memory permanently, then perhaps a mnemonic is all that stands between St Ambrose and oblivion, and all that he deserves in the unmanageable plenitude of so much else that is worth knowing.'

On that argument, of course, it is always possible that if civilization continues on its present trend (holocaust apart), *The Cantos* will be all that is left of our understanding of the classics, of Dante, of Cavalcanti, of Provence. For that matter, according to McLuhan, the book will disappear altogether, and we shall be, are already, living in an audio-tactile culture of electrical media. But even on this supposition *The Cantos* are more likely to survive as a transition from the old fashioned book to the art of instantaneous apprehension of multitemporal and multinational facts.

It is as well to remember, however, that Pound himself

[1] *Poet as Sculptor*, London 1965, pp. 144–5. I do not think that these mnemonics are all that Pound meant by 'gists and piths', cp. *Guide to Kulchur* p. 31 on St Ambrose and *captans annonam*. See Hugh Kenner, *The Poetry of Ezra Pound* (London 1951, Part III, ch. 21, *Gists and Piths*).

makes a very clear-cut distinction—even within this type of effortless residual knowledge—between 'ideas which exist and/or are discussed in a species of vacuum, which are as it were toys of the intellect, and ideas which are intended to "go into action", or to guide and serve us as rules (and/or) measures of conduct.' By way of illustration he adds :

'Note that the bloke who said : all flows [Heraclitus], was using one kind, and the chap who said : nothing in excess [Confucius], offered a different sort.' *Guide to Kulchur*, 1938 (p. 34).

I pause here to reflect that, out of the three aspects of Pound which form part of this culture or paideuma business, I have allowed (1) excernment and (2) polyglottism to lead me on (or back) to knowledge—with or without paraphernalia—a dangerous topic, and that therefore I have not yet got on to (3) personae.

Which might as well have a chapter to themselves.

CHAPTER THREE

'But Sordello, and my Sordello ?'[1]

━━━━━━━━━━━━━

Personae was originally the title of Pound's third volume of poems (1909), into which also went fifteen poems from his first volume *A Lume Spento* (1908).

It is also the title of the Collected Poems which came out in 1926, and there a great many of the early poems, from *A Lume Spento* to *Canzoni* (1911), were dropped, though from *Ripostes* onwards almost everything was included.

But Sordello . . .

For 'personae' is also a critical term which has been applied to the Pound method. Or, if you prefer, it is what Pound has developed as part of his method, so that the critics then etc.

The word 'critics' depresses me, even though I am one myself pro tem, it is one of my personae. So much has been written on this aspect of Pound that my raft is being overwhelmed by the flux and I desperately need a bikini.

Ah. Hugh Kenner shall be my Leucothea. If he doesn't object. I think I know him well enough to feel sure he won't.

The opening of this chapter looked as if I might at last be going to start at the beginning and deal with the early poetry and move on to etc. 'Patience, I will come to the Commissioner of the Salt Works / in due course. . . .' Or (C.46) : 'you who think you will / get through hell in a hurry. . . .' (That is a famous line, and everybody always quotes it. So I'm glad I got it in, now I can forget about trying to. I mean students must be told what's famous and what isn't. Then they can forget it too if they wish, or let it float 'easily in the mind'.)

The last phrase is from Kenner re paraphernalia. There is

[1] C.2.

reason in my method. I wish I could just tell you to go and read Kenner's two vital essays, *Leucothea's Bikini: Mimetic Homage*[1] and *Blood for Ghosts*.[2] Then I could move on. I can't of course give you Kenner in one mnemonic which would save you reading him in the long run, so I had better paraphrase; his main point being that Pound's extraordinary translation of the word *kredemnon* ('for which there happens not to be a simple English equivalent') into 'bikini' is not a translation (there is no hope of satisfying the professor of Greek anyway), but an act of mimetic homage.

Or, to expand just a bit, we must stop looking at a poem as an object, and its translation as a similar object, each made, in effect, by no one in no particular circumstances, the whole attention shuttling between one object and the other by way of dictionary equivalences, analyzable rhythms, etc. The eighteenth century understood the art of mimetic homage, fetching from the classics what the poet and his age could use and recreate in its own idiom. The nineteenth century lost it, under the influence of the Holy Spirit theory (poetry is untranslatable because the H.S. seized its author and such an event cannot be counterfeited). Pound has had the nerve to 'translate' in the more eighteenth-century sense and has incurred considerable abuse. In Kenner's words : 'if, as Wyndham Lewis once put it, whole landslides from other times and tongues are coming onto his pages, it is into the twentieth century that they are sliding, at the bidding of a twentieth-century poet.' (*Leucothea's Bikini, op. cit.*)

We tend too much, says Kenner, to look on a poem as a statue, but it is a drama, 'enacted in time, before our minds, by the single actor, its maker'. In other words, restore the *person* and the *occasion*, and we can begin to talk sense. 'Here is the Greek, or the Latin, or the Chinese; someone like and unlike us wrote it in a time like and unlike ours. . . . Here is . . . a somewhat similar English poem. It is the printed record of a *perform-*

[1] In *Ezra Pound: Perspectives*, ed. Noel Stock, Chicago 1965.
[2] *The Texas Quarterly*, X/4 Winter 1967, and in *New Approaches to Ezra Pound* (ed. Eva Hesse, Faber & Faber 1969).

ance, a mimetic record by a certain man, not concealing his traces, who in our own time and place was moved (why?) to pay in this manner his tribute to a former mastery . . .' (*ibid.*).

This mimetic homage 'located in time and place and stirring to life models that will not die' is the central Poundian act. It is crucial to our understanding, not only of small points like the bikini, but of all *The Cantos*, e.g. 'in the China Cantos, where we find, superimposed, three things: (1) a bare high chronicle manner moving to the clash of oriental cymbals and drums, paraphrase of some dynastic record that does not exist, being generated in (2) the imagination of an American who is (3) exiled in twentieth-century Italy and leafing through a multi-volumed history published in eighteenth-century France'[1] [example follows].

Paraphrase of some dynastic record *that does not exist*. . . . I want to stress that, because this point has been all too insufficiently understood by critics of Pound who will go on insisting that since he is dealing with history (and Pound has himself misled them by his own insistence on his view of history), he must be judged *in that respect* as a bad historian, *though* (maybe or maybe not, according to the critic) a 'great' poet. Here comes Form and Content again, rearing its ugly two-pronged head. 'Lie quiet', dinosaur, I'll deal with you later.

For instance: Noel Stock, who has run the gamut from belief in every word Pound has ever said to the sad discovery that alas, Pound is fallible and all too human, tends to track down sources in order to discover, not what good poetry Pound makes

[1] *op. cit.* The history is Joseph Anne-Marie de Moyriac de Mailla's *Histoire Générale de la Chine*, 12 vols (Paris 1777–83), usually referred to in works on Pound simply as Mailla. As it happens I had also pointed out this layered view in an essay *Lay me by Aurelie*, written in 1965 (*22 Versuche über einen Dichter*, ed. Eva Hesse, Frankfurt 1967, and in English in *New Approaches to Ezra Pound*, Faber 1969). The same applies to the *Chou King* in *Rock-Drill*, seen via the nineteenth-century Jesuit Fr. F. S. Couvreur + Pound, and *The Sacred Edict* via the Victorian Baller + Pound in *Thrones*. Or, a better known example, Canto 1, Homer via the Latin Renaissance translator Divus (which is why Pound says towards the end of the Canto: 'Lie quiet, Divus'), + Pound in a rhythm based on the Anglo-Saxon *Seafarer*.

out of them, but how he has misunderstood them, or used them to the exclusion of more acceptable sources. He even accuses him of taking seriously and literally every evasive letter from every important person he wrote to on subjects he held dear: e.g. Arthur Griffith, the Sinn Fein leader, is quoted in C.19 as saying of people in the mass, 'Can't move 'em with a cold thing like economics' [this phrase is recurrent in *The Cantos*], a reply suggesting polite evasion which Pound is said to have turned into a nugget of wisdom. Is it not, however, true? Or again in C.95: 'Something *there!* sd. Santayana'—a phrase barely corresponding to the letter in question.[1]

But this is just what a good poet—indeed, even a mere novelist—does: he gives to things uttered carelessly and trivially a funny or serious (or funny / serious) meaning unintended by the originator. I once created a 'character' out of two contradictory remarks made at a year's interval by a friend. Of course I am not concerned with traditional characters but with their resultant textuality, still, by the time I had finished he had nothing to do with the 'original'. I find what Pound does with Santayana's remark much more funny and (ending as it does with Odysseus again and his raft) much more moving than anything Santayana may or may not have intended:

> 'O World!'
>> said Mr Beddoes.
> 'Something *there,*'
>> sd / Santayana.
> Responsus:
>> Not stasis /
>> at least not in our immediate vicinage.
> a hand without face cards,
>> the enormous organized cowardice.

[1] *Poet in Exile—Ezra Pound* (Manchester Un. Press 1964). I must add that Mr Stock's combination of admiration and disappointment has produced an impressively honest book, more useful however on the early poetry than on *The Cantos*. His later *Reading the Cantos* suffers from a lack of critical demonstration, falling too often into personal opinions that this or that is pointless as far as he can see, etc.

And there is something decent in the universe
   if I can feel all this, *dicto millesimo*
At the age of whatever.
I suppose St Hilary looked at an oak-leaf.
(vine-leaf? San Denys,
   (spelled Dionisio)
Dionisio et Eleutherio
Dionisio et Eleutherio[1]
   the brace of 'em
that Calvin never blacked out
         en l'Isle)
That the wave crashed, whirling the raft, then
Tearing the oar from his hand,
         broke mast and yard-arm
And he was drawn down under wave,
     The wind tossing,
Notus, Boreas,
      as it were thistle-down.
That Leucothea had pity,
      'mortal once
who now is a sea-god :
      νόστου
γαίης Φαιήκων, . . .'
[return to the land of the Phaeacians]

                        C.95

So closes *Rock-Drill*, drawing us into the Greek text (Od.
V/333 : But Ino saw him, daughter of Cadmus, with fine ankle,
who once a mortal woman gifted with voice, became Leucothea
of the deep seas and holds rank among the gods. She took pity
on Odysseus' suffering, thrown adrift, and in the shape of a
sea-gull came out of the wave and sat on the raft . . .; V/343 :

[1] Two missionary martyrs who according to legend were decapitated
in Montmartre in 273 (Gregory of Tours, *Historia Francorum* I/31).
The church of St Denis was built on the same spot in the twelfth century.
Calvin is said not to have blacked them out because the Huguenots were
put to flight at the Battle of St Denis on Nov. 10th 1567. For further
comment on this passage see pp. 145–6.

remove those clothes, leave your raft and swim for it, try to reach the coast of that Phaeacian land where lies your salvation).[1] Odysseus is drawn down into the black water and *Thrones* opens with Κρήδεμνον (Kredemnon) repeated, the veil or 'bikini' which saves him.

Clearly Pound was haunted very early by this doubling and trebling of 'reality' in the 'personae' behind which he hid, or through which he talked, or which he tried to bring to life :

> Hang it all, Robert Browning,
> > there can be but the one 'Sordello'.
> But Sordello, and my Sordello?
> Lo Sordels si fo di Mantovana.
>
> > > > > > C.2

There are in fact six Sordellos here : Browning's, as re-created in his poem (1840) on the Italian troubadour (*c.* 1180–*c.* 1255); Pound's Sordello, as re-created in *Troubadours, their Sorts and Conditions* (*Quarterly Review*, 1913, *Lit. Essays*, 1954) and of course in Cantos 6, 29, 36; the 'real' Sordello, if we can get at him; Sordello as we have him in his poetry, about which Pound has also written (*Essays*, p. 103); then, in the last line, Dante's Sordello, met in *Purgatorio* (VI & VII), who introduces himself to Virgil with the phrase 'O Mantovano, io son Sordello / Della tua terra' (VI/74–5), which Pound echoes with the stock-phrase from the early 'lives' or *razos* of the Troubadours (e.g. Peire Vidals si fo de Toloza', though the actual phrase Pound uses here is not in any of the extant versions of the Sordello *razo*, only variants); in other words here is a sixth Sordello, of the *razo*, the closest 'document' we have (though unreliable, partly apocryphal etc.) to Sordello himself, and from which Pound gets the story of his great love for Cunizza da Romano, wife of

---

[1] ἐπιμαίεο νόστου / γαίης Φαιήκων has in fact caused editorial trouble and Victor Bérard in his French bilingual edition argues that νόστου (return) is an error, partly from a misunderstanding of the old spelling (no long vowels or digraphs) in ΕΠΙΜΑΙΕΟ ΕΦΑΠΣΑΙ (ἐφάψαι) and partly repeated visually from l. 349 since one cannot 'touch' a return. He translates 'toucher au rivage'. But Bailly's dictionary gives ἐπιμαίεο νόστου in Od. V/344 as figurative for 'faire l'effort pour le retour'.

the Count Ricciardo di San Bonifazzio, so that he had to flee to Provence after abducting her at her brothers' requests (for political rather than amorous reasons).[1]

This opening of C.2 has been much commented on. Hugh Kenner[2] calls it a condensation of the poem *Near Perigord* (*Lustra*, 1915, *Coll. Poems*, 1962), which is an elaborate investigation of the Provençal poet Bertrans de Born via his poem in which he assembles qualities from seven Provençal ladies to make up an ideal one. Pound, finding the stray facts too stray, suggestive and impenetrable, begins Part II with 'End fact. Try fiction. Let us say we see / En Bertrans . . . etc.' But Kenner (rather oddly in view of his later essays) comes to the conclusion that for Pound here, things that really happened are more interesting and complex than anything he can imagine, Browning's truth being an abstraction from fact, like the abstract lady (this last may well represent Pound's view of Browning). Dekker[3] also emphasizes the appeal to the Provençal biography as the most nearly contemporary report we have, and refers us to Acoetes' reply, later in C.2 (one of the most beautiful and justly famous passages in all *The Cantos*, based on *Metamorphoses* Bk. III), when asked to explain what has happened to him : 'I have seen what I have seen', and later, to Pentheus (the communication gap being absolute) : 'And you, Pentheus, / Had as well listen to Tiresias, and to Cadmus, / or your luck will go out of you.' Or Dekker : 'If other civilizations, particularly that of the troubadours, have something to say to us, then we must be prepared—as Browning was not—to listen carefully and humbly to the voice of first-hand experience.' (*op. cit.* p. 51).

Yes, but we must also add to it, re-create, or, as Pound does,

---

[1] The story recurs in C.29, Cunizza going off with a soldier later and 'Greatly enjoying herself / And running up the most awful bills. / And this Bonius was killed on a sunday / and she had then a lord from Braganza / and later a house in Verona.' In her old age she freed her slaves in the house of Cavalcanti Senior. (Cp. C.6 'freed her slaves on a Wednesday' & *Guide to Kulchur* p. 107.)

[2] *The Poetry of Ezra Pound* (1951) ch. 12.

[3] *Sailing after Knowledge* (1963) pp. 49–52.

pay our mimetic homage, learning as well as adding. Or as
Kenner says: 'we can write nothing except with reference to
what has been written before, if only because we cannot set
down two words without stirring a whole language into life.
And we can write nothing except as we, whoever we may be,
write it. And we cannot possibly write it except here and now.'[1]
And in *Blood for Ghosts*—which I cannot possibly paraphrase so
you will have to read it[2]—Kenner insists that personae may
also possess. He returns to the well-known Homeric passage in
C.1—the rhythm and presentation of which are the result of
Pound's long preparation, for he brings us Homer through a
distant echo of Anglo-Saxon via Divus ('Lie quiet, Divus').
There Odysseus makes blood sacrifice to call up the shades of
the dead and make them *speak*. For this is, I must insist, what
Pound is so frequently doing (one of his early collections, in
which he reprints poems from *Personae*, *Exultations*, *Ripostes*,
Canzoni, is called *Umbra*—1920). And Kenner ends his essay
with a brilliant analysis of the passage in C.80 and on to C.81
when Pound, bookless in his cage at Pisa and undergoing an
anxious self-interrogation as to his worthiness and that of his
craft, seems incredibly to fall back into the pentameter he had
taken a lifetime to 'break'.[3] In fact he is re-creating, in a few
pages, 'the history of English versification from Chaucer to
1945', miming (as a ghost in itself) even 'the English tradition
of weighty moral utterance, a grave didacticism that finally
returns to paraphrased Chaucer as to its tonic.' These are the
famous 'What thou lov'st well remains' and 'Pull down thy
vanity' passages, always (ironically enough) quoted by even
adverse critics, and for the wrong reasons, as Pound's 'greatest'
poetic 'bits' (though *The Cantos* are a failure etc.). But
as Kenner says: 'Is there another passage in literature that
can number among the protagonists in its drama the metre
itself?'

[1] *Leucothea's Bikini, op. cit.*
[2] *op. cit.*
[3] Cp. 'to break the pentameter, that was the first heave' (C.81), cp.
also: 'and as for those who deform thought with iambics' (C.98).

BUT SORDELLO, AND MY SORDELLO?

This, to me, is ultimately what is meant by the 'personae' of Pound : his endeavour, so early, long before *Ripostes* even, 'to undergo purposefully a multiplicity of influences'[1] in order to achieve, painfully, slowly, and by no means always or consistently, that perfect balance of subjective and objective, presence and absence, ghost and full-blooded flesh, past and present, fact and fiction, high seriousness and humour. Or as he says (of John Adams and his brother as it happens) :

there is our norm of spirit

our 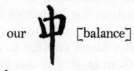 [balance]

whereto we may pay our

homage

C.84

In the light of which it may now be appropriate and revealing to turn to the 'personae' in the very early poetry, by way of transition to the next chapter where I shall (at last) begin at, I mean go back to, the beginning.

There is no doubt that Browning's dramatic monologues on the one hand, and (much more tenuously) Yeats' 'masks' on the other, are the main influences on the young Pound's development of 'personae'. Both Yeats and Pound were emerging (Yeats before Pound) from the so-called 'poésie pure' stage, from the late nineteenth century drift into a vague symbolic dream-world, towards a harder poetry, though Yeats went much further in Symbolism than Pound ever did, developing his own non-rhetorical version of it, but later becoming more colloquial and less dreamy under the influence of Pound.

This colloquial tone Pound learnt mainly, in his early phase, from Browning. The Yeats 'mask' barely affects him and I shall

[1] N. Christoph de Nagy : *The Poetry of Ezra Pound: The Pre-Imagist Stage* (The Cooper Monographs 4, ed. R. Stamm, Francke Verlag, Bern), 1960, rev. 1968, ch. 5, p. 111.

44

not go into it here.[1] But certainly the Browning influence (though later Pound tried to slough it off) accounts for the striking difference between two kinds of poems in Pound's very early verse: the 'archaic', 'dreamy' poetry with its tendency towards what I prefer to call *poésie purée* (not all *poésie pure* being ipso facto bad, cp. Mallarmé); and the tougher, harder, colloquial Browningesque poems like *Cino* (the poet Cino da Pistoia):

> Bah! I have sung women in three cities,
> But it is all the same;
> And I will sing of the sun.
>
> from *A Lume Spento* (1908)
> (*Coll. Shorter Poems*, 1962)

But Cino doesn't stick to this excellent resolution and keeps remembering 'Eyes, dreams, lips . . .' and imagined snatches of conversation about him. The poem 'mimes' his state of mind, including a facetious Cantico del Sole as he really tries to sing of the sun: ' " 'Pollo Phoibee, old tin pan, you / Glory to Zeus' aegis-day. . . ." '

The best known early poem for this 'tough' note is *Sestina-Altaforte*, the portrait of the rumbustious, war-loving poet Bertrans de Born:

> Damn it all! all this our South stinks peace.
> You whoreson dog, Papiols, come! Let's to music!
> I have no life save when the swords clash . . .
>
> For the death of such sluts I go rejoicing;
> Yea, I fill all the air with my music . . .[2]
>
> from *Exultations*, 1909 (*Coll. Sh. Poems*, 1962)

[1] Cp. de Nagy (*op. cit.* ch. 5) who finds a link in *La Fraisne* with *The Madness of King Goll* (*Wind among the Reeds*, 1899). He points out however that Yeats did not develop his actual *theory* of self, anti-self & mask until 1917 (essays *Per Amica Silentiae Lunae*) and that Yeats uses merely symbolic personages (Aedh, Michael Robartes, Owen Aherne) who only exist as masks of Yeats. Pound's personae already in 1908 are 'objective revivications' as well as masks.

[2] The subtitle goes: Loquitur: En Bertrans de Born [En = Seigneur, contracted from domine] (cont. p. 46).

Or there is the dramatic 'miming' that ends *Piere Vidal Old*, when Vidal, 'the fool par excellence of all Provence', who in his madness disguised himself as a wolf for the love of the Lady Loba and was hunted by men and dogs through the mountains of Cabaret and brought back half dead. He is shouting his abuse at the world in general, then suddenly realizes that much more particular 'stunted followers' are upon him:

> O age gone lax! O stunted followers,
> That mask at passions and desire desires,
> Behold me shrivelled, and your mock of mocks;
> And yet I mock you by the mighty fires
> That burnt me to this ash.
>
> Ah Cabaret! Ah Cabaret, thy hills again!
> *(sniffing the air)*
> Take your hands off me!
> Ha! this scent is hot!
> from *Exultations*, 1909 (*Coll. Sh. Poems*, 1962)

Christoph de Nagy, in the only thorough examination we have of Pound's pre-Imagiste poetry, devotes an excellent chapter[1] to the Browning influence, and distinguishes four main groups of poems which function as 'personae', the groups forming a gradation (not, however, chronologically in Pound's development but for us as we face the texts) from translation to dramatic monologue:

(1) the translations
(2) poems whose form is so akin to that of other poets as to approach the condition of a mask
(3) poems in which Pound is speaking through someone else but which are not monologues

---

> Dante Alighieri put this man in hell
> for that he was a stirrer up of strife.
> Eccovi!
> Judge ye!
> Have I dug him up again? . . .

[1] *op. cit.* ch. V, also as *Pound and Browning*, in *New Approaches to Ezra Pound* (ed. Hesse, Faber & Faber 1969).

(4) the personae proper, more or less consistent dramatic
monologues which, even when they voice the words of a
poet, go beyond mere translation.

This is useful, though Mr de Nagy throughout his book
constantly falls into the Form versus Content trap which still,
incredibly, bedevils so much modern criticism. E.g.: 'Pound
consciously and purposefully clothes the emotional content he
wants to express into [sic] the form of one of his ancestors, thus
using their *form* as a mask' (p. 110). 'Lie quiet,' dinosaur, I'll
deal with you later.

The first three sections in fact cover most of the poems which
Mr de Nagy has already dealt with before coming to the Brown-
ing influence, and which I shall also examine in the next chapter.
In order to analyze the similarities and differences between
Browning and Pound, de Nagy here confines himself to the
seven poems 'that practically make up' the last group (4):
*La Fraisne, Cino, Marvoil, Piere Vidal Old, Sestina: Altaforte,
A Villonaud: Ballad of the Gibbet* and *Villonaud for this Yule.*[1]

For the detailed analysis you will have to go to de Nagy's
ch. V. But as he is a little obfuscating at times, I will try to
bring out a few points. First, the order of the poems given above
is not fortuitous, for even within this fourth section the poems
reveal the same gradation from (4) to (1): i.e. (apart from the
slightly Yeatsian *La Fraisne*) *Cino* is the nearest to 'the
Browning pole', *Marvoil* the second nearest and so on, *Sestina:
Altaforte* approaching the 'translation pole' and the Villonauds
being even closer to translation; for instance 'Wining the ghosts
of yesteryear' echoes both Villon's famous ballad and Rossetti's
translation of it (and of course foreshadows the blood given to
the shades in C.1).

Secondly, two important differences (which in fact can be
treated as one): (i) all the above except *La Fraisne* ('For I was

---

[1] *La Fraisne, Cino* and the two *Villonauds* first appeared in *A Lume
Spento* (1908); *Marvoil* in *Personae* (1909); *Piere Vidal Old* and *Sestina:
Altaforte* in *Exultations* (1909). All are in the *Collected Shorter Poems*
(London 1962).

a gaunt, grave councillor') are of poets. (ii) Browning's high degree of 'oral realism'. This is a confusing term de Nagy has taken from Fuson,[1] which *sounds* as if it means Browning's capacity for 'miming' the voice of his characters but in fact is used to mean just the opposite, and even so it is defined as *if* it meant the first: 'The language serves exclusively to embody the dramatic conflict in which the speaker is involved'. This however is taken to mean that in Browning's *The Glove—Pierre Ronsard loquitur* 'we do not expect—and do not get—a poem written in anything like Ronsard's manner' (de Nagy p. 112). What is really meant is that Browning uses his own voice, but impersonally, i.e. he re-creates in his own terms the dramatic conflict, but 'first and foremost the monologue is objective; the personalities evoked in Browning's monologues are severed from the poet's own; he takes no moral responsibility for the attitudes and reactions of his created speaker; one does not expect to find any existential connections between Browning and Fra Lippo Lippi, Abt Vogler or the Italian in England. He, as Pound puts it, brings the dead to life—trying to present them as he thinks they were.'

Yes, well, that last phrase begs the whole question of objectivity and responsibility.

However, it is true that although Pound does not write these particular poems 'in the manner of' Marvoil etc.,[2] he does fill them with allusions and details from the biographies, and even (end of *Marvoil*, Villonauds) quotations.

Moreover, all the poets 'dug up' except Bertrans are in some sort of trouble, in exile, banished. There is a definite semi-identification, an understanding, a compassion. De Nagy links this with the 'poète maudit' or 'perennial outsider' theme of several other early poems, notably the dichotomy of 'we' (poets)

---

[1] Benjamin Willis Fuson, *Browning and His English Predecessors in the Dramatic Monologue*, Iowa City 1948.

[2] In *Cino* there is hardly any reference to Cino da Pistoia's poetry, *Marvoil* is written in irregular lines inconceivable in a troubadour, and *Sestina: Altaforte* is written in the intricate and lyrical sestina form which Bertrans never used, preferring (for the purpose that Pound expresses) the more political and abusive *sirventes*.

versus 'you' (society) in *Li Bel Chasteus, Purveyors General, The Flame*.[1] In these poems Pound was still in the Ivory Tower phase of the 'Decadent' movement, and the six poems about Provençal poets that form part of the true 'personae' group are a testimony to the healthy fusion of this aspect with the more colloquial or shall we say socially integrated Browning influence.

For this is the point of Pound's interest in Browning, already expressed in his direct and facetiously unsatisfactory miming tribute, *Mesmerism* (which is more of a parody than a dramatic monologue):

> Aye you're a man that! ye old mesmerizer,
> Tyin' your meanin' in seventy swadelin's,
> One must of needs be a hang'd early riser
> To catch you at worm turning. Holy Odd's body-kins![2]

Browning's own *Mesmerism* has little to do with magnetic healing, but everything to do with raising souls and shades: 'Herself, now: the dream is done / And the shadow and she are one.' And if Browning here implies that *his* version, his 'dream' vanishes so that only the objective 'she' remains, this seems to me the essential point of difference. In Pound, *his* Sordello, his dream, his poetic soul, is part of the result, so that not only does he become the poet in search of truth, who in C.1 can speak with 'Tiresias Theban', but these shades, these ghosts, acquire—in *The Cantos* at least—mythic dimensions. Or as he said already in *The Spirit of Romance* (1910), a propos of Apuleius:

'We are in the era of "once upon a time" . . .

'The mood, the play is everything; the facts are nothing. Ovid, before Browning, raises the dead and dissects their mental processes; he walks with the people of myth; Apuleius, in real life, is confused with his fictitious hero.'

I shall return to myth and metamorphosis in *The Cantos* later —how can I not? Meanwhile, however, let us have a look at that long preparation.

[1] See de Nagy pp. 38 ff. These poems appeared in *A Lume Spento* (1908), *A Quinzaine for this Yule* (1908), *Canzoni* (1911). Only *The Flame* was reprinted in *Personae* (1926) and *Coll. Shorter Poems* (1962).

[2] In *A Lume Spento* (1908), also in *Collected Shorter Poems* '1962'.

CHAPTER FOUR

'The mastery of any art is the work of a lifetime'[1]

————————◆◆◆◆◆————————

The first poem in *A Lume Spento* is so awful one can hardly believe it:

Lord God of heaven that with mercy dight
Th'alternate prayer wheel of the night and light
Eternal hath to thee, and in whose sight
Our days as rain drops in the sea surge fall,

As bright white drops upon a leaden sea
Grant so my songs to this grey folk may be:

As drops that dream and gleam and falling catch the sun,
Evan'scent mirrors every opal one
Of such his splendor as their compass is,
So, bold My Songs, seek ye such death as this.[2]

I give it all, not by way of digging up in order to castigate Pound who has repudiated most of these poems; but first, to show the contrast, the contradiction, between this and his other, Browningesque vein, already apparent as we have seen even in this same volume; and secondly to emphasize, precisely, the

[1] *Pavannes and Divisions* (1918) parts of which (including this, *Credo*) were reprinted in *A Retrospect* (*Lit. Essays*, 1954).

[2] *Grace before Song.* Reprinted in *Personae*, 1909, omitted from *Personae*, 1926 & *Coll. Shorter Poems*, 1962. Pound finally consented to a reprint of *A Lume Spento* in 1965, adding a sour foreword in which he called it 'a collection of stale creampuffs': 'As to why a reprint? No lessons to be learned save the depth of ignorance, or rather the superficiality of non-perception—neither eye nor ear. Ignorance that didn't know the meaning of "Wardour Street". EP.'

fantastic progress from this to the creation of a modern poetic language for which all subsequent poets are indebted to Pound, even if they have never read him. Also because the poem, despite its wrong 'tone', reveals Pound's early attitude to poetry as something pure, evanescent, 'drops that . . . falling catch the sun' and *die*, lost in the 'leaden sea', which is immediately paralleled with 'this grey folk' i.e. us, the pharasaic public, society, the world.

It might of course have been interesting to trace this development chronologically, so that in one book you would have as it were an accelerated version of a lifetime, like those films of Disney that speed up the blossoming of a flower, which takes days, into a few seconds. But if anything it is Pound's early poetry that is a full-blossomed and even already faded bloom, which metamorphosed itself, not without pain, into a hard huge tree. Disney couldn't do anything with that. I showed you branches of the tree first, to make you feel in your bones and nerves and veins a metamorphosis which can hardly be filmed or demonstrated.

I cannot, in the space of one chapter, go into the details of the early influences, since this has been done by de Nagy[1] and is discussed to a greater or lesser extent by many critics.[2] What I want to bring out here are certain tensions and contradictions which not only reveal the young Pound in mid-struggle but which produce, like all his contradictions, some confusions in his critics.

De Nagy, for example, cites *Salutation the Second* (*Lustra*, 1916, also in *Personae*, 1926 and *Coll. Sh. Poems*, 1962) to show that Pound was able to comment ironically on his early verse. Certainly it is a 'post-*Ripostes*' poem, light, conversational:

[1] *The Poetry of Ezra Pound: The Pre-Imagist Stage, op. cit.* Also, for the influences of critical ideas with reference to the later early poetry: *Ezra Pound's Poetics and Literary Tradition—The Critical Decade* (The Cooper Monographs 11, Francke Verlag, Bern, 1966).

[2] Notably Donald Davie in the early chapters of *Poet as Sculptor* (1965), Noel Stock, *Poet in Exile* (Manch. U.P. 1964), G. S. Fraser in *Ezra Pound* (Writers and Critics Series, London 1960), M. L. Rosenthal, *A Primer of Ezra Pound* (New York 1960).

You were praised, my books,
　　because I had just come from the country;
I was twenty years behind the times
　　so you found an audience ready.
I do not disown you,
　　do not disown your progeny.

Here they stand[1] without quaint devices,
Here they are with nothing archaic about them.
Observe the irritation in general :
'Is this', they say, 'the nonsense
　　that we expect of poets ?'
'Where is the Picturesque ?'
　　'Where is the vertigo of emotion ?'
'No! his first work was the best.'
　　'Poor Dear! he has lost his illusions' . . .

　　And yet, after Pound has sent his 'naked and impudent songs'
to 'Greet the grave and the stodgy', to Rejuvenate even 'The
Spectator', how does he end ? Like this :

　　But, above all, go to practical people—
　　Say that you do no work
　　　　and that you will live forever.

　　The last two lines express the inherent contradiction that was
to haunt Pound throughout his poetry : in the first we have the
remnant of the Aesthetes and their art for art's sake, the poet
being an outcast, poetry having no function in society, no
'utility'—an idea which much of *The Cantos* repudiates but which
some of *The Cantos* in practice endorse; while the last line is, of
course, a direct contradiction of that first poem about evanescent
drops, which ends 'So, bold My Songs, seek ye such death as
this.'
　　And indeed already *Personae* (1909) contains *Revolt against
the Crepuscular Spirit in Modern Poetry*, in which Pound wants
to 'shake off the lethargy of this our time, and give / For
shadows—shapes of power / For dreams—men', and is against

[1] i.e. the progeny, the later poems.

dreaming 'pale flowers, / Slow moving pageantry of hours that languidly / Drop as o'er ripened fruit . . .' etc.[1] But the poem itself is still influenced by the very vocabulary it has to mention in its rejection, and the apparent 'vigour' of the four times repeated 'Great God' (the last one, 'Great God, if these thy sons are grown such thin ephemera' giving an echo of Whitman) seems more rhetorical than vigorous.

For the influences are numerous, and above all complex. There is, way back, Keats and Shelley, with the idea of the poet reaching up to some spiritual sphere beyond ordinary mortals, and Shelley's contradictory notion of poets as 'legislators', having a definite influence on the lives of men and the shaping of the world. There are the Pre-Raphaelites, Swinburne, Rossetti and Morris, already out of date by the nineties and moreover reaching Pound as it were 'pruned' or 'corrected' by Dowson and other poets.[2] There is Fiona McLeod (William Sharp),[3] and of course Yeats as he moved along his erratic line from dreamland via *poésie pure* to Symbolism. There is Whitman too, and Noel Stock has even found a peculiarly unilluminating trace of the Canadian poet Bliss Carman in *Famam Librosque Cano*.[4]

The poetry, in fact is a mass of echoes, not all of which have been noticed, e.g. I can hear the distinct pawings of Thomson's *The Hound of Heaven* in *The Flame* :

> There canst thou find me, O thou anxious thou,
> Who call'st about my gates for some lost me . . .[5]

[1] Not included in later collections. The poem is given in its entirety by de Nagy (*Pre-Imagist Stage, op. cit.*), who analyzes the polarity of dream versus life on which it is constructed.

[2] De Nagy, *Pre-Imagist Stage, op. cit.* p. 75. De Nagy shows that there is very little direct influence of Swinburne on Pound—though he echoes Eliot's assumption that there may have been in his unpublished verse, since *A Lume Spento* was a selection from a large mass of equally heterogeneous material (a speculation which seems to me pretty fruitless).

[3] De Nagy, *op. cit.* p. 94. I shall not go into these influences here.

[4] *Poet in Exile, op. cit.* p. 9. Also in a poem from *Ripostes*.

[5] *Canzoni*, 1911 (where it is part VIII of a long love-sequence called *Und Drang*. The sequence from VII onwards (*The House of Splendour* to *Au Jardin*) is reprinted in *Personae*, 1926 and *Coll. Sh. Poems*, 1962, but

Admittedly the 'thou' is 'Thou hooded opal' or the soul of the poet (the flaming gem image is from Pater), so that the poet is talking to his soul instead of creating a dialogue between God and himself, as in *The Hound of Heaven*. All the same, the vocabulary and rhythm is pure Thomson and the echo seems singularly out of place in a poem which is ostensibly rejecting even the influence of Symons and 'impressionist' poetry, with its nostalgically fleeting urban scenes:

> 'Tis not a game that plays at mates and mating,
> 'Tis not a game of barter, lands and houses,
> 'Tis not 'of days and nights' and troubling years,
> Of cheeks grown sunken and glad hair gone gray;
> There *is* the subtler music, the clear light
> Where time burns back about th'eternal embers.
> We are not shut from all the thousand heavens:
> Lo, there are many gods whom we have seen . . .
>
> *The Flame*

The 'days and nights' is an allusion to Arthur Symons' poem *Days and Nights* (see de Nagy p. 41), and 'glad hair gone gray' presumably to Yeats' version of Ronsard's sonnet ('When you are old and gray . . .').[1] The last line quoted gives a curious foretaste of *The Cantos*, so full of the gods from the very beginning ('Aye, I, Acoetes, stood there, / and the god stood by me . . .' 'I have seen what I have seen'—C.2).

For that matter, I can hear an echo of my favourite poem by Wyatt (*Vixi Puellis Nuper Idoneus* or 'They flee from me that sometime did me seek', *Oxford Book of Engl. Verse*) in the poem *In Durance*, and this despite the allusion to Coleridge:

with no indication that it was once a sequence. This in itself doesn't matter but Mr de Nagy analyzes *The Flame* purely as a poem about poetry, whereas in the sequence it could be about love and poetry, or even about love-poetry.

[1] This is the poem Pound refers to frequently in *The Cantos*, from *Pisan* onwards, one of which references occurs in the passage from C.98 I quoted: 'Uncle William two months on ten lines of Ronsard'. Or in C.80, after a vivid and moving evocation of his Paris days: 'and there was also Uncle William / labouring a sonnet of Ronsard'.

When come *they*, surging of power, 'DAEMON,'
'Quasi KALOUN.' S.T. says Beauty is most that, a
'calling to the soul'.
Well then, so call they, the swirlers out of the mist of
my soul,
They that come mewards, bearing old magic.

There is the 'they' (here of course, poets) and the 'mewards'
which, though ugly and unnatural, reminds me of the (to
Wyatt natural) inversion 'And she me caught in her arms long
and small'; and the conversational pause and change of rhythm
in 'Well then' and 'But for all that' which recall : 'Thanked be
fortune, it hath been otherwise / Twenty times better.'

Oddly enough, the allusion to Coleridge contains a weird
contradiction for Pound the Milton-hater. It comes from an
essay on aesthetics, *On the Principles of Genial Criticism*, based
partly on Kant and partly on Plotinus, which ends with a dialogue
between Milton and a prejudiced Puritan. It is Milton as beauty-
lover who utters the words quoted by Pound, and *to kalon*
simply as beauty (the 'quasi kaloun' etymology is fanciful)
often recurs in *The Cantos*.[1]

Pound's attitude to his early masters is, in fact, highly
ambiguous. He can announce a rejection in a poem still
thoroughly imbued with what he is rejecting—almost speaking
through it, by way of a mask. His *Donzella Beata*, for instance,
de Nagy regards as an 'anti-Blessed Damozel' on the grounds
that the title is taken from the Italian translation of the Rossetti
poem, and that the second of the two stanzas asks for a less
passive woman, not one who merely waits as 'the incarnation of
a romantic type of love which corresponds to a perpetual longing

---

[1] The 'Milton' passage says that 'the Beautiful arises from the perceived harmony of an object, whether sight or sound, with the inborn and
constitutive rules of the judgement and the imagination : and it is always
intuitive. . . . Hence the Greeks called a beautiful object καλόν quasi
καλοvν, i.e. *calling on* the soul, which receives it instantly, and welcomes
it as something connatural'. There follows a quotation from Plotinus,
Ennead I. Lib. 6. (*Biographia Literaria*, ed. J. Shawcross, O.U.P., London
1958, vol. ii, p. 243).

for a union beyond earthly existence'.[1] That's fine, but the
only words in the stanza which do the rejecting are 'bolder . . .
than'; all the others still describe, in Rossettian terms, the
woman than whom Pound's would be bolder. The result is as
pre-Raphish as the first stanza (with its 'oer', its 'rose-hued
mesh' and its 'gold-white' light) :

> Surely a bolder maid art thou
> Than one in tearful, fearful longing
> That should wait
> Lily-cinctured at the gate
> Of high heaven, star-diadem'd,
> Crying that I should come to thee.[2]

Parody, all right, but parody creates nothing of its own. One
could go on for ever (and many do), giving Pound the benefit
of the doubt as to whether these are 'masks' or not. Certainly it is
true that he never went the whole way with the Pre-Raphaelites,
nor with the incense-laden-sin aspect of the Decadent movement, pale though much of it seemed by the time it gets to
Symons via Verlaine ('The pink and black of silk and lace /
Flushed in the rosy golden glow' etc.—*Silhouettes*, Symons).
Even Pound's poem *The Decadence* (*A Lume Spento*, 1908), with
its naïvely proud adoption of the label (as in France), sounds
relatively healthy through the parody element which can never
be quite dismissed : 'Tarnished we! Tarnished! Wastrels all!
/ And yet the art goes on . . .'. Nor did Pound go all the way
with Yeats, or indeed with anyone, probably because of his
technical interest in the Provençal poets, the Tuscan poets,
Villon and Browning, his own inevitable if hated roots in
Whitman and even, possibly, his early admiration for the folksy
and colloquial American poet James Whitcomb Riley (1853–
1916), and for the then very popular Canadian poet Bliss
Carman.[3] And of course his own very individual temperament.

[1] de Nagy, *op. cit.* p. 67.
[2] *A Lume Spento*, 1908. Not reprinted.
[3] See Noel Stock, *Poet in Exile* (*op. cit.*) pp. 3–9 for these last two
tentatively made suggestions. They do not seem to me to account for the
tone of more than a few stray lines here and there.

I cannot imagine Pound going all the way with anyone, not even Confucius. He himself was saying, already in 1913 :

'The artist's inheritance from other artists can be little more than certain enthusiasms, which usually spoil his first work; and a definite knowledge of the modes of expression, which knowledge contributes to perfecting his more mature performance. This is a matter of technique.' *Troubadours—Their Sorts and Conditions* (Quart. Rev.), *Lit. Essays*, 1954.

At the same time, Pound has never been one to conceal his debts, if anything he is over-generous with homage, whether overt or by way of translation and mask. Even Walt Whitman, whom he had so deliciously parodied in *The Spirit of Romance* (1910) in the course of a somewhat irresponsible comparison with Villon :

> Lo, behold, I eat water-melons. When I eat water-melons the
>   world eats water-melons through me.
> When the world eats water-melons, I partake of the world's
>   water-melons.
> The bugs,
> The worms,
> The negroes, etc.
> Eat water-melons; All nature eats water-melons . . .

nevertheless got some sort of ambiguous homage in *A Pact* :

> I make a pact with you, Walt Whitman—
> I have detested you long enough.
> I come to you as a grown child
> Who has had a pig-headed father;
> I am old enough now to make friends.
> It was you that broke the new wood . . .
>
> *Lustra*, 1916 (*Coll. Sh. Poems*, 1962)

I think it is this generosity and this honesty which have led critics into such a flurry of source-hunting and barrel-scraping and updigging of rejected poems. And, with the source-hunting, the booby-trap of Form and Content.

Here it comes. The two-headed monster. 'Lie quiet,' dinosaur, I'll deal with you later. For the moment I only want to show how it mars the criticism of Pound's early poetry in Mr de Nagy's otherwise excellent book. This is not in order to castigate Mr de Nagy, who has done a fine job, but because it is crucial to an understanding of Pound's poetry, the whole of Pound's poetry, not only in itself but as interpreted by some of his critics, to reject the outworn division of Form and Content.

As a literary historian, Mr de Nagy is necessarily concerned with tracing similarities of attitudes, of 'content', but when he has found one it tends to blind him to the quality (good or bad) of the poem he is discussing, and I do not think the two can be so ruthlessly separated, even in literary history. He spends five pages (69–74), for instance, paraphrasing and quoting from *Salve O Pontifex* (Pound's homage to Swinburne), simply and solely to show that Pound's attitude to Swinburne was at that time one of admiration and awe. It never occurs to him to tell us—or to demonstrate critically—that *Salve O Pontifex* is a lousy poem, justly consigned to oblivion by its author.[1]

Or, to look at something more interesting in a bit more detail, Mr de Nagy finds, quite rightly, the same 'Ivory Tower', negative attitude to life in early Yeats, *The Shadowy Waters* (Forgael's speech), as in Pound's poem *In Durance*.[2] He might have shown that the Yeats he quotes is every bit as bad as the passage he quotes from Pound (*if* that is what he means about Pound), my point being that he does not tell us what he thinks. Here is the Yeats quotation (de Nagy p. 48) :

[1] *A Lume Spento*, 1908, reprinted in *Ripostes*, 1912 but not in later collections. It does of course appear in the 1965 reprint of *A Lume Spento*. In *Ripostes* a note is added at the end of the poem : 'This apostrophe was written three years before Swinburne's death' [i.e. in 1906]. The note sounds a bit apologetic to me, as if Pound were reprinting the poem out of honesty but with doubts.

[2] *Personae*, 1909, *Personae*, 1926, *Coll. Sh. Poems*, 1962. *The Shadowy Waters* appeared in Yeats' 'Poems 1899–1905'.

ART IS THE WORK OF A LIFETIME

> All would be well
> Could we but give us wholly to the dreams,
> And get into their world that to the sense
> Is shadow, and not linger wretchedly,
> Among substantial things; for it is dreams
> That lift us to the flowing, changing world
> That the heart longs for.

The namby-rambling rhythm, the run-on blank verse enjambement without, even, the courage of its enjambing, the repeated 'and', the thrice-repeated 'that' as a relative, all contribute to the dreary but hesitant drone. The 'content' is of course idiotic. But this is my point: when the so-called 'content' is bad or nil, so is the form, the one is nil because the other is and vice versa. Add to that the fact that Mr de Nagy has wrenched this out of a play, ignoring the dramatic element.

On the other hand *In Durance* as a whole is one of Pound's better early poems and I doubt whether Mr de Nagy has fully understood it, though he traces the ' "These sell our pictures" ' to Browning's *Pictor Ignotus* and the 'Quasi Kaloun' to Coleridge and the line in quotes ('All they that with strange sadness') back to Pound's early poem *Masks*.[1] But when he gets down to the 'we / ye' dichotomy he had found in *The Flame* and a few other poems, he fails to bring out the complex shift of personal pronouns in this poem: i.e. abruptly from 'But I am homesick after my own kind' to ' "These sell our pictures!" Oh well, / They reach me not', to 'thee. / "Thee"? Oh, "Thee" is who cometh first / Out of mine own soul-kin', to 'When come *they*, surging of power, "DAEMON". . .' to 'so call they, the swirlers out of the mist of my soul, / They that come mewards, bearing the old magic', to ' "All they that with strange sadness" . . . /

---

[1] *Masks* appeared in *A Lume Spento*, 1908 and in *Personae*, 1909, but not in *Personae*, 1926 or *Coll. Sh. Poems*, 1962. Oddly enough *In Durance*, although it appeared in *Personae*, 1909, is reprinted in *The Coll. Sh. Poems* and in *Personae*, 1926 with the mysterious date (1907) below the title. Both were probably written in 1907 so that if, as de Nagy suggests, *Masks* was connected with a concrete situation in Pound's life, then so was *In Durance*.

My fellows . . . ye, that hide / As I hide most the while . . . Oh ye, my fellows . . . we are one. / Yea thou, and Thou, and THOU . . .'

In other words, although the 'we' that Mr de Nagy found before is there, the 'ye' has made a volte face: we and ye are one, against they, but even 'ye' are *first* introduced as 'they', while the first 'they' which follows 'my own kind' *ought* to mean 'my own kind' but means the opposite, the sellers of art. The student may decide himself whether this is a point for or against, by reading the whole poem. Either way it is interesting in relation to Pound's very idiosyncratic use of pronouns in *The Cantos*.[1] All I want to stress here is my own personal view that insofar as the 'content' of Pound's poem is a bit less idiotic than that of Yeats, it is also, despite bad patches, better poetry.

Or again, Mr de Nagy (p. 65) examines *'Fair Helena' by Rackham*[2]—a very bad poem—and notes that the sub-title, given as 'What I like best in all the world' is from Browning's *De Gustibus* and that the picture in question by Arthur Rackham —an illustration for *A Midsummernight's Dream*—is a very pre-Raphish painting of 'a pathetic Helena standing under a starry sky in the forest . . . her hair . . . filled with light and producing the effect of a fine cloud' etc. But he fails to consider the question-mark after the sub-title. A small point, no doubt, but which might mean either irony or that Pound is simply cheating, unable to decide whether he does like it best or not. Whereas, on the other hand, a mere semi-colon in *Anima Sola*—'the only Swinburnian poem Pound ever printed'—sends Mr de Nagy into a splutter of incomprehension by way of exemplifying 'the subordination of meaning to sound' (p. 79):

> My love is the light of meteors;
> The autumn leaves in flight.[3]

[1] See ch. 8, pp. 137 ff. ch. 10, pp. 189 ff.

[2] *Exultations*, 1909, rejected from all subsequent collections except *Provença*, 1910.

[3] *Anima Sola*, *A Lume Spento*, 1908, rejected from all subsequent collections.

Mr de Nagy comments :

'The second line—separated from the first by a semi-colon—either stands by itself and makes no "sense" at all, or it may be dependent on "My love", but is in this case totally unrelated to the preceding cosmic image; "flight" seems to have been chosen because it rhymes with "light", and "leaves" because of the "l" which carries on the alliteration of the preceding line.'

These may well have been the reasons, and they may well, in this case, not be very good ones, though that is, oddly enough, how poets work. But the triple metamorphosis of love = meteors = autumn leaves is a perfectly intelligible metaphor, and, I think, a reasonably effective shift from the visible but unreachable to the visible but less unreachable. It is moreover achieved by straightforward syntactic means : a strong copula 'is' for the more unreachable part, an apposition for the less unreachable, the more obvious.

Mr de Nagy is not much more satisfactory when he is hunting similarities of so-called 'form' or what Pound would call technique. He is happy to note (pp. 77–8) that the rhythm of *Ballad for Gloom* is the same as that of several Swinburne ballads, notably *Les Noyades*, 'despite the fact that in "Ballad for Gloom" every second line is shorter'. Yet it would be extremely odd if a ballad did not have a ballad rhythm. Or again he spends quite a time on the Morris-like 'decorative' words, in particular the jewels, in *Guillaume de Lorris Belated*.[1] But the 'multiplex jewel, of beryl and jasper and sapphire' in *Sandalphon* is somehow O.K. because 'if one examines . . . the source of the poem, the "Talmud", which attaches hidden powers to the various gems, one realizes that this "multiplex jewel" is more than mere ornament . . . he uses them as symbols of the magic powers with which they are connected' (p. 84). Similarly on p. 102 the jewels in *Guillaume de Lorris Belated* (as in Davidson's *Fleet Street Eclogues*) are 'mere ornament and serve to create an atmosphere of delicate elegance'. But in Yeats's *The*

---

[1] *Personae*, 1909 (sub-title 'A Vision of Italy'), a pretentious poem in which the cities of Italy are treated as personifications, as in *Le Roman de la Rose*. Not reprinted.

Shadowy Waters they are 'given an occult symbolical [I nearly wrote symbological, one of Pound's favourite derogatory words] significance.' There follows a quote from Yeats : 'and she and I / Shall light upon a place in the world's core, / Where passion grows to be a changeless thing / Like charmed apples made of chrysoprase [ugh!], / Or chrysoberyl, or beryl, or chrysolite.' Mr de Nagy goes on to say that this is why Pound uses those very stones in *The Flame*, 'when he evokes the visions of which the initiate-poets, those "of the Ever-Living", partake' :

> places splendid,
> Bulwarks of beryl and of chrysoprase.

Mr de Nagy then tells us that the beryl, because of the prophesying spirits living in it, is the most mysterious of precious stones, and that the chrysoprase imparts the magic powers of poetry. This may be so, but I don't see that it makes the lines any better, as such, than jewels used 'to create an atmosphere of delicate elegance' (what's wrong with that, if intended and if well done?). And apart from that I prefer 'bulwarks of beryl' (especially in the *fuller* context : 'Lo, there are many gods whom we have seen, / Folk of unearthly fashion, places splendid . . .') to Yeats' 'passion . . . Like apples made of chrysoprase'—a pretty loathsome concept. Or even concetto. Precious stones, incidentally, play a fairly important role in *The Cantos*, which Mr de Nagy would presumably find O.K. if symbolical but not if decorative. In fact they do have a magical connotation[1] but this is subordinated to the part they play in making up the colour-and-light prism whenever we get a glimpse of the lost 'forma', the sunken beauty that re-emerges every few centuries or so, or a glimpse of paradise. We do not have to know any mysterious symbolic significances unless we want to.[2]

I hope I have given enough detailed textual criticism of these

[1] Boris de Rachewiltz, *L'Elemento Magico in Ezra Pound* (Milano 1965), and in English, *Pagan and Magic Elements in Ezra Pound's Works*, in *New Approaches to Ezra Pound*, ed. Eva Hesse (Faber & Faber, 1969).

[2] See also J. Espey, *Ezra Pound's Mauberley* (London, Faber & Faber 1955, p. 78).

(mostly unreprinted) early poems as dealt with by Mr de Nagy to show how dangerous and pointless the distinction between Form and Content can be as a mode of thought. For one thing it leads, inevitably, to a purely personal (or fashionable) judgment of 'content': some 'themes' are suitable for poetry, others are not, some are in vogue, etc., and this is more often than not unconscious in the critic (e.g., above, 'an atmosphere of delicate elegance' is a *bad* 'content' but extraneous symbolic meanings from esoteric books are all right. One might just as well say the opposite.

Moreover, the division usually leads to critically meaningless phrases and even contradictions. E.g. on p. 82 Mr de Nagy tells us that the taboos on various themes laid down by the *poésie pure* boys, notably Valéry, but also Yeats, 'really had to mean an elimination of content, and consequently an enhanced importance given to form . . .'. A paragraph later: 'although many traditional themes had been cast out, quite a number of new ones appeared, in particular the theme of the demi-monde in the big cities, and of the strata below it.' This, however, 'was motivated by anything but a social protest' but 'served . . . as means to [sic] generate certain moods of futility . . .' etc. The implication being, presumably, that social protest is an acceptable theme but futility is not. On p. 85 : 'Impressionist poetry, however, meant more than merely an innovation in technique. The themes themselves the new technique was mainly applied to, represented, as the above stanza of Symons shows [the pink and black lace quoted on p. 56] something quite new in English poetry : the bustling life of the city, and, in particular, the life of the *demi-monde*, the cabarets and music-halls, and also the figure of the street-girl.' I would hardly call that an 'elimination of content'.

The poetry of Dowson, however, 'represents a further step in the process of subtilization characteristic of the fin-de-siècle : it lives, emptied of almost all content, mainly by its musical quality' (how then, by Mr de Nagy's standards, can it live?). As for Pound's *Praise of Ysolt*[1] (the 'content' of which Mr

[1] In *Personae*, 1909; *Collected Shorter Poems*, 1962.

de Nagy has just acutely described as 'a praise of a demand for the praise of Ysolt . . . The first half represents an echo in the poet's mind of an ever-present demand for praise' etc.), it has no 'palpable content', but is nevertheless beautiful: 'This beautiful poem is as "contentless", as near "poésie pure" as anything written by the Symbolists in England—and perhaps even in France.' Earlier in the book (ch. 2, p. 15) he had quoted an early review of *Personae* by the poet Edward Thomas, who said about *Praise of Ysolt*: 'The beauty of it is the beauty of passion, sincerity and intensity, not of beautiful words and images and suggestions. . . . The thought dominates the words and is greater than they are. . . .' Personally I think that both these directly contradictory views are wrong. The poem is quaintly fey ('And little red elf words crying "A Song" / Little grey elf words . . . Little brown leaf words' etc.) rather than 'beautiful' and the 'content' is of course quaintly fey with the form, rather than either passionate or non-existent.

It never seems to occur to Mr de Nagy that 'poésie pure' can be as excellent in quality as poésie impure, or as poetry content-ful of social protest or of any other 'theme': for example Mallarmé, whose 'theme' (if we must use the word in this sense) is the very act and impotence of engendering a text, but so integrated into his 'form' as to make the distinction impossible (even his 'emptied' use of the adjective *blanc* is much more powerful than Yeats' 'white beauty' or for that matter Pound's 'white words as snow flakes' in *Praise of Ysolt*). That is why I have coined the phrase 'poésie purée', to distinguish *within* that particular school. Bad verse is bad throughout, whatever its school or period or genre. When Pound (or anyone else) is bad, his 'form' and 'content' collapse together, and this applies throughout his work. The best is good all through, the form expresses, follows, mimes the thought, the emotion, 'content' etc. The form is the content. Pound knew this, as every creative artist knows it, deep down, though not all can express it:

'When this rhythm, or when the vowel and consonantal melody or sequence seems truly to bear the trace of emotion which the poem . . . is intended to communicate, we say that this part of the work is good. And "this part of the work" is by now "technique". That "dry, dull, pedantic" technique, that all bad artists rail against . . .

[later]

'On closer analysis I find that I mean something like "maximum efficiency of expression"; I mean that the writer has expressed something interesting in such a way that one cannot re-say it more effectively.' *The Serious Artist* (*Egoist,* 1913) (*Lit. Essays,* 1954).

Of course it is true that at the time of these early poems Pound had, on the whole and with obvious exceptions, 'nothing to say'. Few young men under twenty-five have. But he *also* had not found a way of saying whatever he might have had to say. He had nothing to say because he hadn't found a way of expressing what was burning inside him, and what was burning inside him couldn't come out because he hadn't found the way. The two go together. In his remarkable essay on Cavalcanti (*Make It New,* 1934, *Lit. Essays,* 1954) he tells us that when he 'translated' (his quotes) Guido 18 years before, he did not see Guido :

'What obfuscated me was not the Italian but the crust of dead English, the sediment present in my own available vocabulary —which I, let us hope, got rid of a few years later. You can't go round this sort of thing. It takes six or eight years to get educated in one's art, and another ten to get rid of that education.

'Neither can anyone learn English, one can only learn a series of Englishes. Rossetti made his own language. I hadn't in 1910 made a language, I don't mean a language to use, but even a language to think in.'

CHAPTER FIVE

'I believe in technique as the test of a man's sincerity' [1]

————————————⚹————————————

I seem to have used Mr de Nagy as a poisoned spear to kill the monster with, and I apologize, for both his books are extremely useful (as I hope I have made clear and will continue to make clear in the next chapter). But it was necessary, because his division between Form and Content is typical of its constant misapplication to Pound's later work; indeed, Mr de Nagy is in good company, for instance with T. S. Eliot: 'In each of these influences [of English predecessors and of Provençal and Italian on the early poems] we must distinguish between influence of form and influence of content' (*Introduction to Selected Poems*, 1949).

So before going on, I think I might as well lay that monster now, for it is still alive, though in theory everyone apparently agrees that it is dead. And if I seem, to some, to be reiterating critical banalities, or to *enfoncer des portes ouvertes*, it is only because so many critics, of Pound especially, still keep them resolutely closed. Or as Susan Sontag puts it in her essay on *Style*:

'It would be hard to find any reputable literary critic today who would care to be caught defending *as an idea* the old antithesis of style versus content. On this issue a pious consensus prevails. Everyone is quick to avow that style and content are indissoluble, that the strongly individual style of each important writer is an organic aspect of his work and never something merely "decorative".

[1] *A Retrospect (Credo)* in *Pavannes and Divisions* (1918), *Lit. Essays*, 1954.

'In the *practice* of criticism, though, the old antithesis lives on, virtually unassailed. . . .'[1]

Miss Sontag then specifies the two main ways in which the antithesis lives on: '[in] the frequency with which quite admirable works of art are defended as good although what is mistakenly called their style is acknowledged to be crude or careless. Another [way] is the frequency with which a very complex style is regarded with a barely concealed ambivalence . . . it is clear that such a style is often felt to be a form of insincerity. . . . Indeed, practically all metaphors for style amount to placing the matter on the inside, style on the outside [e.g. Whitman's "curtain" which he declared would not "hang between me and the rest"]. It would be more to the point to reverse the metaphor. As Cocteau writes: "Decorative style has never existed. Style is the soul, and unfortunately with us the soul assumes the form of the body." '[2]

I should perhaps make it clear at this point, if it isn't already, that by 'form' I do not mean merely a sonnet as opposed to a sestina (which is maybe what Eliot meant), or a tragedy as opposed to a comedy, even an epic poem as opposed to a play or a novel as opposed to a poem. These are *genres* and *sub-genres* (and even so, these have become pretty useless distinctions and modern criticism speaks simply of 'a text'). No, I mean the whole play, novel, poem, including the rhythm, the vocabulary, the pace, the order of presentation, the texture and so forth (what Pound covers by 'technique'), *not* separated from the paraphrasable 'plot' or 'subject' or 'theme' or 'content'. Miss Sontag calls this totality 'style' and thus avoids the above confusion with *genre*, but the word 'style' leads her into another duality which on her own terms could, I think, have been avoided: that of style and stylization—the latter for what she calls 'creative mistreatment', i.e. when the material of art is being treated as subject matter: ' "stylization" ', she says, is needed, 'precisely when an artist does make the by no means

[1] In *Against Interpretation*, London 1967.
[2] Cp. Pound's 'mnemonic' for Plotinus: 'A soul, said Plotinus, the body inside it' (C.98).

inevitable distinction between matter and manner, theme and form . . . when style and subject are . . . played off against each other, one can legitimately speak of subjects being treated (or mistreated) in a certain style. Creative mistreatment is more the rule. For when the material of art is conceived as "subject matter" it is also experienced as capable of being exhausted. And as subjects are understood to be fairly far along in this process of exhaustion, they become available to further and further stylization.' Hence Valéry's inversion 'What is "form" for everyone else is "content" for me' hardly solves the problem. I feel, however, that this 'stylization' expresses the same inner need, is as much the 'soul', the 'content', as 'style' is, and we are quite free to criticize it *in toto* (e.g. if the 'sincerity' or emotion is empty or banal, or tortuous, etc., so is its expression). As Miss Sontag herself says : 'The antipathy to "style" is always an antipathy to a given style.'

I am well aware that a quarrel does not go on for so long unless there is something to be said for the other side, nor would the antithesis have survived so long unless it had its uses. I have used it myself as a journalistic short-cut in novel-reviewing —the lowest form of activity. But it doesn't work in serious criticism. For as Miss Sontag says : 'what is inevitable in a work of art is the style. To the extent that a work seems right, just, *unimaginable otherwise* [my italics, cp. Pound in *The Serious Artist*, quoted p. 65, end of last chapter] without loss or damage, what we are responding to is a quality of its style.'

Certainly creative writers (and I prefer their testimony to that of critics) have written against the division. For example Robbe-Grillet (deploring still the need to do so) : 'Hasn't that old leaking ship—the academic distinction between form and substance—sunk yet?'[1] Ortega y Gasset wrote against it already in 1926.[2] So have many others. Above all, and more to the point, Pound wrote against it :

[1] *Towards a New Novel*, transl. Barbara Wright, London 1965, pp. 70 ff. But the whole trend of the French Nouvelle Critique which, like its American equivalent, derives from Linguistics, is also against it.

[2] In *The Dehumanization of Art* (transl. by apparently no one, Double-day Anchor Books, New York 1956).

THE TEST OF A MAN'S SINCERITY

'. . . There is a distinct decadence when interest passes from significance—meaning the total significance of a work—into DETAILS of technique.

'That sentence must not be taken to contradict my sentence of 30 years ago [actually 20] that technique is a test of a writer's sincerity. The writer or artist who is not intolerant of his own defects is a smear.

'But the aim of technique is that it establish the totality of the whole. The total significance of the whole . . . As in Simone Memmi's painting. The total subject is the painting.' *Guide to Kulchur*, 1938, pp. 89–90.[1]

Of course Pound has contradicted himself on this, as on many things. *Guide to Kulchur* is relatively late criticism. Earlier he often speaks of the two as separate, e.g. in *A Retrospect* (*op. cit.*, 1918) he speaks of the need for a knowledge of technique, adding 'of technique of surface and technique of content'. In *Troubadours —their Sorts and Conditions* (1913) he tells us: 'The three devices tried for poetic restoration in the early thirteenth century were the three usual devices. Certain men turned to talking art and aesthetics and attempted to *dress up* [my italics] the folk song. Certain men tried to make verse more engaging by *stuffing it with an intellectual and argumentative content* [my italics]. Certain men turned to social satire . . .' (*Lit. Essays*, 1954). Or, in *Retrospect* again: 'I think there is a "fluid" as well as a "solid" content, that some poems may have form as a tree has form, some as water poured into a vase. That most symmetrical forms have certain uses. That a vast number of subjects cannot be precisely, and therefore not properly rendered in symmetrical forms.'

Critics have pounced on this to show that the early poetry is a vase whereas *The Cantos* are a tree. I seem to have called *The Cantos* a tree myself some way back, and later I shall call them a spiral. But Pound is here using 'form' in the sense of 'genre', opposing 'symmetrical forms' such as sestinas and sonnets to non-symmetrical ones. And clearly Pound was groping his way

[1] Simone di Martino, thirteenth-century Sienese school.

69

out of the then prevalent dichotomy. For even the idea of a tree (which cannot really be divided into a ' "solid" content' and a 'form') totally contradicts that of a 'fluid' content being *poured* (from outside) into a vase. Similarly the phrase quoted earlier from *A Retrospect* shows that although he mentions them separately as techniques of surface and techniques of content, both are necessary and the very term 'technique of content' implies a unified view.

Or again, in 1918 :

'And one tends to conclude that all attempts to be poetic in some manner or other defeat their own end; whereas an intentness on the quality of the emotion to be conveyed makes for poetry.

'Another possible corollary is that the subject matter will very nearly make the poem. Subject matter will, of course, not make the poem; e.g. compare Mangan's *Kathleen ni Houlihan*, with Yeats' *Song that Red Hanrahan made about Ireland*, where the content is almost identical.' *The Hard and Soft in French Poetry*, 1918 (*Lit. Essays*, 1954).

The following year he said of Browning :

'His weakness in this work [translation of Aeschylus' *Agamemnon*] is where it essentially lay in all of his expression, it rests in the term "ideas".—"Thought" as Browning understood it—"ideas" as the term is current, are poor two-dimensional stuff, a scant, scratch covering. "Damn ideas, anyhow". An idea is only an imperfect induction from fact.

'The solid, the "last atom of force verging off into the first atom of matter" is the force, the emotion, the objective sight of the poet. In the *Agamemnon* it is the whole rush of the action, the whole wildness of Kassandra's continual shrieking. . . .' *Translators of Greek: Early Translators of Homer*, *Egoist* Jan.–April 1919 (*Lit. Essays*, 1954).

In other words, action, pace, order of incident, dialogue, vocabulary, rhythm, the lot, is one with 'the force, the emotion', one *form* + *content* whole, in which neither the 'technique' *nor* the 'ideas' or 'thought' or 'content' must stick out.

But it was in *The Serious Artist* (1913), from which I quoted at the end of the last chapter, that Pound really tried to get to grips with the dichotomy—possibly without realizing that the dichotomy existed; indeed he is primarily concerned at this point with the difference between prose and poetry. There too he speaks of poetry as an energy, and says (my italics for what seems to me to bear on the problem in hand) :

'And "Good writing" is perfect control. And *it is quite easy to control a thing that has in it no energy*—provided that it be not too heavy and that you do not wish to make it move . . .

'. . .

'The prose author has shown the triumph of his intellect and one knows that such triumph is not without its sufferings by the way, but by the verses one is brought upon the passionate moment. This moment has brought with it nothing that violates the prose simplicities. *The intellect has not found it but the intellect has been moved.* . . . In the verse something has come upon the intelligence. In the prose *the intelligence has found a subject for its observations. The poetic fact pre-exists.*' Lit. Essays, 1954, p. 49, pp. 53–4.[1]

Whether these distinctions between poetry and prose are valid or not (I think not), Pound here is also groping for the (at the time) obscure identity of supposedly outer style and inner content, or, as Susan Sontag prefers to put it, the outer content (subject matter) and the inner style. Both divisions are confusing, in fact I would say that much of the confusion is due to 'content' so often being thought of as either some external, factual, 'reality', or as some internal but extractable, paraphrasable 'plot', 'theme' etc., whereas Pound (surely like most artists) clearly thinks of it as the poetic fact, which is also the emotion, the 'passionate moment', which pre-exists but is given perfect expression and thus re-created. And anyone who does not do this has 'nothing to say' and is *therefore* not a technician, not a stylist :

'As the most efficient way to say nothing is to keep quiet, and

[1] This is a mystical assumption, which many poets would reject, for whom poetic facts are created, not found. But the pre-existence of the material is part of Pound's aesthetic (see chs. 10 and 11).

as technique consists precisely in doing the thing that one sets out to do, in the most efficient manner, no man who takes three pages to say nothing can expect to be seriously considered as a technician. To take three pages to say nothing is not style, in the serious sense of that word' (*ibid.*, p. 54).

For if Pound never explicitly repudiated the Form and Content dichotomy, in practical criticism he treated the two as one, *even* when apparently separating them (unlike modern critics who repudiate the dichotomy but go on etc.). By 1938 the apparent separation seems to be no more than a nervous tick, a habit hard to get rid of.

For example in his essay on Johnson's *The Vanity of Human Wishes* (*Guide to Kulchur*) he still uses phrases like 'You are never for an instant permitted to forget that the thought is in full dress uniform' and 'In a highly superior and accomplished way the WHOLE of the eighteenth century was a cliché'—both of which phrases imply that nothing is being said but very well. In practice, however, Pound is hard on the 'manner' because he is hard on the 'matter':

'. . . Johnson has enough thought to carry the uniform *to a reader searching* for the thought and the technique of its expression. Almost nothing suffers by being excerpted, line, distich or four lines at a time.

'The cadence comes to an almost dead end so frequently that one doesn't know the poem is going on . . .

'. . . taking it by and large the poem is buncombe. Human wishes are not vain in the least.

'The total statement is buncombe. The details acute and sagacious. . . .[1] Johnson's verse is not as good prose as that often found in Thomas Jefferson's letters. There is probably no couplet in the two reprinted poems that has the quality of Jefferson's. . . .'

And he ends up, quite unambiguously: 'The "often thought

---

[1] By which he does not mean 'technical' details but smaller 'statements', locally well expressed. He had previously called Gongorism an excess of attention to high-coloured detail, and eighteenth-century English verse a very superior kind of intellectual Gongorism.

yet ne'er so well express't'' angle very often means that the idea is NOT thought at all by the expressor during or preceding the moment of expression. It is picked up and varnished, or at best, picked up and rubbed, polished etc. . . . thought remembered in a moment of lassitude.'

By unambiguously I do not mean that he does not still express himself in terms of the dichotomy (thought picked up and polished etc.), but that he makes it quite clear that if the thought is a cliché so will be the expression of it, however neatly the rules are observed.

I suppose that while I am riding this unfortunately not dead horse I had better make a brief digression into 'approval' or 'non-approval' of the 'content' as well. When *The Pisan Cantos* won the Bollingen Prize in 1947, the American edition came out with a big splash to the effect that at last it was possible to acclaim great poetry without endorsing the poet's views. I can't remember the exact phrasing but it emphasized a further division.

For great poetry, and even good poetry, is great, or good, whatever the poet's views. One can admire Milton's qualities without accepting his concept of the Fall, or of God the Father, and one can also say that insofar as his notions were petty or banal or anthropomorphic his language suffered and insofar as they were humane or generous or perceptive it did not. Pound need not accept the whole Christian dogma of Dante, who, as he said, 'était diablement dans les idées reçues' (essay on Cavalcanti), in order to think him a great poet. Nor, to take a smaller example, can we possibly infer that Pound approves of war when he praises Bertrans de Born's vigour, realism, 'premeditated thrust', and says that 'De Born writes songs to provoke war, and they were effective'.[1]

For that is my point: when Pound's views are vulgar, so is his language, when they are not, it is not. Everything collapses together. Or as he saw himself, about metre and language:

'WHEN the metre is bad, the language is apt to be poor.

[1] *The Letters of Ezra Pound*, ed. D. D. Paige (London 1951). Letter 190, to Felix E. Schelling, Paris, 8 July 1922.

THE TEST OF A MAN'S SINCERITY

'WHEN the metre is good *enough*, it will almost drive out all other defects of language.' *The Townsman*, July 1938.

So one might continue : when the language is poor, the thought is apt to be poor. (Or vice versa.) When the language is good *enough*, it will almost drive out all other defects of thought. (Or vice versa.)

For by 'technique' Pound never means *just* rules, or the rhymes of a sestina etc. He means the whole activity. Or, as he says on music :

'Good old Richter, ripe with years and with wisdom, has the sense to interlard his treatise on theory, counterpoint, harmony, with the caution that "these are the laws and they have nothing to do with musical composition which is a different kind of activity".' *Guide to Kulchur*, 1938, p. 29.

Or—to get back to 1913—at the end of A FEW DON'TS :

'. . . "*Mais d'abord il faut être un poète*", as MM. Duhamel and Vildrac have said at the end of their little book, "*Notes sur la Technique Poétique*".'[1]

Which makes as good a transition as any from the dinosaur (I hope layed for the rest of this book at least) back to Pound as a young man of twenty-five trying to find a language, not only to use, but to think in.

For as Eliot has justly said : 'the situation of poetry in 1909 or 1910 was stagnant to a degree difficult for any young poet of to-day to imagine. Pound himself had a long way to go : and he has gone it.'[2]

[1] *A Few Don'ts* (Poetry I, 6, March 1916) reprinted as part of *A Retrospect* in *Pavannes and Divisions* (1918), and *Literary Essays*, 1954.

[2] Introduction to *Literary Essays*, 1954.

CHAPTER SIX

'An artist is always beginning'[1]

———※———

What happened? In 1909 we still have the mixed bag, best and Ivory Towerish worst, of *Personae* and *Exultations*; in 1910 the quaint translations of *Canzoniere* in *Provença*, reprinted in *Canzoni* (1911), which is also a mixed bag. Then comes what many critics, including Mr de Nagy, regard as a turning point (though I do not) in *Riposte* (1912), and, more important, the planning of the *Imagiste Manifesto* in 1912, printed in 1913—the same year as *The Serious Artist*—and Pound talking of poetry as a science, a chemistry, a study of 'man considered as a thinking and sentient creature'.

What happened was Imagisme, as well as T. E. Hulme, Ford Madox Hueffer (later Ford Madox Ford), and the French prose tradition of Flaubert, the French poets Théophile Gautier, Tristan Corbière, Jules Laforgue, the French critic Remy de Gourmont; the first acquaintance with the Fenollosa papers (1913); Eliot, met in 1914; the correspondence with Joyce (from 1913); Wyndham Lewis and *Blast* (1914–15). During this decade Pound published *Lustra* (1915) and the translations from Chinese poetry (*Cathay*, 1915). By 1917 he had written three Cantos (later withdrawn). In 1919 came *Homage to Sextus Propertius* and in 1920 *Hugh Selwyn Mauberley*, which some critics consider his best poems. By 1924 he had published the first sixteen Cantos.

[1] From *How I began*, T.P.'s Weekly, June 6 1913 : 'If the verb is put in the past tense there is very little to be said about this matter.

'The artist is always beginning. Any work of art which is not a beginning, an invention, a discovery, is of little worth.'

AN ARTIST IS ALWAYS BEGINNING

During this decade moreover (between *Canzoni* in 1911 and the publication of Cantos 5–7 in August 1921, *Dial* LXXI/2), Pound wrote more criticism than at any other time in his life. As Mr de Nagy points out: 'from 1912 onwards until 1921 the yearly output of critical articles never drops under 13; only two articles are published in 1911—in 1918 the peak is reached with 102 articles.'[1]

Of course it wasn't an overnight change. The new influences were gradual. Ford Madox Ford for example, as critic and editor of the *English Review* (1908–10) had a decisive influence on Pound from the moment they met soon after Pound's arrival in England in 1908. And Pound himself describes Ford's mirth at his earlier efforts:

'And he felt the errors of contemporary style to the point of rolling (physically, and if you look at it as a mere superficial snob, ridiculously) on the floor of his contemporary quarters at Giessen when my third volume displayed me trapped, flypapered (possibly hyphen), gummed and strapped down in a jejune [sic] provincial effort to learn, *mehercule*, the stilted language that then passed for "Good English" in the arthritic milieu that held control of the respected British critical circles, Newbolt, the backwash of Lionel Johnson, Fred Manning, the Quarterlies and the rest of 'em.'[2]

There has been quite a critical tussle as to whether Ford or T. E. Hulme was the main influence on Pound in those days.

[1] *Ezra Pound's Poetics and Literary Tradition—The Critical Decade* (The Cooper Monographs, Francke Verlag, Bern 1966).

[2] Obituary on FMF: *Ford Madox (Hueffer) Ford; Obit* (The Nineteenth Century and After, August 1939). The 'third volume' would be *Canzoni*, since Pound refers to himself in *The Spirit of Romance* (1910) as 'the author of "Personae" and "Exultations" ', obviously disregarding *A Lume Spento* and *A Quinzaine for this Yule*, and *Provença* was merely a reselection; since, also, Pound visited FMH at Giessen in the summer of 1911. I should add that it is of course as a critic and novelist that Ford won Pound's admiration. Pound evidently thought little of Ford's verse. His DON'TS of 1913 says 'Don't use such expressions as "dim lands of peace". It dulls the image.' The expression is taken from one of Ford's early poems. But he fell over backwards to praise him in *The Prose Tradition in Verse* (*Poetry*, 1914, *Lit. Essays*, 1954).

AN ARTIST IS ALWAYS BEGINNING

Sir Herbert Read took up Hulme's case,[1] Mr de Nagy and others Ford's. Personally I agree with de Nagy. Pound himself has been relatively silent on Hulme (apart from the brief and ambiguous *This Hulme Business*), but expansive about Ford, and in retrospect Hulme fades away into insignificance. One of the few times that Hulme expressed himself in print was on the Image, and his ideas were borrowed almost verbatim from Remy de Gourmont, whom Pound was of course also reading.[2] Apart from the question of Imagisme, neither Hulme's so-called 'classicism' nor his Bergsonian ideas on time seem to have anything to do with Pound; and as for the five poems which Pound printed at the end of *Ripostes* under the title 'The Complete Poetical Works of T. E. Hulme', with prefatory note,[3] they offer only the slenderest evidence of talent or leadership: slight 'images' in the sense of impressionistic fleeting analogies, typical of most Imagiste poems, the conversational tone which everyone, including Ford and for that matter Yeats, and even to some extent Dowson and Symons, had been trying to capture for poetry since the Nineties.

However that may be, the interesting fact remains that (except perhaps for *Portrait d'une Femme* and *The eyes of this dead lady speak to me*) there is hardly a single poem in *Ripostes* (1912) which can really be said to bear the stamp of Ford's influence in the sense of Ford's insistence on the prose tradition in verse, on Flaubert and *le mot juste*, on precision and the demand that poetry must be at least as well written as prose. Yes, there is the attempt at colloquialism with exclamation marks and line splits:

No, no! Go from me. I have left her lately.

A Virginal

But does or did anyone then actually say 'Go from me'? And the iambics are still heavily with us, either in the song-based

[1] *The True Voice of Feeling* (London 1953) ch. VI.

[2] See de Nagy, *op. cit.*, pp. 67 ff. for a clear statement of the whole position. Also John Press, *A Map of Modern English Verse* (O.U.P. 1969) ch. 3.

[3] Reprinted in *Collected Shorter Poems*, 1962.

lyrics like *An Immorality* ('Sing we for love and idleness, /
Naught else is worth the having'); or in the thudding pentameter which mars the 'conversational', cynical tone of *Portrait
d'une Femme* (a first adumbration of many a *vers de société* in
Lustra):

> Your mind and you are our Sargasso Sea,
> London has swept about you this score years
> And bright ships left you this or that in fee . . .

And although Pound is trying to vary it with, precisely, the
conversational tone, the pentameter is very much there, under-
neath, marking time in its heavy-handed nineteenth-century way
(for that is what blank verse had become):

> You have been second always. Tragical?
> No. You preferred it to the usual thing:
> One dull man, dulling and uxorious,
> One average mind—with one thought less, each year.

Even when he seems to hit on the basically dactylic rhythm
that was to lead him out 'to break the pentameter', as in Δώρια,
he falls back, despite the printed break in the lines—a favourite
device of Pound's to make the lines at least look different:

> Be in me as the eternal moods
>   of the bleak wind, and not
> As transient things are—
>   gaiety of flowers . . .

And when he tries to get away he echoes Whitman (in
'N.Y.') or even Wordsworth (*A Girl*).[1] And the archaisms
are still there (hath, Twas, thee etc.), and he is still much too
fond of the word 'soul': 'Now! for the needle trembles in my
soul!' (*The Needle*), or 'I am thy soul, Nikoptis . . . See, the light

---

[1] Eliot praised the 'feeling' of this as 'original in the best sense'. But
as Alvarez has pointed out (*Craft and Morals, op. cit.*) the idea of a girl as a
tree is a cliché and the last stanza has been faked. 'Wordsworth's "violet
by a mossy stone" is half-hidden in it' ['Tree you are, / Moss you are, /
You are violets with wind above them . . .'].

grass sprang up to pillow thee, / And kissed thee with a myriad grassy tongues; / But not thou me' (*The Tomb at Akr Çaar*, still vaguely echoing *The Hound of Heaven*); or 'Thou keep'st thy rose-leaf / Till the rose-time will be over, / Think'st thou that Death will kiss thee?' (*Echoes* II [of Shelley?], reprinted in *Coll. Sh. Poems*—without *Echoes* I—as *The Cloak*).

The student can check his own judgment against mine more easily than with the earlier volumes, since all of *Ripostes* except four poems is reprinted in *The Collected Shorter Poems*. One of the poems omitted is *Salve O Pontifex*, which Pound reprinted in *Ripostes* from *A Lume Spento*—somewhat unnecessarily I think—with that apologetic-sounding little note about its date (see p. 58, ft. 1).

It seems to me that *Ripostes*, far from being a turning-point, is a sort of queer regression, marked by the new ideas, certainly, but also very confused, with the archaic animal dying no doubt but still giving convulsive shakes.

For Pound's best and most obviously individual early poems —let us not forget it—had already appeared in what I called, for that reason, the 'mixed bags' (this is a personal selection, maybe the student can find others) : in *A Lume Spento* (*The Tree, La Fraisne, Cino, Masks, Plotinus, In Tempore Senectutis*); in *Personae* (*Marvoil, In Durance*); in *Exultations* (*Sestina: Altaforte, Piere Vidal Old, Planh for the Young English King*); in *Canzoni* (the five last poems from the sequence *Und Drang*, i.e. from *The Flame* to *Au Jardin* in the *Collected Shorter Poems*).

In other words, what sets him apart from all 'influences' is his interest, on the one hand, in Browning, on the other, in the 'hard' quality and disciplined technique of his favourite latins— and I say latins advisedly, for we forget too easily Pound's very early interest (already as a student at Pennsylvania and Hamilton) in Catullus, Horace, and Martial;[1] and the 'hard-

---

[1] Cp. *Notes on Elizabethan Classicists* (1918) : 'and the Greeks might be hard put to it to find a better poet among themselves than is their disciple Catullus. Is not Sappho, in comparison, a little, just a little Swinburnian?' See also Peter Whigham, *Ezra Pound and Catullus* in *Ezra Pound: Perspectives* (ed. Noel Stock, Chicago 1965). Mr. Whigham

ness' which he wrote about later with reference to Gautier, Corbière and Laforgue,[1] he also found in the Provençal poets, and above all in Cavalcanti, on whom he worked for well over twenty years.[2] And what fascinates Pound in Cavalcanti is a certain quality of mediaevalism which has nothing to do with Christianity or with paganism, a quality which 'has not been in poetry *since*', for 'the gulf between Petrarch's capacity and Guido's is the great gulf, not of degree but of kind', that between Guido's 'intelletto d'amore', as vibrantly expressed in his sharp, mimetic lines and metamorphic rather than ornamental figures, and Petrarch's sentimentality larded with ornament: 'the prettiest ornament he could find, but not an irreplaceable ornament, or one that he couldn't have used just about as well somewhere else. In fact he very often does use it, and them, somewhere, and nearly everywhere, else, all over the place.' Pound goes on:

'We appear to have lost the radiant world where one thought cuts through another with clean edge, a world of moving energies *"mezzo oscuro rade"*, *"risplende in sè perpetuale effecto"*, magnetisms that take form, that are seen, or that border the visible, the matter of Dante's *paradiso*, the glass under water, the form that seems a form seen in a mirror, these realities perceptible to the sense, interacting, *"a lui si tiri"*. . . .' *Cavalcanti* (1910–34), *Lit. Essays*, 1954, p. 154.

I shall return to other aspects of this essay in later chapters, but for the moment I want to relate this particular idea of clarity

<hr/>

also tells us that Horace is quoted more frequently in *The Cantos* than any other Roman poet. Martial's epigrammatic quality was of course to come out in *Lustra*.

[1] *The Hard and Soft in French Poetry* (*Poetry* XI, 5, Feb. 1918); *Irony, Laforgue and some Satire* (*Poetry* XI, 2, Nov. 1917). Both reprinted in *Lit. Essays*, 1954.

[2] The first sign of interest in Cavalcanti appears in *Guido invites you thus* (*Personae* and *Exultations*, 1909), a curious non-translation (i.e. it refers to Dante's *Guido vorrei* but instead of being Cavalcanti's reply (which Pound translates in *The Sonnets of Guido Cavalcanti*) it is Pound's own answer, taking up Dante's imagery. The essay on Cavalcanti, though it did not appear until 1934 (*Make It New*) is dated 1910–31 (*Lit. Essays*, 1954).

and clean edge to Pound's archaism, which, as we have seen, still occurred in the poems of 1912, but, more curiously, lingered on in the translations, even of Cavalcanti. Especially of Cavalcanti. Pound himself is well aware of the problem by the end of his essay:

'There is no question of giving Guido in an English contemporary to himself, the ultimate Britons were at that date unbreeched, painted in woad, and grunting in an idiom far more difficult for us to master than the Langue d'Oc of the Plantagenets or the Lingua di Si.'

This shows not only a curiously misinformed or perhaps intentionally comic notion of late thirteenth-century England, but also an even more peculiar notion that one ought at all to translate into the same period (an idea he does not for a moment entertain with regard to ancient Chinese, since it really would be impossible). He goes on to say that 'if, however, we reach back to pre-Elizabethan English, of a period when the writers were still intent on clarity and explicitness . . . our trial, or mine at least, results in:

Who is she that comes, makyng turn every man's eye
And makyng the air to tremble with a bright clearenesse[1]
etc.'

He quotes it all, and rightly comments: 'The objections to such a method are: the doubt as to whether one has the right to take a serious poem and turn it into a mere exercise in quaintness; the "misrepresentation" not of the poem's antiquity but of the proportionate feel of that antiquity, by which I mean that Guido's thirteenth-century language is to twentieth-century Italian much less archaic than any fourteenth-, fifteenth-, or early sixteenth-century English is for us. It is even doubtful

[1] *Chi è questa che vien, ch'ogni uom la mira, / Che fa di clarità l'aer tremare.* You only have to say the words aloud, even without understanding them, to hear how crisp and sharp and swift they are, and how Pound misses this as well as the vibrancy of the thought they reflect. His variation in *Canzoni* is no better ('Who is she coming, that the roses bend / Their shameless heads' etc.). The same applies to *Donna mi prega*, including the version in *Canto 36*.

whether my bungling version of twenty years back isn't more "faithful", in the sense at least that it tried to preserve the fervour of the original. And as this fervour simply does not occur in English poetry in those centuries there is no ready-made pigment for its objectification.'

Quite. This passage contains the essence of Pound's ambivalent attitude to language and to translation : even the expectation of a ready-made pigment is a self-contradiction; at the same time, the translation must not be an exercise in quaintness, *yet* one must somehow represent the feel of the original's 'antiquity'—not, mark you, its extraordinary modernity, its hardness and 'clean edge', but at most its 'fervour' (a curiously loose term which could equally apply to, say, Francis Thomson : presumably what he means is 'intentness', for Cavalcanti's *intenzione*). In other words Pound is still only concerned with the effect that Cavalcanti has on us, compared with modern Italians (its feel of antiquity, which is relative), rather than with the effect it must have had at the time. This feel of antiquity he seems to equate in the essay with the poem's quality. At best he is trying to achieve a telescoping of both effects, the 'betweenness' of ancient and modern which makes the tension of the *Canzone*. But he has not yet grasped—as indeed no one had at the time—the real art of 'mimetic homage', or the fact that it is into the twentieth century that these poems must landslide. This, from a poet who later translated a Chinese character (exclamatory particle) as 'bi-gosh', is a strange paradox, and one which was to pursue him throughout his work.

At this stage, however, and on his own terms, I should have thought that if a period style had to be chosen, the style of Donne's *The Ecstasy* would have been a better equivalent, on Pound's own later admission. But Pound was not really interested in Donne, he did not 'imitate' him or put himself through that particular mastery, partly from a dislike of argumentative verse, partly from a dislike of Baroque. Or as he said of Binyon's Dante translation :

'The devil of translating medieval poetry into English is that it is very hard to decide HOW you are to render work done

82

with one set of criteria in a language NOW subject to different criteria.

'Translate the church of St Hilaire of Poitiers into Barocco?'
Hell (*Criterion*, April, 1934) *Lit. Essays*, 1954.

The idea of translating into period, not modern, is still there. And his attitude to the masteries which did influence him swerves, even at the very start, from the tough re-creations of the 'personae', as in *Cino*, to the namby-pamby softening of even Villon in the two early Villonauds, both also attempts to re-create 'between-ness' of two traditions.[1] In *Lustra* he not only disowns the archaic poems (see p. 52) but also partly the 'tough' ones :

> O my fellow sufferers, songs of my youth,
> A lot of asses praise you because you are 'virile',
> We, you, I! We are the 'Red Bloods.'! ...
>
> ... We are compared to that sort of person
> Who wanders about announcing his sex
> As if he had just discovered it.
> Let us leave this matter, my songs,
>   and return to that which concerns us.
>
> The Condolence, Lustra, 1916
> (*Coll. Sh. Poems*, 1962)

This division (quaintness and toughness, both repudiated) was nevertheless to pursue him throughout his life, though in *The Cantos* they are made to function with a purpose, ritualistic or comic. But it was not until *Homage to Sextus Propertius* (1917) and, eventually, the much later translations (Confucius, *The Women of Trachis*, and the idiosyncratic treatment of sources in *Rock-Drill* and *Thrones*) that Pound really fulfilled himself as a 'creative translator' or 'creative mistranslator' in the sense which is commonly applied to him.

[1] Cp. *ABC of Reading*, p. 104: 'Villon, the first voice of man broken by bad economics, represents also the end of a tradition, the end of the mediaeval dream, the end of a whole body of knowledge, fine, subtle, that had run from Arnaut to Guido Cavalcanti, that had lain in the secret mind of Europe for centuries. ...'

And I don't just mean the howlers. He has been well defended on this score.[1] Similarly, 'worldly riches' is not the same as Anglo-Saxon *weorldes rices* in *The Seafarer* BUT is so much truer to the original than earthly kingdoms or realms, since these words have later connotations and the Anglo-Saxon lord or treasure-giver really was just a local sort of chap, handing out riches. So Hugh Kenner, in *Blood for Ghosts* comments on 'wuniath tha wracan ond thas woruld healdath / brucath thurh bisgo. Blaed is gehnaeged' etc., which Pound translates 'Waneth the watch, but the world holdeth. / Tomb hideth trouble. The blade is laid low.' Every word has undergone a 'sea-change' (*wracan* is not 'watch' but 'weaker', *wuniath* is not 'wane' but 'dwell', *Blaed is gehnaeged'* means 'Glory is humbled' etc.). Kenner reminds us that this translation made possible the idiom in which the ghost of Divus speaks in C.1 ('Bore sheep aboard her' etc.), 'a familiar point, and by 1967 a commentator's staple'. His aim is to show not only that Pound's 'mistranslation' does not in fact falsify, but that Pound was chiefly interested in the ninth-century sounds, 'beyond philology, in how a bard breathed: in the gestures of tongue and expulsions of breath that mimed, about A.D. 850, the emotions of exile.' That's fine. I agree, even allowing for the fact that many of Pound's errors cannot be justified in this way: e.g. 'God that madst her well regard her', in *Ripostes*, 'translates' Charles d'Orléans' 'Dieu! Qu'il la fait bon regarder', but is little more than a nonsensical misunderstanding of Old French syntax (= 'Dieu qu'il fait bon la regarder'), and does not seem to me to contribute much in the way of poetry, except a silly pun on *regarder* and *regard 'er*—unless I'm being obtuse. But my point is rather this :

Pound's archaism in translation, which lingered long after he had got rid of it in his own poetry, and which affects certain passages in *The Cantos*, does not always or inevitably produce a better poem than the original, or even a good poem in itself, a new equivalent etc.

[1] See especially *J. P. Sullivan: Ezra Pound and Sextus Propertius* (*A Study in Creative Translation*), London 1965.

AN ARTIST IS ALWAYS BEGINNING

I realise that ultimately this is a matter of personal opinion. And Pound himself varied enormously on this very point. For instance, as late as 1920, in his very odd versions of Arnaut Daniel:

> Doutz brais e critz,
> Lais e cantars e voutas
> Aug del auzels qu'en lur latins fant precs
> Quecs ab sa par . . .

comes out good and hard and crisp, only to collapse in the third line:

> Sweet cries and cracks
>   and lays and chants inflected
> By auzels who, in the Latin belikes,
> Chirm each to each . . .

though it picks up later, and the rhythm—as in all these translations—prepares *The Cantos* (cp. C.9: 'One year floods rose, / One year they fought in the snows . . .').

Similarly *Can chai la fueilla | Dels ausors entrecims, | El freitz s'ergueilla* . . . is not caught by 'When sere leaf falleth / from the high forkèd tips, / And cold appalleth . . .' etc. As for the incredibly difficult *L'aura amara*, with its brief lines (three two-syllable lines and two one-syllable lines in each stanza, and most lines have only four), Pound veers crazily from archaism ('Amor, look yare!' for the truly colloquial *Amors, gara*) to the absolute success of 'No debates / Shake me, nor jerk . . . etc.':

> Amor, look yare!
> Know certainly
> The keys:
> How she thy suit receives;
> Nor add
> Piques,
> 'Twere folly to annoy.
> I'm true, so dree
> Fates;

AN ARTIST IS ALWAYS BEGINNING

No debates
Shake me, nor jerk.
My verities
Turn terse,
And yet I ache.[1]

We have already seen this wide variation in the early poems. The archaism is particularly marked in the early translations, of the troubadours, of Cavalcanti,[2] most of which I think do not render for one moment the particular quality that Pound admired in these poets, but lose it in a curious mush that is not integrated with or mitigated by the occasional God-damn-you bits of toughness. And I now want to concentrate solely (and briefly) on *The Seafarer* and *Donna mi prega*, since they both affect *The Cantos* (C.36 is a newer version of *Donna mi prega*, and echoes of it occur later in *The Cantos*).

Pound's translation of *The Seafarer* has been praised by many as a poem in its own right, and 'more important to the twentieth century than the original superb poem'.[3] Certainly parts of it are very effective, the bits that everyone always quotes ('the blade is layed low', or 'Lordly men are to the earth o'ergiven', the latter phrase recurring on its own in *The Pisan Cantos*). But personally I do not think that the original poem is superb, and I find a great deal of Pound's version ridiculous. Without actually obeying the complicated Anglo-Saxon rules of scansion (which would be undesirable in modern English and in fact impossible), it contrives nevertheless to remain close enough for

[1] The Daniel translations appeared in the essay *Arnaut Daniel*, *Instigations*, 1920. *Lit. Essays*, 1954, and *The Translations of Ezra Pound*, ed. Hugh Kenner (Faber & Faber, London 1953, Paperback 1971).

[2] See *The Translations of Ezra Pound*, ed. Hugh Kenner, *op. cit.*

[3] Tom Scott, *An Appreciation* (in *Ezra Pound: Perspectives*, ed. Noel Stock, Chicago 1965). I hesitate to disagree with a poet on this, especially since I agree with everything else Mr Scott says. G. S. Fraser, in his short book *Ezra Pound* (London 1960), praises *The Seafarer* but rather, and I think rightly, for (*a*) its strong influence on Pound's own versions from Chinese, and (*b*) for its 'more muscular, vigorous quality of language, a greater complexity of feeling brought over, when one compares it with some of the earlier translations'. Fair enough.

absurdity, bringing in as well some serious faults such as alliterating on the fourth stress (which in Anglo-Saxon was always left non-alliterating, as a kind of neutral ground towards the next line); or alliterating on the same sound two lines running, or alliterating on one sound in the first half-line and on another, twice, in the second; all of which faults exaggerate the alliteration and produce an effect of heaviness.[1] And of course, there are the archaisms, the inversions etc. :

> This he little believes, who aye in winsome life
> Abides 'mid burghers some heavy business,
> Wealthy and wine-flushed, how I weary oft
> Must bide above brine.
> Neareth nightshade, snoweth from north,
> Frost froze the land, hail fell on earth then,
> Corn of the coldest. Nathless there knocketh now
> The heart's thought that I on high streams
> The salt-wavy tumult traverse alone.
> Moaneth alway my mind's lust
> That I fare forth, that I afar hence
> Seek out a foreign fastness.
> For this there's no mood-lofty man over earth's midst,
> Not though he be given his good, but will have in his youth
>   greed . . .

It is perhaps not quite so ridiculous as William Morris' famous rendering of *flota fāmig-heals fugle gelīcost* (foam-throated vessel most like a bird, *Beowulf* 218) as 'the foamy-neck'd floater most like to a fowl' (though Pound's 'Bitter breast-cares have I abided', elsewhere in the poem, comes pretty close). What is interesting about it—as about so much of Pound's

---

[1] Cp. Pound, praising Binyon's Dante (*Hell, Criterion*, April 1934, *Lit. Essays*), 'Mr B. says in preface that he wanted to produce a poem that could be read with pleasure in English. He has carefully preserved all the faults of his original.

'This in the circumstances is the most useful thing he could have done. There are already 400 translations of Dante carefully presenting the English reader with a set of faults alien to the original, and therefore of no possible use to the serious reader who wants to understand Dante.'

earlier verse—is that it forms part of the long preparation, not only as Fraser says for *Cathay*, but for the magnificent rhythm of Canto 1 and ultimately, for the breaking of the pentameter.

Anglo-Saxon metre was quantitative, not syllabic, and based on four main stresses (or 'lifts') to the line. As long as the four lifts were there, you could put (within reason) as many syllables as you liked between the lifts, or in the 'dips' as they are called, though of course the syllables had to be relatively unimportant: nouns in the main took the lifts (hence the 'static' 'majestic' quality of the verse), then verbs, sometimes pronouns, adverbs or adjectives, but all these latter could also go into the dips, as did prepositions, relatives, articles etc.

The important point is that the first 'half-line' could be in a different metre from that of the second, and usually was. E.g. a type A (falling : ́ x ́ x) could be followed by a Type B (rising : x ́ x ́) or a type C (rising/falling : x ́ ́ x).[1] These are the three basic types, the cross representing the dip. Hence a Type A could have several syllables in either of its dips, e.g. : ́ x x x ́ x; and similarly a B could have a long run-in : x x x ́ x x ́.

Now since, from the point of view of weight, the dip could consist of more than one unaccented syllable, it follows that in practice the two dips could not come together, or they would merely count as one dip of several unaccented syllables and the line would be too light. In other words, the following three combinations could not make up a correct half-line : ́ x x ́, ́ ́ x x ; x x ́ ́.

For the same reasons, the two lifts couldn't come together either, except as in C above, flanked on either side by a dip. However, there are two more types of half-lines, D and E, which are in fact the first two forbidden combinations above, but with one of the dips changed into a half-lift. In other words, two dips could come together, provided that one of them was in fact half-stressed, i.e. given a more weighty word that would count as a half-lift: e.g. Type E is really the first forbidden half-line above, but with a half-lift on one of the dips :

[1] I am using the old descriptions from Sievers for simplicity and because nothing else would have been available to Pound at the time.

′ x x̣ ͟ or ͟ x̣ x ͟. While Type D is the second forbidden half-line with a half-lift on one of the dips : ͟ ͟ x x̣ or ͟ ͟ x̣ x. The third forbidden half-line cannot be thus redeemed because it would mean starting with a half-lift, which would not be weighty enough.

I apologize for this sudden brief excursion into Anglo-Saxon prosody, but it is necessary for grasping just how Pound evolved his rhythms. The fact that two half-lines could be and should be of different types meant that the total line was extremely varied and supple, within the rigid rules. If, say, a falling half-line can be followed by a rising one, or by a rising/falling one (A + B or C), or by the variations D or E, clearly the result is nothing like a pentameter. Secondly, the same applies to combinations of half-lines in which the 'dips' can contain two or three or four unaccented syllables. Lastly, the fact that Pound breaks the rules and constantly uses the forbidden half-lines, in which the two lifts come together and the two dips merge, did produce, by way of error, what was to become the characteristic Poundian line, ending in either a spondee (two stressed syllables together), or, on the contrary, in several unaccented syllables (i.e. the last two forbidden half-lines above : x x x ͟ ͟ and ͟ ͟ x x x x). I say produced, but really it confirmed him in what he was already doing, now and again, as early as *Cino* (e.g. the spondee : 'and the night goes'; 'beneath the sunlight'; 'to our way-fare'; 'the new laid rast-way' etc.). Or in *The Return* (*Ripostes*), the poly-syllabic endings : tentative, hesitate, Inviolable. All of which enabled him to find a more natural rhythm, which can be heard, for instance, in the last two lines of the passage quoted from *The Seafarer*, though they are longer than his normal line (and of course too long for Anglo-Saxon). The pentameter is never-theless totally broken with either a long run-in or with a dip of several run-in small syllables. And those two particular lines end on two consecutive stresses.

Despite all this, I believe that the static quality of this Anglo-Saxon translation also influenced Pound retrogressively, or rather, to put it more accurately, also served to express the characteristically passive, receptive, feminine aspect of Pound which is there from the very first together with the masculine and aggressive force. The feminine aspect may perhaps be more or less equated with the traditionalism, and the masculine with the innovation; the feminine with the strain of pure aestheticism, the masculine with the iconoclastic rough and tumble. These are merely categories which obviously overlap, not only in Pound's but in anyone's psyche, and I emphasize them here as a guide-line to the constant and deep contradictions with which Pound presents us throughout his life's work. For these in fact are not so much contradictions as complements or what the Chinese call non-antagonistic pairs, and of course, like most people, Pound has antagonistic ones as well. It is obvious that at his best what I call the feminine strain is not only fused with the masculine but is itself a strength, a 'still centre', or, to use Pound's term for the Confucian axis of harmony or golden mean, an 'un-wobbling pivot'. But Pound's pivot could wobble dangerously. He is a poet of extremes, he took all the risks, he 'lived his poetry' as the Provençal poets he admired 'lived their poetry'. Hence his yearning for and insistence on the Confucian balance. And unless we understand this basic contradiction of extremes which forms the essence of his genius we shall continue to veer into critical extremes ourselves, the falling-over-backwards-to-find-all-perfect by the cultist who is pro, and the hysterical attack of the critic who is con (if you will excuse the French pun).

On this bisexual note let us return to the early translations. It is interesting that Donald Davie, in a careful analysis of Pound's Cavalcanti translations, and in particular of *Donna mi prega* as published in the Cavalcanti essay, comes to the con-clusion that it is static, and mainly for metrical reasons (though without reference to Anglo-Saxon). Since Cavalcanti used internal rhyme (*d'un accidente che sovente é fero . . . e sua potenza | L'essenza . . .* etc.), Pound breaks up his line typographically into smaller members to stress the rhyme, which is just one other way of breaking the pentameter. Pound has tended to develop the one-line-one-statement rhythm anyway, avoiding the epic Miltonic enjambement. But Cavalcanti *does* run on, all the time. Or as Davie puts it:

AN ARTIST IS ALWAYS BEGINNING

'This explains why this poem which is so concerned with energy is so unenergetic. . . . In either of Pound's versions the last thing we would ascribe to Cavalcanti's poem is impetus, momentum. The same thing is true of "Who is she that comes, makyng turn every man's eye", just as it is true of *Cathay*. And, indeed, how could it be otherwise? The metrical sign of kinetic energy, of impetus, is inevitably the enjambement, which swings or whirls the reader on a torrent of feeling out of one line and into the next. Yet Pound the translator, as we have seen, had to eschew enjambement, for in no other way could that breaking of the pentameter which his originals forced upon him, the rhythmical dismemberment of the verse-line from within, be brought about. . . .'[1]

Donald Davie goes on to relate this striking paradox (that so dynamic a character as Pound should produce such undynamic poetry as in these translations) to the dregs of the Aesthetic Movement within him—though he puts it more elegantly: 'the deliberate prolongation of what Walter Pater calls the "intervals of time" in which aesthetic perception occurs . . . in a tranced stillness'. And he ends by saying that this kind of poetry is 'a poetry that characteristically moves forward only hesitantly, gropingly, and slowly; which often seems to float across the page as much as it moves down it; in which, if the perceptions are cast in the form of sentences, the sentence is bracketed off, and, as it were, folded in on itself so as to seem equal with a disjointed phrase; a poetry (we might almost say) of the noun rather than the verb.'

This hardly seems to describe the poetry with which we began this book. And indeed insofar as Davie seems to be extending his censure from C.36 to the whole of the Cantos it simply does not apply, it ignores the layers of time which Pound explores both

---

[1] *Ezra Pound: Poet as Sculptor* (London 1965) ch. VI. Oddly enough, Donald Davie has himself experimented with Anglo-Saxon metre, and very successfully, breaking up the line into half-lines, in his poem *The Forests of Lithuania*, which is based on bits of the Polish epic *Pan Tadeusz*, by the Romantic poet Mickiewicz. Auden's attempt to reproduce Anglo-Saxon metre in *The Age of Anxiety* was to my mind pretty disastrous.

vertically and horizontally (see ch. 10) as well as Pound's dynamic use of verbs, with which he often opens a sentence, and many other features. But it does undoubtedly describe an aspect of Pound which runs parallel to the other, 'virile' and aggressive poetry, all the way from the early days, sometimes fusing to perfection, sometimes pulling him apart. Pound has himself described the movement in phrases like 'Ply over ply' (C.4)— which recalls Mallarmé's *pli selon pli*, 'phase over phase' (C.97) or even, in C.91, which we shall examine later, 'over harm / over hate'.[1] This end-stopped, one-statement-one-line tendency was moreover necessary to his poetics of juxtaposition, as we shall see. And the very influences, beneficial or not, show this up. For the one thing which was not really allowed in Anglo-Saxon—the heavy end-stopping of a line with two lifts—is precisely what Pound took over in error, blending it, at his best, with his more thorough knowledge and feeling for Greek cadences, and above all with his delicate ear for the cadences of natural speech. But the end-stopping is there, and can give a static effect. Moreover, Anglo-Saxon too was a poetry of the noun rather than of the verb (the noun took precedence in alliteration and stress). Which makes as good a transition as any to Fenollosa and (ah yes) the ideogrammic method. Not to mention Imagisme which I suppose I can't avoid either.

[1] Mallarmé, *Remémoration d'amis belges* : 'Toute la vétusté presque couleur d'encens / Comme furtive d'elle et visible je sens / Que se dévêt pli selon pli la pierre veuve.' Cp. ch. 10, my examination of the Stonehenge and Laʒamon passage in C.91, where layers of prehistory are folded one over the other; and, in the earlier discarded Cantos : 'Ancient in various days, long years between them; / Ply over ply still wraps the earth here.'

CHAPTER SEVEN

'The natural object is always the adequate symbol'[1]

━━━━━━━━━━━◆━━━━━━━━━━━

This famous phrase from *A Few Don'ts* seems to have thrown more confusion on Imagisme—that much epitaphed movement as Hugh Kenner calls it somewhere or other—than any of Pound's other definitions.

I doubt whether I can disentangle it. I shall only try to simplify. At this distance of time I don't think the student should bother himself with the relation of Pound's 1912 version of Imagisme (with an *e*, for Pound clearly linked it back to France and Remy de Gourmont) to the 'earlier' Hulme version of 1909 which died an early death anyway, or to the diluted stuff which Pound came to call 'Amygism' (after Amy Lowell).[2] The full sentence in which my chapter heading occurs goes like this :

'Don't use such an expression as "dim lands *of peace*". It dulls the image. It mixes an abstraction with the concrete. It comes from the writer's not realizing that the natural object is always the *adequate* symbol.'

Four possible confusions here : Pound seems to be against metaphor, of which he gives a bad example; then he calls it an image; then he seems to be against mixing abstract and concrete, whereas any glance at his poetry shows that he does this all the time; finally he calls the natural object a symbol, and yet he rejected Symbolism at this very time.

To take these one at a time—though they are all part of the

[1] *A Few Don'ts*—Poetry I, 6 March 1913. Also in *A Retrospect* (*Pavannes and Divisions*, 1918, *Literary Essays*, 1954).
[2] See de Nagy, *Critical Decade, op. cit.* for detailed treatment of influences.

same thing ultimately in Pound's actual poetics and practice : I shall deal with the last one first, to get it out of the way and because the others will lead me straight on to the ideogram.

The 'natural object' or referent can never in itself be a symbol except as man makes it so via language or other cultural codes, so presumably Pound means the word for the natural object; in which case by 'symbol' he must mean more than mere 'sign' (the word for the thing). Unless he means in fact 'image' (see below). Certainly he rejected Symbolism, without, it seems, having a very clear idea of what it had become in the hands of Mallarmé or even of Yeats. His well-known statement on this is only partly helpful and partly true :

'Imagisme is not symbolism. The symbolists dealt in "association", that is, in a sort of allusion, almost of allegory. They degraded the symbol to the status of a word. They made it a form of metonymy. One can be grossly "symbolic", for example, by using the term "cross" to mean "trial". The symbolist's *symbols* have a fixed value, like numbers in arithmetic, like 1, 2 and 7. The imagiste's images have a variable significance, like the signs *a*, *b* and *x* in algebra.'[1]

This perhaps throws more light on the 'image' than on Symbolism, and hardly fits in with the so-called 'private'—in fact, contextually engendered—symbols of the Symbolists (and many of Pound's 'images' in *The Cantos* are really private, as well as contextually engendered); nor does it fit in with the Symbolists' emptying a word of its normal associations (e.g. Yeats' 'white beauty'). But it does at least get rid of that coded chrysoprase.

Secondly (going backwards still), on the question of abstract and concrete, this is only a dictum, enounced with reference to 'dim lands of peace'. Pound in fact mixes abstract and concrete all the time, as we shall see, but in a very particular way, that of ideas *in action*. Even when he equates Dante's *directio voluntatis* with Confucius' will or direction of the will (chih[4], 'the officer

[1] *Vorticism*, The Fortnightly Review, New Series, Sep. 1, 1914, and in *Gaudier-Brzeska—A Memoir*, London 1916, p. 97.

standing over the heart' 志 ⁽¹⁾), or Cavalcanti's *virtu* with 'the total light process', the sun and moon together 明 ⁽²⁾),

it is their function which interests him, the way they work out in praxis or even in mimesis. Whereof more later.

Thirdly (and back to the beginning of the statement), he is not against metaphor. He has cited with approval Aristotle's dictum that metaphor is a sign of genius.⁽³⁾ And of course his own early poetry is full of it :

> The light became her grace and dwelt among
> Blind eyes and shadows that are formed as men;
> Lo, how the light doth melt us into song :
> The broken sunlight for a healm she beareth
> Who hath my heart in jurisdiction . . .
>
> *Ballatetta* (*Canzoni*, 1911, *Coll. S. P.*)

Here metaphor is achieved by the normal traditional means of syntax : a metaphoric verb can change the nouns it is attached to (light *dwells* among blind eyes, *melts* us into song : i.e. light

⁽¹⁾ Mistake by Pound : the lower component does mean 'heart', but the seals show that the upper component 士 as used here is a growing plant 屮, not 士.

⁽²⁾ 'The sun and moon, the total light process, the radiation, reception and reflection of light; hence the intelligence' (Pound, *Confucius*, New Directions 1951). The ideogram can be taken to represent either the sun and moon or the bright moon shining through windows.

⁽³⁾ 'But the greatest thing by far is to be a master of metaphor. It is the one thing that cannot be learnt from others; it is also a sign of genius, since a good metaphor implies an intuitive perception of the similarity of dissimilars.' (*Poetics* XXII. 9, Loeb Transl.) Or Fenellosa : 'Metaphor, the revealer of nature, is the very substance of poetry.' And Pound's footnote to this : 'Compare Aristotle's Poetics : "Swift perception of relations, hall-mark of genius." ' (I shall come to Fenellosa later in this chapter.)

becomes human or animal, eyes become a dwelling-place; light becomes a fire, 'us' becomes wax or something meltable, 'us' also becomes song, C makes A into B); or the nouns are changed into other nouns by means of a verb or verb + preposition (A is or becomes B, A are formed as B, C beareth A for a B, C has A in B).

Fourthly (the second part of the statement), his use of the word 'image' for metaphor is the use of the time, as derived by both Hulme and Pound from de Gourmont, though admittedly de Gourmont is very contradictory on this aspect and has no doubt, via Hulme and Pound, and later Eliot, been responsible for the frequent modern use of the term 'image' to mean a literal fact that is given emotive or even symbolic associations by the poet (Yeats' 'symbols' and Eliot's 'objective correlative', *representing* an emotion or a complex of emotions, rather as a delegate represents a constituency); and later still, it came to mean almost anything the poet happens to mention.[1] De Gourmont, for instance, in *Le Problème du Style*, stresses mainly the visual and/or sensual quality of the image, dividing poets into *visuels*, who render an experience with an image, and *ideo-émotifs*, who merely remember and render the emotion roused: 'une idée n'est qu'une sensation défraîchie, une image effacée' (p. 69).[2] On the other hand, in *Esthétique de la langue française* (p. 43), he deals with dead metaphors that lie dormant in language and the way in which all languages continually create new metaphors spontaneously, and he calls this 'l'art de "créer des images" '. But in *La Culture des Idées* he tells us that any unusual combination of words makes a new image, even if unintentional.

Pound was not really interested in de Gourmont's philosophic and psychological treatment of the image, that is, in de Gour-

---

[1] Cp. also Ford : 'Any very clear and defined rendering of any material object has power to convey to the beholder or to the reader a sort of quivering of very definite emotions.' (*Les Jeunes et Des Imagistes* (The Outlook, XXVIII/850, May 16, 1914).

[2] This is no doubt the source for Pound's 'An idea is only an imperfect induction from fact' (re Browning, quoted p. 70).

mont's reconciliation of Locke's *Nihil in intellectu quod non primus in sensu* (nothing in the intellect that is not first in the senses) with Schopenhauer's 'idealism'—a reconciliation he thought he had achieved via subjectivity: i.e. although the outside world conditions or even creates our organs of perception and therefore must be 'real', the image of it as seen by one man is different from that seen by a dog or by another man.

I shall therefore not wander into this dangerous territory. For Pound has been fairly explicit on the subject, in one of his most important essays, *Vorticism*,[1] which is unfortunately not reprinted in the *Literary Essays*, where he says: 'The point of Imagisme is that it does not use images as ornaments.' He describes his experience in the Paris Metro (at the Concorde) when he suddenly saw a beautiful face, then another, then another, and wrote a 30 line poem about it, which he destroyed 'because it was what we call work of the second intensity'; six months later he wrote a poem 'half that length' and a year later [1912], he made 'the following *hokku*-like sentence':

> The apparition of these faces in the crowd:
> Petals on a wet, black bough.[2]
>
> *Lustra*, 1916 (*Coll. Shorter Poems*, 1962)

He says later that the Japanese have understood the beauty of this kind of imagistic as opposed to lyric writing, and evolved

[1] *Vorticism*, The Fortnightly Review, New Series, Sep. 1st 1914. Also in *Gaudier-Brzeska* (1916).

[2] Pound described the experience slightly differently a year earlier in *T.P.'s Weekly* [T. P. O'Connor], July 6 1913, *How I began*, in which he says he waited three years to find the words for *Piccadilly* (an 8-line poem at the end of *Personae*, 1909, and not reprinted): 'Beautiful, tragic faces, / Ye that were whole and are so sunken ... O wistful, fragile faces, few out of so many ... Who hath forgotten you?'. And how he was then told it was 'sentimental', and how for another year he had been trying to make a poem of a very beautiful thing that befell him in the Paris metro, and how, after thinking that 'in Japan, where a work of art is not estimated by its acreage and where sixteen syllables are counted enough for a poem if you arrange and punctuate them properly', he finally got it.

the form of the hokku. He quotes Moritake's well-known hokku:

> The fallen blossom flies back to its branch:
> A butterfly.

He comments: 'The one image poem is a form of super-position; that is to say it is one idea set on top of another. I found it useful for getting out of the impasse left by my metro emotion.'

The whole question of the hokku or haiku's influence on Pound's technique is admirably described by Earl Miner,[1] who shows how important this concept of super-positive structure is for understanding Pound's poetry. The first part of a haiku (and of the Metro poem) 'consists of a relatively straightforward, unmetaphorical statement. The second part is a sharply defined metaphorical image. . . . In its simplest form, as here, the connection between the "statement" and the striking image is one of seemingly simple contrast. There is a *discordia concors*, a metaphor which is all the more pleasurable because of the gap which must be imaginatively leaped between the statement and the vivid metaphor. . . . Pound used the super-pository method, as it may be called, as a very flexible technique which provides the basic structure for many passages and many poems.' Professor Miner adds that the discovery of this technique in a poetic form written in a language he did not know is one of the insights of Pound's genius, and he gives many examples, not only from the shorter poems (*April*—a particularly good one—*Liu Ch'e, Gentildonna, Alba*, and, adapted to comic effect, *The Bath-Tub*, or to love—a subject alien to the haiku, which is nature-poetry, *Fan-piece*); but also in *Mauberley, Near Perigord*, and in *The Cantos*, to focus the meaning of a passage in one vivid and sudden image such as 'In the gloom, the gold gathers the light against it' (C.11); or in C.83, after the portrait of Yeats:

[1] *The Japanese tradition in British and American Literature*, Princeton Univ. Press 1958, ch. V, reprinted in revised form in *22 Versuche über einen Dichter*, ed. Eva Hesse, Frankfurt 1968.

did we ever get to the end of Doughty :
The Dawn in Britain ?
perhaps not
'Summons withdrawn, sir.'
(being aliens in prohibited area)
clouds lift their small mountains
before the elder hills.

The most important development, however, is that of the
two-term technique of the haiku or one-image poem into a
complex, pluralistic technique which holds the vast material
together, and Professor Miner quotes from the same *Vorticism*
essay : 'I am often asked whether there can be a long imagiste or
vorticist poem. The Japanese, who evolved the hokku, evolved
also the Noh plays. In the best "Noh" the whole play may
consist of one image. I mean it is gathered about one image. Its
unity consists in one image, enforced by movement and music.
I see nothing against a long vorticist poem.'

And from Pound's note to *Suma Genji*, one of the plays he
translated (1916) : 'At least, the better plays are all built into
the intensification of a single image : the red maple leaves and
the snow flurry in Nishikigi, the pines in Takasago, the blue-
grey waves and wave pattern in Suma Genji, the mantle of
feathers in the play of that name, Hagoromo.'

Here Pound, and Earl Miner, seem to be using 'image' in the
more literal sense of one visual thing, rather than in the
metaphoric sense, as in the haiku. In this sense the unifying
images in *The Cantos*, as Earl Miner says, are many and well-
known (the Odyssean and Dantesque journey, the raising of the
dead, the sacred influence of light, the heavenly visitor—indeed
the *tennin* of the *Hagoromo* is actually fused with the moon
nymph, the Virgin Mary and Venus in C.80—and the word
hagoromo is juxtaposed in the margin of C.36, Cavalcanti's
Canzone). The concentration, the separation of the image from
the abstract statement, the emphasis on natural images (qualities
stressed in *A Few Don'ts*) are, Miner tells us, all outstanding
characteristics of Japanese poetry, and he relates these to

Pound's definition of an image as 'that which presents an intellectual and emotional complex in an instant of time' (*A Few Don'ts*, 1913, *Lit. Essays*, 1954).

Elsewhere Pound says : 'The Image can be of two sorts. It can arise within the mind. It is then "subjective". External causes play upon the mind, perhaps; if so, they are drawn into the mind, fused, transmitted, and emerge in an Image unlike themselves. Secondly, the Image can be objective. Emotion seizing upon some external scene or action carries it intact to the mind, and that vortex purges it of all save essential and dominant or dramatic qualities, and it emerges like the external original.'[1]

This not very helpful division between subjective and objective somewhat confuses the issue, but the last sentence about purging the image 'of all save the essential and dominant or dramatic qualities' really does express what Pound so staunchly stood for and mostly achieved. Even so, not all Japanese haiku poems seem to fall into Earl Miner's definition, nor are all Pound's haiku-like poems equally successful. The Metro poem is often cited as *the* example of the Poundian image, but personally I do not find it all that remarkable, at least, compared with what was to come, though better than *Piccadilly* (where there is no metaphoric idea), and better than a previous version of a similar idea :

> A soul curls back,
> Their souls like petals,
> Thin, long, spiral,
> Like those of a chrysanthemum curl
> Smoke-like up and back from the
> Vavicel, the calyx . . . etc.[2]

This earlier version is of course a simple comparison with 'like' (which is then used twice again). The Metro poem is a double metaphor : faces = petals, crowd = black bough. It is

[1] *And as for Imagisme*, The New Age, XVI/13, Jan. 28, 1915.
[2] *Effects of Music upon a Company of People—I* (*Ripostes*, 1912, fortunately omitted from later collections).

therefore richer and very succinct. And it achieves its effect by means of juxtaposition or apposition with colon, one of Pound's favourite early methods. The apposition avoids the clumsy 'like' or the over-emphatic 'is/are'. But the effect is oddly static. For what is missing is the verb. And here it is worth quoting Donald Davie's comment on two lines cited by Hugh Kenner:[1]

> Swiftly the years beyond recall
> Solemn the stillness of this spring morning.

Kenner quotes Empson on this 'haiku': 'My feelings of transience are held in tension with my desire to linger amid present pleasures, as the flight of time is in tension with the loveliness of this Spring morning.'

Kenner has been considering the classic metaphor 'the ship ploughs the waves', in relation to what Aristotle calls 'analogy' (A is to B as C is to D), and finds four elements (as against the usual modern division of metaphor into 'tenor' and 'vehicle' or 'metaphor' and 'proper term') : the ship becomes a plough, the waves become a field. Donald Davie, however, finds six, i.e. two more in the verb: the action of ploughing, the action of sailing.[2] Kenner comments on the 'haiku': 'The presence of two purely emotional [juxtaposed] components among the requisite four does not differentiate this in principle from the entirely "objective" metaphor, "The ship ploughs the waves".'

Davie says: 'No; but the absence of two components out of the requisite six—this does make a difference. What are missing are the verbs, hence the syntax. Where the verbs should be, the ploughing or the sailing, we have only the yawning vagueness of "held in tension with". Significantly what we get is only a state, an immobile grouping, not an action, a dynamic trans-

---

[1] *The Poetry of Ezra Pound* (London 1951) p. 87. The two lines are misdescribed and treated as a haiku. They are in fact the first two lines of an eight-line poem by T'ao Ch'ien as translated by Arthur Waley (*170 Chinese Poems*, London 1918).

[2] Donald Davie, *Articulate Energy—An Enquiry into the Syntax of English Poetry* (London 1955), ch. IV, 'Syntax as Action: Ernest Fenollosa'.

ference of energy' (*op. cit.*). But of course it could be argued that the dynamic moment of transition is supposed to happen in the reader's mind, being merely suggested.[1]

Three critics plus myself on two lines may seem rather a load of commentary, but it does point up the weakness of the Image as first used by Pound, a weakness which is occasionally apparent also in *The Cantos*, despite Pound's dramatic evolution towards a more dynamic function for the Image. Which brings us, at last, to Fenollosa and the ideogram.[2]

I shall not deal here with the vague nonsense that Fenollosa talked about Shakespeare rarely using the 'weak' copula *is* and using many more transitive verbs than intransitive, the transitive being better.[3] Nor shall I venture into the non-classical sinologue's scorn for Fenollosa as 'a small mass of confusion' (George Kennedy, Yale; or similarly J. Paulhan in *La preuve par l'étymologie*, Paris, 1953). Pound, as has so often been levelled against him, was often influenced by the 'wrong' (i.e. unorthodox) books, and the important thing is what he did with them.

This is not to say that Fenollosa is all nonsense and that Pound miraculously turned him into sense. On the contrary, the point about all Pound's interests and enthusiasms is that he could see what was good, and above all what he could use.

For it has been objected that a modern Chinese would not see or feel the juxtaposed elements in an ideogram as 'alive'

---

[1] I have dealt with this small dispute of the 4 or 6 elements in *A Grammar of Metaphor*, ch. IX, pointing out that although Kenner in a way misses out on the action, Davie over-emphasizes it, since the whole advantage and strength of a verb metaphor like *ploughs* lies in the fact that it relates directly to the noun, 'changing' it, and that we do not have to be aware of the action being 'replaced', as we do have to be aware of what a noun metaphor 'replaces' or 'points back to'. E.g. in 'the meadows *laugh*' we do not have to 'replace' *laugh* with 'are full of flowers', the effect is immediate.

[2] *The Chinese Character as a Medium of Poetry—An Ars Poetica, with a Foreword and Notes by Ezra Pound*, London 1936. Reprinted without the Foreword and Notes in *Instigations*, 1920. Pound was working on the Fenollosa papers during the Winter of 1913–14 and after.

[3] See my *A Grammar of Metaphor*, London 1958.

(e.g. the two legs in 'man' or the four legs in 'horse', or the eye + two legs in 'sees'—the eye moving through space), any more than we 'feel' the original etymologies in most of our words. This objection is simply not valid here. For one thing people vary enormously. I cannot vouch for the Chinese, but many of us are aware of the original meanings of, say, *psychosomatic* or *hydroelectric*, or that *silly* once meant blessed (selig) or that *to be* came from *bhu*, to grow, even if we don't all 'know' that, say, *imbecile* once meant 'not supported by a stick'. And writers tend, in their own dotty way, to be almost as interested in these things as their pet abominations the philologists. Witness Joyce.

Fenollosa saw poetry in the ideogram, and whether Professor Kennedy or a modern Chinese now also sees it or not is irrelevant. He saw that to picture 'Spring' as 'the sun underlying the bursting forth of plants' is beautiful and above all active (even if that is not what the ideogram in question originally represented— and I wouldn't know); he saw that the ideogram ming, for bright, brightness, brightens/shines—one of Pound's favourites,

which, he said, present the sun and moon together (明)[1]

serves as noun or verb or adjective according to context (e.g. the sun-moon of the cup, the cup sun-moons, the sun-moon cup), and said : 'there is no possible confusion of the real meaning, though a stupid scholar may spend a week trying to decide what "part of speech" he should use in translating a very simple and direct thought from Chinese into English'; and he saw that the chief verb for 'is' not only means actively 'to have' but 'shows by its derivation that it expresses something even more concrete, namely "to snatch from the moon with the hand". Here the baldest symbol of prosaic analysis is transformed into a splendid flash of concrete poetry.'

It is this kind of 'seeing' which has enabled Pound to 'translate' Confucius in a way that brings him alive to us instead of making him sound like an idiot. It is not merely a question of

[1] See p. 95, n. 2.

choosing one supposedly original 'concrete' component of an ideogram and translating that literally, but of capturing the poetry in the juxtaposition of components by means of live and active, not dead, words and syntax, even if the juxtaposed elements make up an abstraction. One only has to compare Waley's and Pound's translations of *The Analects* to grasp the principle, even without knowing any Chinese :

Analects, Bk. IX. 30
Waley: The flowery branch of the wild cherry
How swiftly it flies back!*
It is not that I do not love you;
But your house is so far away.
The Master said, He did not really love her. Had he done so, he would not have worried about the distance.†

* When one pulls it to pluck the blossom. Cp. Song 268.1. Image of things that are torn apart after a momentary union. Evidently a verse from some song not included in own Book of Songs.

† Men fail to attain to Goodness because they do not care for it sufficiently, not because Goodness is 'far away'.

Pound: 1. The flowers of the prunus japonica deflect and turn, do I not think of you dwelling afar?
2. He said: It is not the thought, how can there be distance in that?

Which becomes a single line in C.77, flanked by two ideograms[1] :

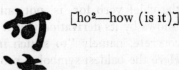

[ho²—how (is it)]

'How is it far if you think of it?'

[yuan³—far]

[1] The line in English recurs later in the Canto, the ideograms alone gloss a passage in C.80.

THE ADEQUATE SYMBOL

Waley's footnotes are of course necessary in a scholarly translation, but the interpretative bits ought not to be, indeed the second line of the poem, superfluously glossed by the footnote, is better than Pound's learned version, yet Pound distils Waley's four lines into one phrase. And in the Master's comment, Pound exactly contradicts Waley (who is no doubt right), or rather, he goes a step further, condemning the idea of distance, and produces, out of the ideogram, poetry, where Waley is flat-footed.

Analects, Bk. I/1
Waley: The Master said: to learn and at due times to repeat what one has learnt, is that not after all a pleasure? That friends should come to one from afar, is this not after all delightful? To remain unsoured even though one's merits are unrecognized by others, is not that after all what is expected of a gentleman?

Pound: 1. He said: study with the seasons winging past, is not this pleasant?
2. To have friends coming in from far quarters, not a delight?
3. Unruffled by men's ignoring him, also indicative of high breed?

Which becomes in C.74:

> To study with the white wings of time passing
> is not that our delight
> to have friends come from far countries
> is not that pleasure
> nor to care that we are untrumpeted?

Analects XV/6
Waley: The Master said, Straight and upright indeed was the recorder Yü!* When the Way prevailed in the land he was (straight) as an arrow; when the Way ceased to prevail, he was (straight) as an arrow. A gentleman indeed is Ch'ü Po Yü.† When the Way prevailed in

his land, he served the State; but when the Way
ceased to prevail, he knew how to 'wrap it‡ up and
hide it in the fold of his dress'.

* Having failed to persuade Duke Ling of Wei to use the services
of Ch'ü Po Yü, the recorder Yü gave directions that when he (the
recorder) died his body should not receive the honours due to a minister,
as a posthumous protest against the Duke Ling's offences. The story is
told in *Han Shih Wai Chuan*, 7, and many other places.

† Ch'ü Po Yü left Wei owing to the tyrannical conduct of Duke
Hsien in 559 B.C. No tense is expressed in the first clause. I say 'is'
because in XIV, 26 Ch'ü Po Yü appears to be still alive. It is, however,
not very probable that he was, as legend asserts, still alive when Confucius visited Wei in 495 B.C.

‡ His jewel; i.e. his talent.

Pound: 1. He said: Straight, and how! the historian Yu.
Country properly governed, he was like an arrow;
country in chaos he was like an arrow.

2. Some gentleman, Chu Po-yu! Country decently
governed, he is in office; when the government is
rotten he rolls up and keeps the true process inside
him.

The first verse appears as one cryptic unpronouned line in C.80:

in Fano Caesaris[1] for the long room over the arches
olim de Malatestis
            wan   caritas   *ΧΑΡΙΤΕΣ*
and when bad government prevailed, like an arrow,
fog rose from the marshland
            bringing claustrophobia of the mist . . .

This insistence on the active elements in juxtaposition is a
key insight of Fenollosa. Every sentence is a 'plot', a trans-

[1] Cp. C.30, letter from Girolano Soncino, printer, to his patron Cesare
Borgia, about new type fonts, from Fano, with a pun on Cesare and on Fano:
'Here working in Caesar's fane' (the Church of Caesar), printing representing the end of the Church's authority based on faith, ritual, magic,
and the Borgias representing the materialistic church (this comes
immediately after the Madame ULE or Madam Matter passage about
Lucrezia Borgia), the Christian distrust of matter having over-emphasized
its importance to the detriment of spirit or 'process'.

ference of force from one unit to another (farmer pounds rice).
'A true noun, an isolated thing, does not exist in nature. Things
are only the terminal points, or rather the meeting points, of
actions. . . .' And later: 'Fancy picking up a man and telling
him that he is a noun, a dead thing rather than a bundle of functions! A "part of speech" is only *what it does*. . . . Like nature, the
Chinese words are alive and plastic, because *thing* and *action*
are not formally separated. . . .'

Thus it is not the supposedly concrete components of the
ideogram which so influenced Pound, as has often been said,
although Pound did insist on the concrete in theory. Fenollosa
admits that the pictorial clue cannot always be traced, and that
combinations now frequently contribute to a phonetic value.
'But I find it incredible that any such minute subdivision of the
idea could ever have existed alone as abstract sound without the
concrete character. It contradicts the law of evolution.' This is
linguistically meaningless, but he goes on: 'Complex ideas arise
only gradually, as the power of holding them together arises.'
Elsewhere in the essay he insists that in order to deal with
abstract thought Chinese passed through exactly the same
process as did every other language, i.e. the process of metaphor, 'the use of material images to suggest immediate relations.'

And this too is another key insight which further developed
Pound's poetics. 'The whole delicate substance of speech is built
upon substrata of metaphor. . . . But the primitive metaphors do
not spring from arbitrary *subjective* processes [his italics]. They
are possible only because they follow objective lines of relations
in nature herself. *Relations are more real and more important than
the things which they relate*' [my italics].

I am not too sure about the first part of that quotation, at least
I think that the poet's metaphor, as opposed to the spontaneous
popular metaphor, is to some extent arbitrary and to a large
extent subjective, but I'll come to that in a minute. The
last sentence, however, is vital to our understanding of *The
Cantos.*

In a more general way, too, there are phrases in Fenollosa
which strike one retrospectively as having surely affected Pound

very deeply: 'poetry, language and the care of myth grew up together'. . . . Or: 'Languages today are thin and cold because we think less and less into them. . . . Nature would seem to have become less like a paradise and more and more like a factory.' Or, on a word which has lost the embryonic stages of its growth because of the feeble cohesive force of our phonetic symbols: 'It does not bear its metaphor on its face. We forget that the personality once meant, not the soul, but the soul's mask. This is the sort of thing one cannot possibly forget in using the Chinese symbols.' Or again: 'Thus a word [in Chinese], instead of growing gradually poorer and poorer as with us, becomes richer and still more rich from age to age, almost consciously luminous. Its uses in national philosophy and history, in biography and in poetry, throw about it a nimbus of meanings. These centre about the graphic symbol. The memory can hold them and use them.'

Nevertheless, there is something in Fenollosa that doesn't quite gell, and I have a feeling that Pound misunderstood it, as have the many commentators who take Pound's statements about it without referring back to Fenollosa. It has to do with logic and the so-called scientific method, and it is important because it affects the very basis of Pound's thinking.

Fenollosa is against mediaeval logic, with which he seems to equate all European logic as 'a kind of brickyard . . . baked into little hard units or concepts', conveniently labelled, which we then pull out and stick together 'into a sort of wall called a sentence by the use either of white mortar for the positive copula "is" or of black mortar for the negative copula "is not". In this way we produce such admirable propositions as "A ring-tailed baboon is not a constitutional assembly." '

Fair enough, as a joke against the scholastics. But he goes on:

'Let us consider a row of cherry-trees. From each of these in turn we proceed to take an "abstract", as the phrase is, a certain common lump of qualities which we may express together by the name cherry or cherry-ness. Next we place in a second table several such characteristic concepts: cherry, rose, sunset, iron-rust, flamingo. From these we abstract some further common quality, dilutation or mediocrity, and label it "red" or "redness". It is evident that this process of abstraction may be carried on indefinitely and with all sorts of material. We may go on for ever building pyramids of attenuated concept until we reach the apex "being".'

This passage—or rather the cherry-rose-flamingo bit—is constantly cited via Pound's use of it in his account of the ideogrammic method (e.g. by Kenner, p. 83):

'By contrast to the method of abstraction, or of defining things in more and still more general terms, Fenollosa emphasises the method of science, "which is the method of poetry", as distinct from that of "philosophic discussion", and is the way the Chinese go about it in their ideograph or abbreviated picture writing . . .

'. . . when the Chinaman wanted to make a picture of something more complicated, or of a general idea, how did he go about it?

'He is to define red. How can he do it in a picture that isn't painted in red paint?

'He puts (or his ancestor put) together the abbreviated pictures of

ROSE	CHERRY
IRON RUST	FLAMINGO

'That, you see, is very much the kind of thing a biologist does (in a very much more complicated way) when he gets together a few hundred or thousand slides, and picks out what is necessary for his general statement. Something that fits the case, that applies in all of the cases.

'The Chinese "word" or ideogram for red is based on something everyone KNOWS.' *ABC of Reading*, ch. 1.

WOW! In fact the Chinese word for red (ch'ih⁴) is composed of man + fire = flushing from anger, but no matter. More important, this was not the point of what Fenollosa was saying. Pound is *praising* this juxtaposition of concrete things for the eventual 'picking out' of an abstract idea, whereas Fenollosa (somewhat contradicting his earlier ecstasies about the ideogram) is castigating the whole process: 'we may go on for ever building pyramids of attenuated concept. . . .' And he goes on, very clearly: 'At the base of the pyramid lie *things*, but stunned, as it were. They can never know themselves for things until they pass up and down among the layers of the pyramids. . . . We take a concept of lower attenuation, such as "cherry"; we see that it is contained under one higher, such as "redness". Then we are permitted to say in sentence form, "Cherryness is contained under redness", or for short "The cherry is red". If, on the other hand, we do not find our chosen subject under a given predicate we use the black copula and say, for example, "The cherry is not liquid".'

Fenollosa gives another (somewhat absurd) example from classical logic and goes on to say that the sheer loss and weakness of this method are flagrant. 'Even in its own sphere it can not think half of the things it wants to think. It has no way of bringing together any two concepts which do not happen to stand one under the other and in the same pyramid.'

And he adds that it is impossible to represent change in this system or any kind of growth, and that, e.g. the conception of evolution could make no headway 'until it [the conception?] was prepared to destroy the inveterate logic of classification'. Far worse, such logic cannot deal with any kind of interaction or with any multiplicity of function. Science, on the other hand, 'fought till she got at the things'. Its work is done at the base of the pyramid, not the apex. It discovers 'how functions cohere in things. . . . The true formula for thought is: The cherry tree is all that it does.'

Clearly Fenollosa is castigating one particular type of logic, which he sets up against the spirit of science, adding that poetry agrees with science and not with logic. And in the sense that the creative spirit works in similarly mysterious ways in both, this is true. It is also true, as Lévi-Strauss has amply demonstrated, that one particular way of classifying phenomena is not the only way and that the so-called 'primitive' logics are not inferior to ours, merely different. Pound certainly tried to break through to a different kind of logic, as when he called poetry 'a sort of inspired mathematics, which gives us equations, not for abstract figures, triangles, spheres, and the like, but equations for the human emotions.'[1]

But this is not really what Fenollosa seems to mean, nor what Pound has derived from him. Moreover, Pound seems to have further misinterpreted Fenollosa on the method of science, if indeed Fenollosa has not himself misunderstood it. For unless the biologist in Pound's example is extremely dim, it is surely quite clear that no true scientist in fact proceeds in the passive way described, but on the contrary, he brings into his observation not only all the accumulated discoveries, data, dicta or tested theories of the past, including prejudices to be overcome, but also a preconceived theory to be tested against the facts. And this surely must be true of any scientist, even one of modest stature. In other words, as regards the mental equipment he has inherited, he is necessarily a man of his time, in advance maybe, but not so much in advance that, for instance, Archimedes could have exclaimed in his bath: 'Eureka! $E = MC^2$'—however much he had observed the facts when out of his bath. More important, the scientist does not merely observe. As Karl Popper says: 'The belief that science proceeds from observation to theory is still so widely and so firmly held that my denial of it is often met with incredulity. . . . But in fact the belief that we can start with pure observation alone, without anything in the nature of a theory, is absurd; as may be illustrated by the story of the man who dedicated his life to natural science, wrote down everything he could observe, and bequeathed his priceless collection of observations to the Royal Society to be used as inductive evidence. This story should show us that though beetles may profitably be collected, observations

[1] *The Spirit of Romance* (1910), p. 5. This passage is said to have sown the seed for Eliot's 'objective correlative'—an object 'stands for' a subjective state (Mario Praz, *T. S. Eliot and Dante*, Southern Review II/3). Presumably Pound means not just the resulting equation ($a = x$), but the whole process that leads to the result. On poetry and different types of logic, cp. J. Kristeva on *Poésie et Négativité*, in Σημειωτική— *Recherches pour une sémanalyse*, Collection 'Tel Quel', Seuil, Paris 1969.

may not.'[1] Popper goes on to tell how he opened a lecture by asking his physics students to write down everything they observed, and how they asked what he wanted them to observe. 'Observation is always selective. It needs a chosen object, a definitive task, an interest, a point of view, a problem. . . .'

One can't help being reminded at this point of Pound's story about Agassiz and the fish (*ABC of Reading*, ch. 1). The biologist Agassiz showed the student a certain fish and asked him to describe it. The student said it was a sunfish. I know that, said Agassiz, write a description of it. The student returned with the textbook description of the Ichtus Heliodiplodokus. . . . Agassiz again told the student to describe the fish. And so on until the fish decomposed. But by then the student knew all about it. One could argue that Agassiz might have given the poor student, apart from 'a chosen object', at least an interest, a point of view, an order to compare the dead fish and its organisms with the live specimen and its habits, for instance. Agassiz influenced Fenollosa and, like Fabre and Frobenius, forms part of Pound's pantheon of model scientific investigators. Similarly Pound quotes with approval somewhere Karl Bruhn's description of Alexander von Humboldt's 'art of collecting and arranging a mass of isolated facts, and rising thence, by a process of induction, to general ideas'.

I have gone into all this in some detail because Pound's misconception, as well as those of some critics, have created confusion. The idea that mere endless juxtaposition of facts (and of course actions) is what makes up *The Cantos* is very prevalent, and in a sense Pound has lent credence to it, not only in his prose *obiter dicta* ('Damn ideas, anyhow. An idea is only an imperfect induction from fact'), but also within *The Cantos*:

[1] *Conjectures and Refutations: The Growth of scientific knowledge* (London 1963) p. 46. Popper was already saying this sort of thing in 1934 (*Logik der Forschung*, Vienna 1934, translated as *The Logic of Scientific Discovery*, London 1959, cp. pp. 30–1 on deductive testing of theories).

THE ADEQUATE SYMBOL

                    as says Aristotle
    philosophy is not for young men
    their *Katholou* can not be sufficiently derived from
                    their *hekasta*
    their generalities cannot be born from a sufficient
                    phalanx of particulars

                                                        C.74

'A sufficient phalanx of particulars' is indeed the mainspring of *The Cantos*. But we might do well to remember the *ABC of Reading* : 'Any general statement is like a cheque drawn on a bank. Its value depends on what there is to meet it. . . . Even if the general statement of an ignorant man is "true", it leaves his mouth or pen without any great validity. He doesn't KNOW what he is saying. That is, he doesn't know it or mean it in anything like the degree that a man of experience would or does.' Pound, when dealing with the abstract or general statement, emphasizes a *quality* of knowledge (cp. 'nothing matters but the quality of the affection'), and this quality consists in its having been lived, experienced. This subjective experience also lies behind his ideogrammic juxtapositions, it forms his 'sinceritas'. And indeed Pound brings the creative artist in immediately after the Aristotle passage :

    lord of his work and master of utterance
        who turneth his word in its season and shapes it.

And it seems to me that Hugh Kenner's emphasis, when quoting the Aristotle passage, on the Lockean 'first in the senses' notion, is misleading, or at any rate has misled. 'The mind', he says, 'lays hold of nothing else but particulars.' 'The mind can't know *one* thing by itself. You have to look at a lot of dogs to extract the idea of 'dog' with any validity.'[1] No doubt, but as applied to *The Cantos* it gives the impression that all Pound is doing is stringing a lot of dogs together. And of course Kenner does not mean this at all, since he has stressed, and brilliantly,

                    [1] *The Poetry of Ezra Pound*, London 1951.
                              113

the *moving* image. But this emphasis of Kenner's seems to have led Ivor Winters to challenge Pound's method on the grounds that it inverts the Lockean notion: 'since all ideas arise from sensory impressions, all ideas can be expressed in terms of sensory impressions. But of course they cannot be: when we attempt this method, what we get is sensory impressions alone, and we have no way of knowing whether we have had any ideas or not.'[1]

Donald Davie has refuted Winters, at least with specific reference to Canto 91.[2] I would like to refute him in more general terms here, with reference to the image and the ideogrammic method I have discussed in this chapter.

For Pound does not, as any glance at *The Cantos* will show, merely juxtapose one sensory impression after another. It is true that he insists on the particular, so that it is, for instance, from documents that the portrait of Sigismundo Malatesta— one of Pound's 'factive personalities', an 'entire man'— emerges in Cantos 8–11; so that his Odyssean journey is called a *periplum* [for *periplus*], from the discovery that the geography of Homer's *Odyssey* seemed absurd when referred to a map, but turned out to be accurate by the *periploi* of the Phoenician travellers:[3]

> periplum, not as land looks on a map
> but as sea bord seen by men sailing
>
> C.59

But these particulars are all of actions, of things that people do, or of things that people say about things that people do. Moreover, it is the juxtaposition that creates the idea, by metaphoric replacement, as for instance in the splendid anecdote of a lady buttonholing Henry James:

[1] *The Function of Criticism* (Denver 1957) p. 47.
[2] *Poet as Sculptor* (London 1965) pp. 217–29.
[3] Victor Bérard, *Les Phéniciens et l'Odyssée* (Paris 1902), *Les Navigations d'Ulysse* (Paris 1927–8).

in those so consecrated surroundings
   (a garden in the Temple, no less)
   and saying, *for once*, the right thing
namely : 'Cher maître'
to his chequed waistcoat, the Princess Bariatinsky,
as the fish-tails said to Odysseus, ἐνὶ τροίη. . . .

C.79

Admittedly this is done with an 'as' and parallel construction, rather than pure juxtaposition (in fact Pound is not nearly so a-syntactical as has been suggested). But the reference is to Odyssey XII. 189, the siren-song, and the fact that this is paralleled to 'Cher maître' as the best way to flatter James is not just a stray particular, it is an idea emerging from two particulars—a small and local idea perhaps (which is why I chose it), but an active and suggestive idea, as well as a very funny one.

And this is surely the point. Pound at his best is not, by any standards, getting together hundreds of slides and waiting for some general statement to emerge. Even in prose he has contradicted himself on this, reminding us that Dante put Aristotle in Limbo, and calling the latter 'Master of those that cut apart, dissect and divide. Competent precursor of the card index' but who 'assembled the collection of state constitutions, seeing clearly that it wd. be *no use unless* someone had the experience and intelligence to know "what to make of it" '. (*Guide to Kulchur*, p. 343—cp. 'not to a schema / "is not for the young", said Arry, stagirite', C.74). Or, 'Academicism is not excess of knowledge; it is the possession of *idées fixes* as to how one shall make use of one's data.' (*Antheil and the Treatise on Harmony*, Paris 1924, p. 16).

Pound shapes his material. It is *his* Sordello, not Sordello. And he shapes it by 'bringing together concepts which do not happen to stand one under the other and in the same pyramid'. It is Pound the poet who sees the similarities in dissimilarities and brings to his material a very individual, and some would say cranky, 'interest, point of view, problem', even a theory, or

115

theories. The fact that, being a poet and not a scientist, he does not *really* test his theories against the facts, but finds what he passionately wants to find, is another question altogether.

Pound is interested in similarities of function, and Fenollosa's essay, had it done nothing else, would have been important for that aspect alone. And it is this 'interest', this 'viewpoint' or 'theory' Pound brings to his observation, which gives his poetry at its best that quality of energy and motion, of going on from one image to the next, the reader unable to pause because the next thing is so unexpected and yet so revealing. And this despite the non run-on lines, the tendency to end-stop, the lines often (but by no means always) representing items to be juxtaposed, an endless 'phalanx of particulars'. The activity in the similarity of function overrides the end-stopping—indeed I would argue that too much running-on in the blank-verse way of straight narrative would completely drown the feeling of separateness, of things from different 'pyramids' being brought together, the feeling, in fact, of the *dis*similarity in similarity which makes the excitement of metaphor as much as does the sense of similarity in dissimilarity. So that when these similarities of function, of ideas in action, fail us (or seem to fail us because something is said in a language we don't understand, or by means of an allusion we do not grasp) the thing goes flat and 'static'. For even the light, dazzling us in the later Cantos with their glimpses of his paradise, is juxtaposed for its function. The neo-platonic 'light' philosophers (Erigena, whom Pound has saying *Omnia quae sunt sunt lumina*;[1] Duns Scotus; Ocellus and others) are often juxtaposed with Cavalcanti's *virtu* of *intelletto d'amore*, and with the ming ideogram, or hsien[3] ('analyzed' as tensile light), as in the image of a priest in green vestments who becomes the stone green scarab over which Egyptian prayers were said :

[1] In fact part of a question : 'Sed fortasse quis dixent : Quomodo omnia, quae sunt, lumina sunt?' from Joannis Scoti Expositiones super Ierarchiam Caelestem S. Dionysii, ch. I (Migne 122, col. 128), as shown by Walter Baumann in *Ezra Pound and Hermann Broch, A Comparison* (Seminar IV, 2 Feb. 1968).

and this day the air was made open
   for Kuanon of all delights,   [goddess of mercy]
   Linus, Cletus, Clement
       whose prayers,
the great scarab is bowed at the altar
the green light gleams in his shell
plowed in the sacred field and unwound the silk worms early
       in tensile 顯 [^1]

in the light of light is the *virtù*
   'sunt lumina' said Erigena Scotus
   as of Shun on Mt Taishan
and in the hall of the forebears
       as from the beginning of wonders
the paraclete that was present in Yao, the precision
in Shun the compassionate
in Yu the guider of water   [the three early Sage Kings]
                   C.74

'The sun and moon, the total light process 明 [ming], the

radiation, reception and reflection of light : hence the intelligence. Bright, brightness, shining. Refer to Scotus, Erigena, Grosseteste and the notes on light in my Cavalcanti.'

                   (*Confucius*, p. 20)

He even makes Ocellus (who said 'To build light') say 'Make It New', the by then well known ideogram Pound adopted as one of his mottoes—'In letters of gold on T'ang's bathtub : As the sun makes it New / Day by Day make it New' (*The Great Digest*, with Pound's footnote about the ideograms representing renew sun sun renew, 'That is to say a daily organic vegetable and orderly renewal; no hang over', the first and last

[^1]: hsien³, two silk threads exposed to the sunlight so that they become visible. The original text has the ming ideogram here (明) in error.

117

ideogram being, according to Pound, 'ax, tree and woodpile').[1]
So already in C.53 :

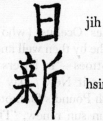

> Tching prayed on the mountain and
>   wrote MAKE IT NEW
> on his bath tub
>   Day by day make it new
> cut underbrush,
> pile the logs
> keep it growing.
> Died Tching aged years an hundred,
> in the 13th of his reign.
>   'We are up, Hia is down.' [2205–1766 dynasty]
> Immoderate love of women
> Immoderate love of riches,
> Cared for parades and huntin'.
>   Chang Ti above alone rules.
> Tang not stinting of praise :
>   Consider their sweats, the people's
> If you wd/ sit calm on throne.

By the end of Canto 94 this has become :

> The boat of Ra-Set moves with the sun.
>   'To build light
>   'To build light

               jih

               hsin

            said Ocellus

[1] The story of T'ang Tching is told in Mailla (*op. cit.*), Vol. XI,
1760 B.C.

CHAPTER EIGHT

'His true Penelope was Flaubert,
He fished by obstinate isles'

———————✦✦✦——————

But how obstinate? Is there a point when *le mot juste* becomes *injuste* when too arbitrarily (or unpregnantly) juxtaposed?

'I am not saying that Baudelaire is nothing but cabbages cast upon satin sofas, but merely that in many poems one "unpleasant" element is no more inevitable than another.' *Imaginary Letters*, Paris 1930 (reprinted from the wartime *Little Review*).

Hugh Kenner has shown that Pound's juxtapositions are not in the least arbitrary or merely incongruous in this way, not 'any decayed cabbage cast upon any pale satin sofa', but based on motion of some kind, a central plot-device such as Aristotle's *peripeteia* or reversal of the situation, e.g. at its simplest: 'Fu I loved the high cloud and the hill, / Alas he died of alcohol' (*Lustra*).[1]

This in fact isn't always so, particularly in *Lustra*, where some of the so-called *hokkus* just don't come off, precisely because of the cabbage/sofa element, e.g. *The New Cake of Soap*:

> Lo, how it gleams and glistens in the sun
> Like the cheek of a Chesterton.

An explicit but feeble comparison. On the other hand it has been argued by Dekker that the fusion of Actaeon (who was changed into a stag for profaning Diana), with Piere Vidal (who disguised himself as a wolf for love of the lady Loba), in C.4 is a bit arbitrary and doesn't come off, but he seems to me to

[1] Hugh Kenner, *The Poetry of Ezra Pound*, London 1951.

ignore the unifying active elements (both hunters become the hunted, Actaeon by his own dogs, Vidal by Loba's husband and his hounds). Some juxtapositions in *The Cantos* no doubt do appear to be arbitrary, but not this one. The fusion is subtly done with a colon, Actaeon's ecstatic vision of Diana being evidently experienced by Vidal in his madness :

> Ivory dipping in silver,
> Not a splotch, not a lost shatter of sunlight.
> Then Actaeon : Vidal,
> Vidal. It is old Vidal speaking,
> > stumbling along in the wood,
> Not a patch, not a lost shimmer of sunlight,
> > the pale hair of the goddess.
>
> The dogs leap on Actaeon . . .[1]

I shall return to the theme of metamorphosis. For the moment, I want to take up another point from Kenner, that of Chêng ming, which he deals with separately, and which at first sight may seem to contradict the whole idea of metaphoric fusion.

The Chêng ming characters (chêng[4] ming[2]) make their first appearance at the end of C.51 and recur five times in the next nineteen Cantos (the China Cantos and the Adams Cantos) which deal with good and bad government. It comes from the *Analects* and means the rectification of language in the sense of using precise verbal definitions :

'If the terminology be not exact, if it fit not the thing, the governmental instructions will not be explicit, if the instructions aren't clear and the names don't fit, you can not conduct business properly.'[2] Digest of the Analects, *Guide to Kulchur* (1938) [chêng ming given].

' "Get the mot juste before action" ' (C.85). Or under Kang Hsi, juxtaposed with France of the Enlightenment :

[1] Cp. *Piere Vidal Old*, described and cited in ch. 3, p. 46.
[2] Cp. *ABC of Reading* (1934) pp. 32–4, where Pound insists that good writers are necessary to keep the language efficient: 'A people that grows accustomed to sloppy writing is a people in process of losing grip on its empire and on itself.'

Gerbillon and Bouvet, done in manchu
        revised by the emperor as to questions of style
A digest of philosophy (manchu) and current
Reports on the mémoires des académies
des sciences de Paris.
Quinine, a laboratory set up in the palace.
He ordered 'em to prepare a total anatomy, et
qu'ils veillèrent à la pureté du langage
et qu'on n'employât que des termes propres
                (namely CH'ing ming)[1]

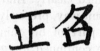
C.60

Or in eighteenth-century America:

to show U.S. the importance of an early attention to language
for ascertaining the language

Chêng[4]
Ming[2]

C.68

Or as Pound expressed it in his final version of the *Ta Hio*
(*Great Digest*):
'The men of old, wanting to clarify and diffuse throughout the
empire that light which comes from looking straight into their
heart and then acting, first set up good government in their own

[1] The French is from Mailla, except that Pound has, reasonably, put
qu'ils for *qui* and omitted *y*: 'Tchang-Tching & Petsin, qui furent
chargés de ce soin, travaillèrent aussi, par ses ordres, à une anatomie
complette, dans laquelle indiquant les diverses sortes de maladies, ils
proposoient des remèdes efficaces pour les guérir; mais ils ne firent
qu'ébaucher cet ouvrage, auquel Patomin (le jésuite *Parennin*), par les
mêmes ordres, donna ensuite toute la perfection dont il étoit susceptible,
avec le secours d'habiles Tartares *Mantchéous*, & de l'empereur même, qui
veillèrent à la pureté du langage & à ce qu'on y employât que des termes
propres. (Mailla XI/p. 365).

states . . . and wanting to rectify their hearts, they sought precise verbal definitions of their inarticulate thoughts (the tones given off by the heart). . . .'

In other words *le mot juste*. Pound comes back to this notion over and over again, equating it with 'the paraclete and verbum perfectum: sinceritas', and even with the Na-khi ceremony of Mùan bpö: 'Without ²muan bpo / no reality' (C.104).[1] Pound was long haunted by the concern for verbal exactitude. Already in 1913 (*The Serious Artist*) he was saying :

'As touching the fundamental issues : The arts give us our data of psychology, of man as to his interiors, as to the ratio of his thought to his emotions, etc. etc. etc.

'The touchstone of an art is its precision.'

So with science :

No science without clear definitions

C.104

Pound does on the face of it appear to believe that the thing exists, and need only be named clearly. And although he does use poetic context in a brilliant way, precisely to shift meanings and effect metamorphoses, part of his mind belongs to the Socratic dispensation, which continued for 2000 years, and in which 'truth' 'beauty' 'justice' etc. were the names of things which were held to exist independently, so that the meanings remained fixed forever. These in the modern view are mystical assumptions.

Well of course Pound is a mystic in a sense. Nevertheless, the

[1] This refers to Baller p. 43. See also *The Muan Bpö Ceremony or the Sacrifice to Heaven as practised by the Na-khi*, article by J. F. Rock, Monumenta servica Vol. XIII, Pechino 1949, Journal of Oriental Studies of the Catholic University of Peking. Boris de Rachewiltz, in *L'Elemento magico in Ezra Pound* (Milano 1965) p. 11, quotes the phrase 'We have not committed the wrong of not calling the objects by their proper names . . .' as coming from this ceremony, but in fact it comes from another, the ²Muan ³nder ³ssu (heaven wrong tell, the confession of sins to heaven). Rock: 'Now follows ²Muan ³nder ³ssu . . . the wording is the same as that chanted at ²Muan ¹bpö, except the following : We have not committed . . . etc.' As usual Pound seems to have got at the essence or gist by instinct.

very people who condemn these assumptions and praise science for ignoring them often fall into the same trap of believing, or saying that scientists believe, that facts remain unaltered by the language they are described in, a belief which is as absolutist as the mystical assumptions condemned. The facts can only be the facts as apprehended by man, and these do alter considerably when a working hypothesis (e.g. Newton's), which *works* for a long time, is upset by a new equation or a new working hypothesis (e.g. Einstein's), just as Einstein's theory has been to a certain extent modified by Heisenberg. Even the principle that the observed thing is altered by the instrument observing it is nearer to the artistic than to any old-fashioned mechanistic view. This is why Pound, with an unerring if ignorant instinct, coupled art with science and even love or 'the quality of the affection' against philosophy, misquoting Thibaut de Champagne to prove his point about 'the conception of love, passion, emotion as an intellectual instigation; such as Propertius claims it; such as we find it declared in the King of Navarre's "De fine amor vient science et beauté" and constantly in the troubadours.'[1]

And this is also why most discussions of Pound which drag in nominalistic points of philosophy seem to me irrelevant, as for instance Hugh Kenner and others on Pound's so-called Cartesianism. If philosophy must be dragged in, Pound seems to me much closer, in some, not all, respects, to Husserl's Phenomenology, which in various ways and with very different repercussions, totally altered the French novel from Sartre onwards—the reason why perhaps writers like Michel Butor and Denis Roche have become interested in Pound. Phenomenology eliminated the old dichotomy between realism and idealism by reducing a world, once regarded as transcendental,

[1] *Remy de Gourmont* (*Instigations*, 1920, *Lit. Essays*, 1954). The poem is by Thibaut de Champagne, King of Navarre, and 'science' should read 'seance', 'fine' should read 'bone': 'De bone amor vient seance et bonte, / Et amors vient de ces deus autresi. / Tuit troi sunt un, qui bien i a pensé ...' (a complex metaphor, further developed, on the Trinity in secular love: God is love, Christ goodness, Holy Spirit grace (seance) (ed. Axel Wallensköld S.A.T.F. 1925).

to its manifestations within the consciousness. Husserl accused Descartes of perpetuating the illusion of a separation between the self and its experience, and distinguished two time-series, 'cosmic' time (that of science and public reference) and 'phenomenological' time (that of individual experience). The traditional novel is written in the former, the Nouveau Roman in the latter, going back to the Platonic belief that imagination is memory, denying chronology, regarding time as an indivisible flux, a duration which consists in constant modifications of the contents of consciousness, one 'now' being intimately connected with past 'nows', the narrator's perceptions therefore being depicted as relations (not I and an object but I seeing/ misseeing, remembering/misremembering an object). Objects are thus intended, i.e. evidence of the mind's intentionality, significant for the consciousness in which they appear, while subjective and objective become fused in this intentionality.[1] The writer does not 'tell' but presents, leaving the conceptualization to the reader. All this has been consistently misunderstood with regard to the Nouveau Roman and I cannot go into it here, but I mention it briefly in order to show that any discussion of Pound in terms of Descartes makes very little sense, since it throws us right back into outdated epistemological dichotomies of a nominalistic/prenominalistic character. William Fleming[2] for example, blames all Pound's errors on the insidious influence of the French language, itself undermined by the Cartesian notion that what is clearly expressed is true. Actually Descartes said clearly *conceived*, a specific activity of what he calls intuition (the undoubting conception of an unclouded mind) which, although or rather because inextricably bound up with language, Descartes was forced to separate entirely from what he regarded as the totally unreliable sense experience, to be doubted systematically. Fleming's essay is hardly worth refuting, but

[1] See John Sturrock, *The New French Novel* (O.U.P., London 1969). The 'newer' Nouveau Roman has moved away from Phenomenology into more complex spheres.

[2] *Pound and the French Language*, in *Ezra Pound: Perspectives*, ed. Stock, Chicago 1925.

Kenner for instance quotes Descartes' *Principles of Philosophy* 1–74:

'We can scarcely conceive anything with such distinctness as to separate entirely what we conceive from the words that were selected to express it.'

and comments:

'It is easy to sense the presupposition that words are at best a makeshift dress for the transcendent. M. Maritain has remarked brilliantly on Descartes' "angelism". Speech has become a mark of man's brutish condition, not, as was held with tireless reiteration from the time of the Stoics to that of Francis Bacon, the sign of his distinction from the brutes. Shakespeare is of the old dispensation. His Prospero taught Caliban to speak instead of giving him a geometrical toy to contemplate.

'These citations may help us to see that there can be no *mot juste* unless there can be a real and supple relation between the world consisting of congeries of intelligible things, and language considered as a structure of directed perceptions. . . .'[1]

Kenner seems to be implying that for Pound the word is the thing, though the word 'supple' just gets him out of it. Nevertheless he goes on to quote Eliot: 'Language in a healthy state presents the object, so close to the object that the two are identical.'[2]

This seems naïve, at odds with philosophy and linguistics, nor does it accord with Kenner's insistence in later essays that Pound's material is constantly affected by the drama of the artist observing it in time and place. It is true that in the quotation from *The Analects* which Pound translates in *Guide to Kulchur*, the terminology must 'fit the thing'. But in the later translation from the *Ta Hio* he clearly means that it must accurately represent the inarticulate thoughts. In *The Serious Artist* he says:

'By good art I mean art that bears true witness, I mean the art that is most precise. You can be wholly precise in representing a

---

[1] *The Poetry of Ezra Pound*, London 1951, p. 98.
[2] T. S. Eliot, *Selected Essays* (on Swinburne).

vagueness. You can be wholly a liar in pretending that the particular vagueness was precise in outline.'

Later in the same essay he goes on :

'Also there are various kinds of clarity. There is the clarity of the request : Send me four pounds of ten-penny nails. And there is the syntactic simplicity of the request : Buy me the kind of Rembrandt I like. This last is an utter cryptogram. It presupposes a more complete and intimate understanding of the speaker than most of us ever acquire of anyone. It has as many meanings, almost, as there are persons who might speak it. To a stranger it conveys nothing at all.

'It is the almost constant labour of the prose artist to translate the latter kind of clarity into the former; to say "Send me the kind of Rembrandt I like" in the terms of "Send me four pounds of ten-penny nails".'[1]

Or :

quand vos venetz al som de l'escalina

$\eta\theta\sigma\varsigma$ gradations

These are distinctions in clarity

ming 明 these are distinctions

C.84

[1] Pound is here groping towards the modern distinction, derived from the English philosopher J. L. Austin, between 'statement' (*énoncé* or *constatatif*, the objective elements of language) and 'utterance' (*énonciation* or *performatif*, the subjective elements in language or Jacobson's 'shifters'). For the performative see J. L. Austin, *How to do Things with Words* (O.U.P., London 1962). For further elaboration see Emile Benveniste, *Problèmes de Linguistique Générale* (Gallimard, Paris 1966, Part 5), Tzvetan Todorov, *Les catégories du récit littéraire* in *Communications* 8 (Seuil, Paris 1966). The simplifications of linguists and literary critics, however, have been much further analysed by the psychiatrist Jacques Lacan, for whom the 'subject', as signifier, though belonging to *énonciation*, is constantly being dislodged and reconstituted by *l'Autre* (as opposed to *l'autre*), that is, Freud's 'other scene', the unconscious. See *Ecrits* (Paris 1967), via the *Index raisonné des concepts majeurs*, under II, *Le moi, le sujet* : esp. II/C, *La structure du sujet*.

In other words, the terminology (and for Pound this includes rhythm, sonority, image, even pictogram as well as *le mot juste*) must *mime* the thing, whether that thing be an emotion, an action, an abstract idea even, a mode of perception, a saying by someone in a certain context, or 'a red glow in the carpet of pine spikes' (C.79).

For not only are form and content indivisible (a banality by now I hope), but they are also one with the perceiver. I could adapt Buffon and say *le style c'est l'homme qui voit la chose*, but this hardly goes far enough. In all communication the recipient as well as the emitter is part of the message (Jacobson), but there is also a constant dissolution of subject and sign, particularly in poetic language (Kristeva) and in the language of the 'subject' or patient in psychoanalysis so brilliantly discussed by Lacan. Hence Lacan's adaptation, *le style c'est l'homme à qui l'on s'adresse* (*Ecrits*, p. 9). But since the 'je' or, in this case the 'on', is constantly shifted by '*la chose*' in the sense of '*la chose freudienne*' (*Wo es war, soll ich werden*, mistranslated as 'Where the id was, there the ego shall be'), i.e., a 'truth' that 'speaks' yet is for ever fleeting and ungraspable; and since '*l'inconscient, c'est le discours de l'Autre*' (Freud's 'other scene', needed by the subject to constitute itself, called also by Lacan *le trésor des signifiants*), it might be possible, in relation to poetic language at least, to adapt both formulae and say *le style c'est l'homme à qui l'on adresse la chose.*[1]

All this may appear to some readers directly to contradict, not only the idea of metaphor (which illogically brings two dis-

[1] Jacques Lacan, *Ecrits*, op. cit., pp. 401 ff (see also *Index raisonné*); Julia Kristeva, *Poésie et négativité*, op. cit., p. 111; Roman Jacobson, *Linguistics and Poetics*, in *Style in Language* (ed. T. A. Sebeok, New York 1960, M.I.T. Paperback 1966). Pound's use of 'personae' is of course very relevant here. On a simpler level, it is interesting that Pound is so often cited by the modern exponents of *lecture-écriture* as having grasped the essentials early. E.g. H. Meschonnic, *op. cit.*, ft. 5: 'La poétique devrait mener vers une pédagogie nouvelle de la littérature : celle que prévoit Ezra Pound dans *Comment lire* et dans *l'ABC de la lecture*—de l'écrit comme un des fonctionnements du langage et non activité esthétique ... , pratique de l'écrivain homogène au vivre, critique homogène à l'écriture.' (pp. 154–5).

similar things together), but also Fenollosa's view (which I did not quote wholly so as not to confuse the issue) that 'languages today are thin and cold because we think less and less into them. We are forced, for the sake of quickness and sharpness, to file down each word to its narrowest edge of meaning. Nature would seem to have become less like a paradise and more and more like a factory.'

Clearly Fenollosa is against paring down a word to its narrowest edge of meaning *because* he is for metaphoric thinking. And so, of course, is Pound, in his own way, for metaphoric thinking. He is in fact much more metaphoric even in the conventional sense than is often realized, as I shall show in a moment, or as 'a red glow in the *carpet* of pine spikes' shows; and it is wholly misleading to speak of a Canto 'consisting, as Mr. Eliot says of Dante's *Commedia*, of an extended metaphor with no room for metaphoric expressions in the detail',[1] especially since Kenner is so very acute on ideogram and metaphor being ultimately identical in function.

On the face of it, for those not used to metaphoric thinking, the bringing together of dissimilar things, whether cabbages and sofas or Helen of Troy and Eleanor of Aquitaine, is not *le mot juste*. Indeed here is Pound himself appearing to confirm this view:

'The Renaissance sought a realism and attained it. It rose in a search for precision and declined through rhetoric and rhetorical thinking, through a habit of defining things always "in terms of something else".' *Gaudier-Brzeska* (1916) p. 141.

This could still mean endless defining of terms. But in the *Cavalcanti* essay he is even more specific:

'Unless a term is left meaning one particular thing, and unless all attempt to unify different things, however small the difference, is clearly abandoned, all metaphysical thought degenerates into a soup. A soft terminology is merely an endless series of indefinite middles.'

Clearly Pound is not here concerned with the poetic image but with very particular philosophical terms in Cavalcanti. In a sense his concern for *le mot juste*, echoed throughout *The Cantos*,

[1] Hugh Kenner, *The Poetry of Ezra Pound*, London 1951, p. 206.

parallels today's Hegelian and anti-Aristotelian stand in stressing difference as opposed to similarity as a basis of thought, while his concern for the image takes up Aristotle's definition of metaphor (similarity in dissimilarity) and at the same time parallels the modern scientific notion of the organism as a whole, as opposed to the object in absolute isolation.

But even without recourse to philosophy, Pound's ideas of language are perfectly clear. In *How to Read* (1928) (*Lit. Essays*, 1954) he had divided poetry into three aspects: *melopeia* (a musical property over and above the meaning of words but bearing upon their meaning); *phanopeia* (the casting of images upon the visual imagination); and *logopeia* or the dance of intellect among words, employing words not only for their direct meaning but taking count in a special way of habits of usage, of the context we *expect* to find with the word, its usual concomitants, of its known acceptances, and of ironical play'. This last prefigures the modern notion of *écart* or deviation, not from a non-existent 'norm' in everyday language, but from the expectation aroused syntactically within the text. [1]

I hope I have made it clear in the last chapter that Pound does in fact 'unify different things', but that each of these things is clear and particular in itself, as is the verbal idea arising out of the union. And what the quotations from *Gaudier-Brzeska* and the *Cavalcanti* essay show is the real reason for Pound's insistence on precision: to avoid soup. Or as he said of poetry in *A Retrospect* (1918):

[1] Leo Spitzer was the first exponent of style as deviation from some undefined 'norm'. See also G. N. Leech, who is traditional in this respect (*Linguistics and the Figures of Rhetoric*, in *Essays on Language and Style*, ed. R. Fowler, Routledge, London 1966). S. R. Levin has divided deviation into quantitative (frequency) and qualitative (agrammatical). (*Deviation—Statistical and Determinate—in Poetic Language*, in *Lingua* 12, 1963, and other essays in *Word* 21, 1965, and *Proceedings of the IXth International Congress of Linguists*, Mouton, The Hague 1964). M. Riffaterre prefers deviation in relation to (*a*) a norm present in the text (syntagmatic) and (*b*) a norm absent from the text (paradigmatic). For these terms see p. 132, ft. n. 1. See also H. Meschonnic, *Pour la poétique* (Gallimard, Paris 1970) who is against the undefined norm outside the text.

'. . . its force will lie in its truth, its interpretative power (of course, poetic force does always rest there); I mean it will not try to seem forcible by rhetorical din, and luxurious riot. We will have fewer painted adjectives impeding the shock and stroke of it. At least for myself, I want it so, austere, direct, free from emotional slither.'

And this is the point. The precision not only kills the *fioritura* and the rhetoric ('Reality and particularization! The Elizabethans themselves began the long series of sins against them') ;[1] but also the sentimental identification with nature of the nineteenth century, the 'pathetic fallacy' of snowdrops pleading for pardon etc. And above all it kills the self-melodramatization, the perpetual comment, as Kenner has so well expressed it in a comparative analysis of passages from Housman, Tennyson and Pound: 'The excitement with which the Pound passage infects us is on the contrary that of inspecting, as it were from behind glass, a new and exotic mode of being. The presentation is not "cold", the Lotus-eater feelings are there. But the passion is attached to cognition, not submersion.'[2]

Pound's ideal is indeed like Flaubert's, that of impersonality, a concept all the more difficult to understand because no one could call his style 'neutral', not in the sense supposedly developed by the modern novelist—in fact Sartre has shown that this is a chimera, that Camus' 'neutral', 'transparent' style is itself a convention and an individual feature. But the critical notion that a poem must be a statement 'about' an emotion personally experienced by the poet simply cannot be applied in a direct way to Pound, who is on the one hand, a bit like the novelist, re-creating other people's emotions, and on the other retelling, as the epic writer retells the old familiar stories, indeed as every writer until fairly recently always did retell: Chaucer, Shakespeare, did not and were not expected to invent their basic plots, nor did the eighteenth-century poets invent their themes, etc. And he is retelling not merely in order to express

---

[1] *Notes on Elizabethan Classicists, Egoist*, 1917–18, *Lit. Essays*, 1954.
[2] *The Poetry of Ezra Pound, op. cit.*, pp. 66–9.

his own emotions (though that too, indirectly), but in order to bring alive the great lost myths within us, the myths of love and beauty and creativity, of destruction, death, decay, in other words the myths of change, the myths of metamorphosis.

'The undeniable tradition of metamorphosis teaches us that things do not remain the same. They become other things by swift and unanalysable process', he wrote in *Affirmations* (1915), and already in a note to a poem in *A Quinzaine for this Yule* (1908) : 'I think from such perceptions as this arose the ancient myths of the demi-gods; as from such as that in "The Tree" (*A Lume Spento*), the myths of metamorphosis.'

This driving-force in Pound has been much written about.[1] I want here to examine how it is effected in practice, through the 'precise verbal definitions'. How, in other words, one thing or person becomes another. 'Let us consider the osmosis of persons' he says in Canto 29 (juxtaposing the phrase with the lethargy of American suburban life), but he starts considering it much earlier. Moreover he is not merely throwing any cabbage *onto* any sofa. If Pound were concerned with cabbages and sofas the cabbage would no doubt have become the sofa, or the cabbage and sofa would have become something else.

And it is this fundamental insight that metaphor *changes* things, that metaphor *is* metamorphosis, which I want to emphasize here, for critics tend to treat metamorphosis as a theme separate from the ideogrammic method. Even in a very simple example, like that of Henry James and the sirens given earlier, James is momentarily changed into Odysseus. These changes are part of the paradigmatic whole, they are integral, not decorative, they do not stop one in one's tracks like a bit of *fioritura*. The wider orchestration or what Pound called the 'great bass' has been dealt with by many critics, notably by

---

[1] e.g. Sister Bernetta Quin, *The Metamorphoses of Ezra Pound*, in *Motive and Method in The Cantos of Ezra Pound*, ed. Lewis Leary, Col. U.P., New York 1954. Also George Dekker, *Sailing after Knowledge* (London 1963), Chs. III & IV.

Kenner, and I shall be touching on it later, but now I want to concentrate on the individual chords, or paradigms. [1]

Since there is no functional force in a mere juxtaposition of a cabbage with a sofa, Pound does not normally touch this kind of thing with a barge-pole. Or even with the churn-stick of his Vorticism (Pound's dots) :

> So-Shu churned in the sea, So-Shu also,
>   using the long moon for a churn-stick . . .
> Lithe turning of water,
>   sinews of Poseidon   C.2

I only quote that to show that Pound uses quite straight-forward syntactic means of turning the crescent moon (Artemis being also a pivotal force in *The Cantos*) into a churn-stick (C using A as B) and waves into sinews (apposition with comma); *as well as* juxtaposition (the two metaphors, one from China and one from the Mediterranean, are juxtaposed with dots, a pause slightly longer than in direct juxtaposition or in apposition with a comma.

More frequent (and ultimately Biblical in origin) is the use of parallel construction, with or without *and*, which implies an equation of terms :

> Builders had kept the proportion,
>   did Jacques de Molay
> know these proportions
> and was Erigena ours ?   C.90

[1] For students still unfamiliar with this now current term, so much more useful and scientific than musical analogies, see Roman Jacobson's seminal essay, *Two Aspects of Language and Two Types of Aphasia*, in *Fundamentals of Language* (The Hague 1956). To summarize : Jacobson developed de Saussure's basic distinction between elements in presence (combination, contiguity) and elements in absence (similarity/difference, selection from a wider code), which in linguistics, semiology, anthropology, psychology etc. works all the way up from the signifier to the signified (in language, from the phonic to the semantic levels). Contiguity, which functions horizontally, is now called syntagmatic (e.g. figures of syntax); selection, which functions vertically, extra- and inter-contextually (e.g. metaphor, allusion) is now called paradigmatic. Poetry is the projection of the paradigmatic axis onto the syntagmatic.

i.e. were they both initiates to the mysteries of perfect proportions? The use of *and* as a link implying similitude is so frequent in Pound, especially in the earlier Cantos, I shall not emphasize it further. To return to apposition, Pound is also fond of apposition with a colon, which is very distinct, as categoric in tone, almost, as the copula (A is B). For instance, at the end of the Wanjina/Ouan Jin passage quoted in ch. 1:

> paraclete or the verbum perfectum : sinceritas

C.74

It is true that by then, through the echoing orchestration, we have already equated sinceritas itself with Kung's call for precise verbal definitions (Chêng ming) through looking straight into the heart, the latter represented either by the ideogram of an

eye with legs 見 = look + heart, contracted to 忄 as

found in shên[4] , or by the ch'êng[3] ideogram for sincerity:

'the precise definition of the word', 'the sun's lance over the precise

spot' as Pound glosses it (誠). Therefore the paraclete

is equated with the verbum perfectum by means of *or*, both are equated with sinceritas by means of colon, and sinceritas is already equated in our minds with Kung's idea of it.

Or again, from Canto 98, also quoted in ch. 1:

> 'By Hilaritas,' said Gemisto, 'by hilaritas : gods . . .

Giorgio Gemistus Plethon was the neo-platonic Renaissance philosopher whom Sigismundo Malatesta met and whose bones he later brought to his Tempio in Rimini. He is one of Pound's 'light' philosophers (cp. *Guide to Kulchur*, pp. 45, 160, 224, 263, 313). It is typical of Pound's attitude to the gods that they must be joyous, funny as well as beautiful and in due season serious. In *Guide to Kulchur* (p. 141) he translates an Italian prayer for 'serenity' (that is, fair weather) as 'shalt show to us through the calm sky the hilarity of thy face' and comments: 'Hilarity. The Italian is just that: *l'ilarità del Tuo Volto.*' At the end of the Fenollosa essay he also explains the ideogram for

Spring 春 as: 'Spring season, hilarity, wantonness—

looks like sun under man and tree, but early forms all show sun under growing branches, profuse branches and grass.'

But with Gemisto too the colon equation has been preceded a few pages earlier by a more unequivocal statement with the copula:

> But Gemisto: Are gods by hilaritas;
> and their speed in communication.   C.98

In fact Pound by no means despises the copula (e.g. 'His true Penelope was Flaubert' from *Mauberley*), and one can see the contrast of the direct copula and apposition in a passage where Pound might seem to fall into a non-organic, non-functional cabbage/sofa type of juxtaposition. This is the famous bit in C.29, which temporarily expresses Pound's view of the female as strong but chaotic until 'formed' by the male force—a notion from de Gourmont[1] which is contradicted throughout the Cantos as we shall see:

> Wein, Weib, TAN AOIDAN [song]
> Chiefest of these, the second, the female
> Is an element, the female
> Is a chaos
> An octopus
> A biological process
>   and we seek to fulfill . . .
> TAN AOIDAN, our desire, drift . . .   C.29

[1] *The Natural Philosophy of Love* (*La Physique de l'Amour*), transl. Ezra Pound, London 1904, 1926, 1957, introd. viii & p. 60.

The female / Is an element, the female / Is a chaos. The subject and copula are twice repeated, and metrically stressed, for the less outrageous equations. The next two, in juxtaposition, are not in themselves outrageous : [the female is] an octopus and a biological process. But these are also juxtaposed to the first. Yet a chaos is not (prosaically) an octopus, nor is an element a chaos. To make them so the poet needs the strength of the copula, hence the early emphasis, which projects forward and holds the contradiction together in a tension more subtle than if he had used the copula throughout.[1]

A successful example of apposition, because helped by parallel construction, is the famous passage of sexual illumination and ritualistic initiation in Canto 47. The parallel construction is the repetition of 'has entered' (the light has entered/have I entered); the apposition is of 'Io!'—a Greek invocation for aid often used by Pound, but also, as it happens, the first person pronoun in Italian—and 'the light' :

> The light has entered the cave. Io! Io!
> The light has gone down into the cave,
> Splendour on splendour!
> By prong have I entered these hills :
> That the grass grow from my body,
> That I hear the roots speaking together,
> The air is new on my leaf,
> The forked boughs shake with the wind.
> Is Zephyrus more light on the bough, Apeliota
> more light on the almond branch?
> By this door have I entered the hill.

The light becomes 'I', and in a way also becomes the instrument prong, so that 'I' *is* the prong, the hill becomes the woman, nature, the gate is the initiation and the physical entry. Or again in the Ouan Jin/Wanjina change quoted in ch. 1,

[1] I note in passing another type of metaphor by means of an echoing phrase : 'Chiefest of these' which echoes St Paul's 'and the greatest of these is charity', thus turning wine, women and song into faith, charity and hope, the usual order altered.

Pound uses the copula 'is' with a conversational 'shall we say'
plus 'or':

> but Wanjina is, shall we say, Ouan Jin
> or the man with an education
>
> C.74

who created the named, and whose mouth was removed etc.,
though this in itself is juxtaposed with Odysseus, whose name
is no-man (see p. 10). The 'shall we say' adds more than a
casually apologetic tone for the preposterous equation, it adds
an impersonal tone as well.

I now want to pass on to one of the main methods of metamorphosis in *The Cantos*, one which is peculiarly Poundian and
which towards the end he refines to a subtle perfection: namely,
the pronouns (use and absence of).

We already noticed the strange, unspecified but also shifting
use of 'they' and 'we' in some of the early poems (ch. 4, *The
Flame*, *In Durance*). Another example is perhaps clearer in *The
Return* ('See, they return ...' where 'they' = Gods of the wingèd
shoe). And there is, of course, the 'I' of the 'personae'. One is
reminded of Fenollosa's description of the five different ideograms for 'I' in Chinese, an emphatic I (spear in hand), a weak
and defensive I (five + mouth, holding a crowd by speaking),
a private I (concealment), an egotistical I (cocoon + mouth, who
takes pleasure in his own speech), and a self used only when
talking to oneself.

Certainly the 'I''s in the *Cantos* are usually someone else,
Odysseus in C.1, Acoetes in C.2 etc., which makes the Poundian
I all the more personal when it does appear: e.g. 'my Sordello'
at the opening of C.2, or of course the very moving personal
break-through in *The Pisan Cantos* and the *Fragments*. Sometimes we are specifically told who the 'I' is, especially when
Pound is quoting from documents, e.g. in *Rock-Drill*, C.94:
'an image that I, Philostratus, saw', from Apollonius of Tyana
by Philostratus; or, very similarly, in C.96, from Paul the
Deacon's History of the Langobards (Bk. III, ch. xii):

> & inviting his wife to drink from her father's skull
> (Cunimundus) a cup which I, Paulus, saw . . .

More usually, however, we are not told who the 'he' or the 'she' or the 'her' etc. is, it is clear only from *what they do or say*. This enables Pound to make extraordinary shifts. You can see what I mean by first going back to the 'said Ocellus' quotation at the end of the last chapter, where, instead of a pronoun we have a named person, Ocellus, who nevertheless *says* 'Make it New' (in ideograms), i.e. he is changed into T'ang, or if you prefer, into Pound quoting T'ang; at the same time what Ocellus actually said, 'to build light', which he also says here, is thereby equated with 'as the sun makes it new, day by day make it new'.

But here is a simpler example with a pronoun. In C.4 the myths of violent destruction through total self-absorption are brought in, and the classical tale of Itys, Tereus, Procne and Philomela is changed into the troubadour story of Cabestan, whose heart was placed on a dish before Soremunda by her jealous husband. Similarly Itys was killed by Procne and served to Tereus as a revenge for seducing Procne's sister Philomela and cutting out her tongue, Philomela later becoming a swallow. After a snatch from Horace, the name Itys is changed into a swallow's cry with a colon. The 'she' who goes to the window is first Procne, then Soremunda, who replies: 'No other taste shall change this' (*Seigner, ben m'avetz dat si bon manjier que ja mais non manjarai d'auctre*, in the Provençal story):

> Et ter flebiter, Itys, Ityn!
> And she went toward the window and cast her down,
> 'All the while, the while, swallows crying:
> Ityn!
> 'It is Cabestan's heart in the dish.'
> 'It is Cabestan's heart in the dish?
> 'No other taste shall change this.'
> And she went toward the window,
> the slim white stone bar
> Making a double arch;

Firm even fingers held to the firm pale stone :
Swung for a moment,
        and the wind out of Rhodez   [in Aveyron,
Caught in the full of her sleeve.   N.W. of Toulouse]
                                          C.4

This is a relatively simple example. Later I shall be analyzing
(for other reasons) a passage from C.91 where one pronoun is
made to work for half a dozen or so metamorphoses. Meanwhile
I would like to attempt a fuller paradigmatic reading by
returning to the Leucothea motif; for although it makes only
brief and fragmentary appearances at the end of *Rock-Drill* and
in *Thrones*, so that Kenner's and my treatment may seem to
have turned it into a major theme, it does have the advantage
that you are already familiar with it. Moreover, Pound's
technique is, precisely, to create such a wide poetic space in
our minds, by constant reference beyond the immediate context,
that every minor theme becomes part of the major.

The first appearance is the 'get rid of paraphernalia' passage
(see p. 16) in C.91, where Leucothea is not so named, except as
a sea-gull and as daughter of Cadmus :[1]

They who are skilled in fire

    shall read   旦   tan the dawn   [sun above horizon]

Waiving no jot of the arcanum
        (having his own mind to stand by him)
As the sea-gull Κάδμου Θυγάτηρ said to Odysseus
KADMOU THUGATER
                        'get rid of paraphernalia'
                            TLEMOUSUNE
                        [distress, patience]

[1] *Odyssey*, Bk. V, 333 ff.; l. 337, αἰθυίη δ'εἰκυῖα (like a seagull).
The Rouse translation, which Pound once checked, has 'shearwater' not
seagull : 'But Ino saw him. She was a daughter of Cadmus, and a beautiful
creature; once a mortal who spoke with a human voice, now she is
Leucothea the white Sea Goddess, to whom the gods have given the honour
of the salt deeps. She pitied Odysseus as he was buffeted about in this

And that even in the time of Domitian
        one young man declined to be buggar'd.
'Is this a bath-house?'   [Philostratus VIII/iii]
ἄλλοτε δ' αὖτ' Εὖρος Ζεφύρῳ εἴξασκε διώκειν   [Odyssey V/332]
      'Or a Court House?'
Asked Apollonius
        who spoke to the lion
           charitas insuperabilis
                          C.91

They who are skilled in fire are the chthonic powers and those
shades in the underworld who nevertheless do not lose sight of
the light, such as Tiresias, who lived both as man and woman
and said that woman gets more pleasure in love, thus causing
Hera to lose her bet against Zeus, so that she put him in Hades,
but to whom Persephone gave the power of prophecy: 'Who even
dead, yet hath his mind entire' of C.47 and—in Greek—C.39,
echoed here in 'having his own mind to stand by him', itself
perhaps an echo of the Chinese ideogram for sincerity which

Pound sees as a man standing by his word (信). Nothing is

left of Tiresias except a thin shade and this power of prophecy
arising out of the full knowledge he had of life. He has got rid
of paraphernalia, as does Apollonius who like Adonis in C.47
had power over wild beasts. And the white sea-goddess (who
in a sense also represents Aphrodite) advises Odysseus to do
the same.

The first occurrence of the line 'my bikini is worth your raft'
is cryptic to say the least, for there is no mention of Leucothea.
It comes twelve lines below the reference to Apollonius and the
Court House and is enfolded, after allusions to Pythagoras and
Porphyrius (which I skip), between Heydon, a seventeenth-
century occultist who saw signatures in nature ('Secretary of
Nature, J. Heydon', see p. 146 n.) and an echo of the four TUAN

miserable way; like a great shearwater she rose on the wing from the
waves, and perching on the wreck she said . . .'

or foundations of C.85 (benevolence, rectitude, manners and knowledge—the latter being the ability to distinguish right and wrong—from p. 4 of Couvreur), the FOUR in itself echoing the four gates of Wagadu: 'now in the mind indestructible, Gassir, Hoooo Fasa, / With the four giants at the four corners / and four gates mid-wall Hooo Fasa / and a terrace the colour of stars', C.74. It is interesting to note in this connection that the psychoanalyst Jung also insisted on the number four as expressing the ultimate divine reality within us, the 'quaternity', adding the Mother Goddess or female force of Santa Sophia or eternal wisdom (beloved of Pound) to the trinity of creator, spirit and word. And of course here too it is a goddess who saves Odysseus:

> Formality. Heydon polluted. Apollonius unpolluted
> and the whole creation concerned with 'FOUR'
> 'my bikini is worth your raft'
> And there be who say there is no road to felicity
>
> C.91

The next reference is at the beginning of C.93, which opens with hieroglyphics followed by a quotation from the Egyptian king Khaty:[1]

> 'A man's paradise is his good nature'
>
> sd/ Kati.
>
> 'panis angelicus' Antef
> two $\frac{1}{2}$s of a seal
> having his own mind to stand by him
> Καδμου θυγάτηρ
> Apollonius made his peace with the animals.

Antef lived at the time of Usertsen I, and left rules such as 'Give bread to the hungry, beer to the thirsty', which fore-

---

[1] Khaty or Nebkeure Akhtoi (2252–2228 B.C., 11th dynasty), who wrote a letter of advice to his son which became a classic. See Clark Emery, *Ideas into Action*, Univ. of Miami Press 1958, p. 157; and de Rachewiltz, see p. 141 n. 1.

shadow those of later religions.[1] This is juxtaposed with Tiresias again, then with an arceviscovo who fumbled under his ample overcloaks and produced a box of LaTour chocolates for Pound's small daughter (a private allusion), which Pound, very impressed, calls here a cornucopia, continuing:

> or as Augustine said, or as the Pope wrote to Augustine
> 'easier to convert after you feed 'em'
>
> C.93

Angelic bread is thus juxtaposed with paradise, which is a man's good nature, or fidelity to his word, or his mind entire, without paraphernalia (Kadmou thugater comes in here), which gives one power over nature (the flux for Odysseus, wild beasts for Apollonius); but which is real bread too, as opposed to dogma, real charity, the basics of life, stripped of paraphernalia. Canto 95, which opens with 'Love, gone as lightning, / enduring 5000 years', deals in a nugget-like way with themes that have recurred throughout *The Cantos* (Van Buren unsmearing Talleyrand, John Adams, Deus as *anima mundi*, guilds in Byzantium, Alexander who paid the debts of his soldiery, etc.), then suddenly:

> Queen of Heaven bring her repose
> Κάδμου Θυγάτηρ
> bringing light *per diafana*
> λευκὸς Λευκόθοε
> white foam, a sea-gull
> And damn it there were men even in my time
> Nicoletti, Ramperti, Desmond Fitzgerald
> (the one alive in 1919)
> That the crystal wave mount to flood surge

近 chin[4]

---

[1] Boris de Rachewiltz, *L'Elemento magico in Ezra Pound*, Milano 1965, p. 33. ' "Panis angelicus" Antef' refers to *Massime degli antichi Egiziani*, ed. de Rachewiltz 1954.

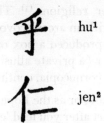

hu[1]

jen[2]

the light there almost solid.

C.95

The Queen of Heaven who is asked to bring her repose is always, for Pound, Diana, with sometimes Christian overtones, as here. In Cantos 74 and 76 the moon-goddess as the voice which comes to him in his tent was juxtaposed with 'la scalza' (the bare-footed one), a real girl perhaps but also Diana on her silver crescent, who says 'and they have broken my house' and 'I still have the mould'; also with Cunizza, Sordello's lady who freed her slaves on a Wednesday and is placed in Paradise by Dante: 'Eurus, Apeliota as the winds veer in periplum / "Io son' la luna"'. Cunizza / as the winds veer in periplum' (C.74); 'Cunizza qua al triedro, / e la scalza, and she who said: I still have the mould. . . . la scalza: "Io son' la luna / and they have broken my house" ' (C.76). In C.80 the same phrase 'Io son' la luna' is identified with the moon goddess on her silver crescent ('disse: "Io son' la luna". / Con piedi sulla falce d'argento'), which is also one of the representations of the Virgin Mary, whose supposed house at Ephesus was found, thus creating a tourist trade for the silversmiths who previously had made money on the cult of Diana: 'At Ephesus she had compassion on silversmiths / revealing the paraclete / standing in the cusp / of the moon et in Monte Gioiosa . . .'. But here the Queen of Heaven is directly juxtaposed with Cadmon's daughter, the white sea-goddess (the moon-goddess as well as Venus being intimately linked with the sea), λευκὸς Λευκόθοε, white Leucothoe—a mistake for Leucothea, see below), 'white foam, a sea-gull', Homer's Ino or Leucothea having arisen out of a crest of foam like a bird; the light she brings is *per diafana*, recalling Cavalcanti's *amore* which 'In quella parte dove sta memora / Prende suo stato si formato chome / Diafan dal lume d'una schuritade', first translated by Pound as 'Formed there in manner as a mist of light / Upon dusk' and later, in C.36, as 'Formed like a diafan from light on shade'. This light of pure memory brings in briefly the names of old friends, among whom Nicoletti, the Prefetto at Gardone (during the Salo republic) who said 'La donna, la donna, la donna' in C.74 and 'this wind out of Carrara / is soft as *un terzo cielo*' in C.76. The crystal wave, brought in as so often with Pound's images of light, with a subjunctive, is thus here both the wave that brings Leucothea and the crystal wave of all ecstatic visions in the Cantos (e.g. the vision of the coral nymph in C.2), the wave, in fact, that bears Aphrodite as she lies about her father at the end of C.23, echoed in C.25: ' "as the sculptor sees the form in the air ... / "as glass seen under water, / "King Otreus, my father ..." / and saw the waves taking form as crystal' (Pound's dots).

Chin[4] hu[1] jen[2] is part of a stock Chinese phrase li[4] hsing[2] chin[4] hu[1] jen[2], meaning 'to act in earnest is near to benevolence' (li[4], strength, for Pound, energy; hsing[2] to act; chin[4] near; hu[1] to; jen[2] benevolence), which Pound gives whole in C.93 and glosses neoplatonically as 'holding that energy is near to benevolence'. There the ideograms come just after the 'Lux in diafana' passage ('Creatrix, oro ... have compassion ... by the horns of Isis-Luna, / Compassion ...')[1] which ends with the child (his daughter) in the basilica:

> J'ai eu pitié des autres.
> Pas assez! Pas assez!
> For me nothing. But that the child
> walk in peace in her basilica,
> The light there almost solid.

Thus energy, even in the sense of governing the world as well as one's passions, is near to benevolence, which is made to

[1] Quoted in full on p. 263.

echo compassion, and *pitié*, and Leucothea who had pity on Odysseus, herself merged with both Aphrodite and Diana (who had compassion on silversmiths) and indirectly the Virgin, revealing the paraclete which is the verbum perfectum which is sincerity, stripped of paraphernalia.

The next reference is the bikini, a page later in the same Canto, and is almost as cryptic as its first occurrence, all the more so because Leucothea has so far only been mentioned in Greek, as Leucothoe, which mistake is repeated here:

> 'Are' as Uncle William said 'the daughters of Memory'
> 'Pirandello,
>> because that is the sort of thing that . . .
> that does go on in one's mind.'
>> Whose mind?
> Among all those twerps and Pulitzer sponges
>> no voice for the Constitution,
> No objection to the historic blackout.
>> 'My bikini is worth yr/ raft'. Said Leucothoe
> And if I see her not
> No sight is worth the beauty of my thought.
>
> C.95

Pound here links the historic blackout he is always complaining about (the facts of finance and others, concealed by experts with vested interests etc.) with the blindness of litterati as well as with the flux that overwhelms Odysseus when Leucothea saves him. The 'her' of 'And if I see her not' is beautifully ambiguous: it seems to refer back to Leucothea (who later vanishes under the dark wave), but the two lines are in fact a quotation from Pound's translation of a poem by Bernart de Ventadorn: *s'eu no vos vei, domna, don plus me cal, negus vezers mo bel pesar no val.* There is thus a quadruple paradigm: Leucothea; a personal love; the Confucian idea quoted earlier, 'how is it far if you think of it'; and finally poetry, which saved Pound in the concentration camp at Pisa when he found Speare's anthology on the lavatory-seat:

That from the gates of death,
    that from the gates of death : Whitman or Lovelace
      found on the jo-house seat at that
in a cheap edition! [and thanks to Professor Speare]
hast'ou swum in a sea of air strip
    through an aeon of nothingness,
when the raft broke and the waters went over me,
Immaculata, Introibo
        for those who drink of the bitterness . . .   C.80

Or as Yeats is said to have said (and Blake did say), 'The Muses are daughters of memory' (C.74). Leucothea herself is daughter of Cadmus, creator of the alphabet. Language and memory are Leucothea's bikini. The Canto (95) ends with a description of Odysseus being overwhelmed :

I suppose St Hilary looked at an oak-leaf
(vine-leaf? San Denys,
    (spelled Dionisio)
Dionisio et Eleutherio
Dionisio et Eleutherio
    the brace of 'em
that Calvin never blacked out
      en l'Isle.)
That the wave crashed, whirling the raft, then
Tearing the oar from his hand,
          broke mast and yard-arm
And he was drawn down under wave,
      The wind tossing,
Notus, Boreas,
      as it were thistle-down.
Then Leucothea had pity,
        'mortal once
who now is a sea-god :
         νόστου
γαίης Φαιήκων, . . .'   C.95

The association between St Hilary and the martyrs Dionysius and the deacon Eleutherius (see p. 40, ft. 1) is elliptical: according to John Heydon, St Hilary looked at an oak-leaf,[1] but Pound, playfully linking truth with the god Dionysus, suggests he might have looked at a vine-leaf. But truth can be blacked out, as Odysseus is drawn down under the wave: Nostou gaies Phaiekon, journey to the land of the Phaeacians (see p. 15). And the next Canto, the first of *Thrones*, opens with 'Kredemnon ... / kredemnon ... / and the wave concealed her, / dark mass of great water,' which leads us into the middle ages, Paul the Deacon's History of the Langobards:

> Thusca quae a thure,
> from the name of the incense, in this province is
> ROMA *quae olim* ...
> In the province of Tuscany is Rome, a city which formerly ...

the dots suggesting Rome's former grandeur and later dogma in a masterly ellipsis.

Kenner in his bikini article says that with Leucothea's disappearance here (the wave concealed her) Pound's dealings with the episode cease. In fact they don't (this of course does not affect his argument about the bikini, though Pound does call it a veil later, then a scarf). Three pages later in the same Canto, an obscure reference to 'that sea gull' and the Phaeacians is sandwiched between the Eparch's book (with which Pound has such fun a little later in the Canto, see below) and the errors of the Britons (dealt with, by allusion, in C.91, see ch. 10):

> And the Eparch's book was down somewhere under all of this,
> ΕΠΑΡΧΙΚΟΝ ΒΙΒΛΙΟΝ
> After 500 years, still sacrificed to that sea gull,
> a colony of Phaeacians θῖνα θαλάσσης   [of the sea]
> ALDFRID, King of Northumbria, Nordanhymbrorum
>   defunctus 7 oh 5,
> Aldhelm, against errors of Britons,
>   pro virginity in hexameters ...   C.96

---

[1] Cp. Walter Baumann, *Secretary of Nature, J. Heydon*, in *New Approaches to Ezra Pound*, ed. Hesse, London 1969.

HIS TRUE PENELOPE WAS FLAUBERT

I confess that the 'pregnancy' of these juxtapositions is here lost, at least on me, in the privacy of Pound's personal reading and associations, but clearly language is still in question. 'Here, surely, is a refinement of language' he exclaims five pages later when dealing with the Edict of Leo the Wise (Leo VI, 886–912) or the 'Eparch's Book' as edited in Greek and Latin by Professor Jules Nicole,[1] then he breaks into sudden prose, as if in a brief gesture of defiant despair :

'If we never write anything save what is already understood, the field of understanding will never be extended. One demands the right, now and again, to write for a few people with special interests and whose curiosity reaches into greater detail.'

And he certainly reaches into the greater detail of Nicole's edition (see ch. 12). But here the sea gull still represents the language which saves him, the paraclete to which (the Christians ? the Phaeacians ?) still sacrificed, the magic veil which carries Odysseus across the engulfing sea. The phrase θῖνα θαλάσσης occurs in Od. IV/779 but is probably also an abbreviation of Pound's old favourite θῖνα πολυφλοίσβοιο θαλάσσης (Iliad I/34).[2] It occurs also in the Odyssey, Bk. XIII/220 when Odysseus, having left Phaeacia (and after the Phaeacian ship which escorted him out has turned into a rock), lands without knowing it in his native Ithaca, wakes up and 'paced along the murmuring sea'. Athene comes to him as a young shepherd and he asks her where he is. Athene is of course Odysseus' constant guide in Homer, appearing in many guises (Mentor, or a girl), and always recognized by her eyes (the bright-eyed). Pound has replaced her with Aphrodite [of the sea], also recognized

[1] *Le livre du Préfet*, Geneva 1893.

[2] Cp. Letter to W. H. D. Rouse, translator of Homer, in 1935 :

'Para thina poluphloisboio thalasses : the turn of the wave and the scutter of receding pebbles.

Years' work to get that. Best I have been able to do is cross cut in *Mauberley*, led up to :

> ... imaginary
> *Audition of the phantasmal sea-surge*

which is totally different, and a different movement of the water, and inferior.' (*Letters of Ezra Pound*, ed. D. D. Paige, London 1952.)

by her eyes but also by her walk, as if a sort of waggle ('as by Terracina rose from the sea Zephyr behind her / and from her manner of walking / as had Anchises' C.74, a reference to the Aenead I/405), who is thus still partly the bitch-goddess Athene fights with in the Iliad (XX), but is also, of course, perfect beauty, 'so difficult', the *forma, intelletto d'amore*, the white goddess who saves Pound from being overwhelmed by the flux.

Canto 98 opens:

> The boat of Ra-Set moves with the sun
> 'but our job to build light' said Ocellus:
> Agada, Ganna, Faasa

新   hsin¹

> Make it new
> Τὰ ἐξ Αἰγύπτου φάρμακα
> Leucothea gave her veil to Odysseus
> Χρόνος
> πνεῦμα θεῶν
> καὶ ἔρως σοφίας
> The Temple (hieron) is not for sale.   C.98

The boat of Ra-Set (an Egyptian goddess invented by Pound out of two male gods, one Good, one Evil—a typical gesture against dualism)[1] is juxtaposed with the second appearance of Ocellus + Make It New—this time less succinct because itself folded round an allusion to the city of Wagadu from Frobenius.[2]

The next line, 'out of Egypt medicine' is from Philostratus VII/xxii (Apollonius of Tyana).[3] It is interesting that

[1] Boris de Rachewiltz, *L'elemento magico in Ezra Pound*, Milano 1965); *New Approaches*, Hesse, *op. cit.*

[2] 'now in the mind indestructible', see ch. 1. The theme is recurrent in *The Cantos*, hence the shorthand here.

[3] Conybeare: 'For you may remember the verses of Homer in which he relates [Od. IV/219] how Helen mingled in the bowl of wine certain drugs from Egypt in order to drown the heart-ache of the heroes.'

pharmaka should here be invoked in connection with Making It New. For Plato, who throughout his works *wrote* (like McLuhan) against writing, calls writing a *pharmakon* (a medicine as well as a poison, a foreign body, a drug which puts live memory to sleep), as opposed to the spoken word, the *logos*, which has an utterer, the father, a visible/invisible sun, origin of being (*onta*), the head, the good (*agathon*) and goods, the capital (*pater* means all these things). Writing, in comparison, is infinitely repeatable, the interest on the capital which becomes invisible, an orphan and a parricide, a substitute which has no relation to live reality but only to itself, as a second-hand, third-hand copy of that live reality.[1]

In the *Phaedrus*, Socrates tells a myth about the father of the logos : in Egypt, a god called Theuth (Thoth, the god of writing and death) was the first to discover the science of numbers, geometry and astronomy, as well as games and dice, and writing (*grammata*). He came to Thebes, to king Thamous of Egypt, whose god was also Ammon. Theuth offered him his arts, saying that here was a knowledge which would make the Egyptians more learned and more capable of remembering : 'memory as well as instruction have found their medicine' (*pharmakon*). But the king, after much reflection, replied ('*O teknikôtate Theuth* / Incomparable master of arts') that Theuth as father of written characters, was giving men the very contrary of what he thought. For this knowledge would have the effect of making their souls forgetful, because they would cease to exercise their memory and would rely on writing, which is external, so that they would remember things thanks to foreign imprints (*dia pistin graphes exothen up'allotriôn tupôn*) and not from within, not from their own efforts. 'It is then not for memory but for memorising that you have found a medicine (*oukoun*

[1] This and the next paragraph are indebted to *La pharmacie de Platon*, in *Tel Quel*, Nos. 32, 33 (*Le Seuil*, Paris, Winter and Spring 1968), by Jacques Derrida, who traces the concept of *pharmakon/pharmakeus* (magician)/*pharmakos* (magician and scapegoat) in connection with writing as well as art (pharmakon also means dye) and life/death throughout the works of Plato. Clearly Thoth has affinities with Cadmus.

mnemes, alla upomneseôs pharmakon eures). As for instruction, it is the semblance of it (*doxan*) which you produce for your pupils, and not the reality (*aletheian*) : for when with your help they will fill themselves with knowledge without having received instruction they will seem able to judge things, whereas most of the time they are void of judgment.' (274e–275b).

Thus pronounces the father. Theuth of course does not reply. Nor has he ever replied : we have gone on reproducing replicas of wisdom, truth, reality, our knowledge being not of things but of their traces. Apollonius too, went to Egypt, and had power over animals, but had to face trial stripped of papers.

Literature, for Pound, is thus a saving medicine : and yet it has also been a poison, a reliance on the printed source, upon which he has tried to breathe life, whose phantoms he has filled with blood, made new. Poetry, though printed today, is nevertheless still the most oral and oracular of the literary arts, closest to the logos : thus the paradox, as well as the personal tragedy of Pound, who also attacked, did he not, undue or 'unnatural' interest on capital, and became a 'pharmakos' or scapegoat (see ch. 10).

'Out of Egypt medicine' is at once equated with Leucothea's veil, followed by Chronos (time), pneuma theon (the soul of god) kai eros sophia (and the wisdom of Eros), the whole ending with an echo of one of Pound's favourite phrases in *Thrones*, 'the temple is holy because it is not for sale', which by now has acquired all connotations, the mysteries, art, creation, language, good government of self and state.

Then the passage quoted in Chapter 1 occurs a page later, so I shall give only the first part here :

> And that Leucothoe rose as an incense bush
> —Orchamus, Babylon—
> resisting Apollo.
> Patience, I will come to the Commissioner of the Salt Works
> in due course.
> Est deus in nobis.   and
> They still offer sacrifice to that sea-gull

est deus in nobis
    Χρήδεμνον
She being of Cadmus line,
    the snow's lace is spread there like sea foam ...   C.98

Leucothoe (as opposed to Leucothea) was daughter of Orchamus, descendant of Baal or Belos of Sumerian Babylon. She resisted Apollo's advances, died and was buried, but the sun drew her out of the earth with his rays, as an incense bush. The similarity of the name (both with 'white') has caused Pound either to confuse them or, more likely, to fuse them (though with two typographical errors), since the two stories are given quite distinctly. Here Leucothoe is clearly juxtaposed as a separate entity, with Leucothea as the sea-gull, the paraclete (god) within us, the saving veil and the alphabet, the whole folded round the Commissioner who as you now know brought the Sacred Edict to the people in simpler terms, volgar' eloquio. 'That sea-gull', as in C.96, has by a very distantly but clearly pointing demonstrative become the paraclete in Pound's sense of 'verbum perfectum : sinceritas'. That particular god is within us (est deus in nobis), and gives us a kredemnon, and is of Cadmus' line, Cadmus having invented the alphabet and built Thebes (in Greece) out of dragon-teeth remaining from a fratricidal struggle. Leucothea herself, as Ino, before she became sea-goddess, has a history of appalling suffering behind her (she was driven mad by Hera after causing her own children to be killed by Themisto, but Dionysus, or in Ovid's version, Aphrodite, took pity on her and changed her into a sea-goddess). The snow's lace recalls the *per diafana* of C.95, already then juxtaposed with 'white foam, a sea-gull' (see pp. 142–3).

The passage then goes on to Yeats, Possum, Wyndham, having no ground beneath 'em (i.e. no true relation of verbal expression to reality). It is wholly repeated, with slight variation and no kredemnon, in C.102, sacrifice being replaced by 'that shrub' (i.e. incense) :

This I had from Kalupso

        who had it from Hermes

HIS TRUE PENELOPE WAS FLAUBERT

'eleven literates and, I suppose,

                      Dwight L. Morrow'
the body elected,

           residence required, not as in England
'A cargo of Iron'

        lied Pallas

           and as to why Penelope waited
keinas . . . e Orgei. line 639, Leucothoe
rose as an incense bush,

              resisting Apollo,

                        Orchamus, Babylon
And after 500 years

           still offered that shrub to the sea-gull
Phaeacians,

        she being of Cadmus line
The snow's lace washed here as sea-foam

      But the lot of 'em, Yeats, Possum, Old Wyndham
      had no ground to stand on

Black shawls still worn for Demeter

      in Venice,

          in my time,

               my young time
     OIOS TELESAI ERGON . . . EROS TE[1]
The cat talks μάω
    (mao) with a greek inflection.

                               C.102

Calypso of course gave Odysseus the clothes Leucothea told
him to get rid of, and gave him also his freedom, by order of

[1] Od. II/272. Athene to Telemachus (a double identification here of
Pound 'in my young time' with both Telemachus and Odysseus) : 'Telemachus you will be wise and brave in life if your father's fine energy is
in you. *What a man to go to the end of his acts and words* (epos, not eros :
οἶος κεῖνος ἔην τελέσαι ἔργον τε ἔπος τε). This journey must bear fruit and
come to an end.' These lines and the next few may be a later interpolation
(see l'*Odyssée*, texte établi par Victor Bérard, Paris 1924, 7th ed.
1967).

Hermes, messenger of the gods, and a skin of red wine, another of water, and provisions, and a fair wind, all of which proved to be a cargo of iron, paraphernalia he had to get rid of.[1] Senator Bronson Cutting, asked by Pound how many literate senators there were, 'sent nine names, ending "and I suppose Dwight L. Morrow"' (*Guide to Kulchur*, p. 260), Dwight Morrow being a great economist and father of Anne Morrow Lindbergh. As to why Penelope waited, the cryptic reference is to the Odyssey Bk. IV/693 (not 639): κεῖνος (not keinas) δ'οὔποτε πάμπαν ἀτάσθαλον ἄνδρα ἐώργει. (But Odysseus has violated/profaned no man.) It is Penelope who says this. A little further (l. 807), when Athene sends a dream to Penelope in the form of her sister's ghost, the apparition says of Telemachus that he must return, for he has never committed any faults towards the gods. Pound seems to have fused these two ideas from memory in *The Pisan Cantos*: 'And old Ez folded up his blankets / Neither Eos nor Hesperus has suffered wrong at my hands' (C.79).

Meanwhile, however, there has been another reference to Kredemnon in C.100 (I put the above two similar quotations together for obvious reasons), which retells how Odysseus swam up-river in Phaeacia and dropped the veil into the water to be carried back to the sea, as instructed by Leucothea (Od. V)[2]:

> So that the mist was quite white on that part of the sea-coast
> Le Portel, Phaeacia
> and he dropped the scarf in the tide-rips
> KREDEMNON
> that it should float back to the sea,
> and that quickly

---

[1] The cargo of iron is a juxtaposed allusion to the beginning of the Odyssey when Athene, as Mentor, tells Telemachus that his ships in the harbour carry a cargo of iron.

[2] Rouse translation: When his breath came back by and by, and his spirit rallied again, the first thing he did was to unwind the goddess's veil: he dropt it into the river, as it ran murmuring seawards and the swell carried it back, until Ino received it into her kind hands.

HIS TRUE PENELOPE WAS FLAUBERT

DEXATO XERSI
[received it into her hands]
with a fond hand
AGERTHE   [gathered back]
But their technique is two lies at once
so there be no profit in conflict C.100

This is incidentally a good example of what happens when
one follows Pound to his source. The passage is perfectly
comprehensible in its own right. But when one looks at the
few lines of the Odyssey in question, one sees that 'with a
fond hand' glosses DEXATO XERSI (δέξατο χερσὶ φίλῃσιν,
Od. V/462), whereas AGERTHE comes from 4 lines above,
when Odysseus lands panting on the Phaeacian shore: φρένα
θυμὸς ἀγέρθη (and gathered back his spirit into his breast);
φρένα means (1) breast, (2) spirit, soul, consciousness, (3)
courage, heart; θυμὸς means soul, spirit, principle of life, feeling,
thought, strength.

By juxtaposing AGERTHE (gathered back), which belongs
to the phrase about his spirit or principle of life, with Ino
receiving the veil into her hands (gathering also), Pound has
either (a) misremembered, thinking that AGERTHE belonged
to Ino gathering the veil, or (b), with the text before him,
identified in his mind the veil and the principle of life. Had this
equation been explicit he would have had to express it by way of
direct metaphor or by way of comparison (he gathered back his
spirit into his breast as Ino received the veil into her hands).
But the juxtaposition is much more implicit and allusive than
that. It is one of the glimpses into the associations of a creative
mind which one can get, often by chance, when following the
process, though of course it is a special kind of pleasure one
cannot indulge throughout.[1]

Then, forward again to C.102, a page after the Kalupso
opening :

[1] Cp. Julia Kristeva, *Poésie et Negativité* (*op. cit.* p. 111 ft. 1) on Lautréa-
mont's misquotations or rephrasings of Pascal, La Rochefoucauld. For a
full paradigmatic reading both texts are necessary.

HIS TRUE PENELOPE WAS FLAUBERT

But with Leucothoe's mind in that incense
all Babylon could not hold it down.
    'for my bitch eyes' in Ilion   [Helen]
                                        C.102

And finally, in C.109, and ending *Thrones* :

Over wicket gate
    INO *Ινώ* Kadmeia
Erigena, Anselm,
            the fight thru Herbert and Rémusat
Helios,
   καλλιαστράγαλος Ino Kadmeia,   [with fine ankle][1]
San Domenico, Santa Sabina,
           Sta Maria Trastevere;
                in Cosmedin
Le chapeau melon de St Pierre
    You in the dinghy (piccioletta) astern there!
                              C.109

Ino daughter of Cadmon is here linked with the idea of tradition (his favourite churches, + an allusion to St Peter's about
whose building John Adams waxed so indignant),[2] and with
Pound's favourite philosophers, those who really 'see', and who
were already in C.100 linked with Rémusat (1797–1875),
friend of Thiers and Talleyrand and author of *Essais de philosophie, Abelard, De la philosophie allemande, St Anselme de
Cantorbéry, Lord Herbert de Cherbury* :

        Until Rémusat : 'Has not', 'Aquinas has not
bien rendu compte
        des connaissances à priori'.
'Want to load' (Cocteau)
        'all the rest of it onto you.'

[1] Actually Ino is introduced as *καλλίσφυρος Ἰνώ*, with fine ankle,
V/333. Pound seems to have got the longer word from Aristotle.

[2] John Adams to Thomas Jefferson, Feb. 2, 1816 (*The Adams–Jefferson
Letters*, ed. Lester J. Cappon, N. Carolina, 1968), echoed in C.31, C.46.

Erigena,
Anselm,
Cherbury,
Rémusat,
Thiers was against income-tax
   'the portal to inquisition'

                C.100

Or again opening C.101 : 'Finding scarcely anyone save
Monsieur de Rémusat / who could understand him . . . M.
Talleyrand . . .'. This mixed bunch are juxtaposed with the sun,
with Ino Kadmeia again, with right-proportioned and possibly
wrong-proportioned architecture, the whole ending on a to-be-
continued note with Dante's piccioletta barca, which takes us
right back to C.7 : 'O voi che siete in piccioletta barca', where
the line appears in an ironic context (see ch. 11).

I hope I have brought out the sheer richness and complexity,
as well as the precision, of Pound's methods. I have of course
totally forgotten to bring in *Lustra, Cathay, Mauberley* and
Propertius. So that :

CHAPTER NINE

'So that :'[1]

In fact, I had no intention of 'dealing with' these last early poems in the usual sense, unless they happened to barge into Chêng ming and Cabbages on Sofas, the theme of my last chapter—which they didn't. Some critics feel that *Propertius* and *Mauberley* are Pound's finest achievements, after which he failed to steer between Scylla and Charybdis, and drowned; or after Canto 7; or after Canto 17; or 30; or 47; or after *The Pisan Cantos*; or after *Rock-Drill*—such are the varying views. Personally I think that Pound stands or falls with *The Cantos*, or rather, that he stands, and that although he is sometimes submerged there is always a Leucothea (if we are going to sail this metaphor to death) to save him, even in the post-*Thrones* fragments.

I did spend some time on the very early poems, partly because they are not all easily available, but more especially to show the enormous leap (in practice a long and painful discipline) as well as the undoubted genius that was already there from the start. But the later poems, including *Cathay* are available and well known, and straightforward. As for *Mauberley* there is a definitive study of it by J. J. Espey, and many other interesting commentaries.[2] There is a thorough study of

[1] End of Canto 1.
[2] J. J. Espey, Ezra Pound's *Mauberley* (London 1955); D. Davie, *Ezra Pound's 'Hugh Selwyn Mauberley'* (Pelican Guides to Literature 1961); F. R. Leavis in *New Bearings in English Poetry* (London 1932, 1950); Hugh Kenner in *The Poetry of Ezra Pound* (London 1951); George Dekker in *Sailing after Knowledge* (London 1963, Ch. VII); M. L. Rosenthal in *A Primer of Ezra Pound* (New York 1960); G. S. Fraser in *Ezra Pound* (London 1960). Espey is the most helpful and the nearest, I believe, to a correct interpretation.

Propertius by J. P. Sullivan, and it seems pointless for me to paraphrase them here. The student can also (I hope) read the poems, and see for himself how in *Lustra* Pound has achieved, via *Cathay* and Martial's epigrams, the modern, colloquial tone and considerable elegance, but at some cost, the depth of feeling too often jettisoned for the superficial irony of *vers de société*. And here I agree with Eliot who rather disliked this aspect of Pound.[1] This is a matter of individual taste. I wish, for instance, that Pound had not written quite so many ironic poems addressed to his poems (O my songs, Come my songs, etc.).[2] I only like some of the epigrams, and I laugh at the take-off on Yeats's *The Lake Isle of Innisfree*:

> O God, O Venus, O Mercury, patron of thieves,
> Give me in due time, I beseech you, a little tobacco-shop . . .

which ends:

> Lend me a little tobacco-shop,
>   or install me in my profession
> Save this damn'd profession of writing,
>   where one needs one's brains all the time.   *The Lake Isle*

Lustra also contains the remarkable *Near Perigord* (the attempt to reconstruct Bertrans de Born which I mentioned earlier: 'End fact. Try fiction'), and some poems which, though not all that interesting in themselves, adumbrate certain themes of *The Cantos*, e.g. *The Coming of War: Acteaon*, τὸ καλόν, *Tempora* (for the line 'Io! Io! Tamuz!'), *The Spring* ('Maelids and water girls, / Stepping beneath a boisterous wind from Thrace / . . . And wild desire / Falls like black lightning').

The elegance was re-united with depth of feeling in *Mauberley*, where all influences so far undergone by Pound seem to meet in an exquisite explosion of passion full of poised restraint: the carved verse of Théophile Gautier, the *mot juste* of Flaubert, the

---

[1] *Introduction to the Selected Poems* (London 1928).
[2] E.g. 'Come my songs, let us speak of perfection— / We shall get ourselves rather disliked . . .' (*Salvationists*. See also *Commission, Further Instructions, Ite, Salutation the Second, The Condolence, Coda, Epilogue*).

intricate rhymes of Laforgue, Remy de Gourmont's ideas on sexual love from *La Physique de l'Amour* and other works, the hesitant rhythms of Bion, the brevity and the juxtaposition of the *haiku*, the aesthetic ideals of the Pre-Raphaelites, the Jamesian struggle of cultivated barbarian as against decadent civilization. It is full of direct echoes, which yet manage to be, as always, idiosyncratically Poundian. J. J. Espey has examined and analyzed all these in his admirable study (*op. cit.*), which Pound has admitted is the correct interpretation, and I shall therefore not imitate other critics and add any other. The poem is still being misunderstood by those who, it seems, refuse to read Espey. But apart from one fairly obscure section (Part II/ii —Mauberley realizing he has missed his chance of renewal through active passion), which functions on two levels, one sexual and one aesthetic (orchid/ὄρχις = testicle, iris/irides or diastiasis of eyes as invitation), the poem is straightforward and divided clearly into two parts that balance each other almost point by point, the first part distinctly an ironically diminished self-portrait of Pound (the first poem is called 'E.P. Ode pour l'élection de son sépulchre'), the second, equally distinctly, entitled 'Mauberley', a devastating portrait of the minor artist in the very society castigated throughout Part I—at most a portrait of what Pound might have become if he had stayed in London. *Mauberley* in fact marks Pound's decision to become a committed writer and not just a social epigrammatist.

And yet I wonder whether—Espey apart—it deserves such a wealth of comment. Part of its interest, surely, lies in that it foreshadows certain elements in *The Cantos*. It introduces the Odyssean theme for the first time, and that of usury, and at the very end of *The Cantos*, in the last fragment, Pound returns to acknowledge Laforgue, not as a Symbolist poet but for the 'deeps in him':

> And Laforgue more than they thought in him . . .
> And I have learnt more from Jules
> > (Jules Laforgue) since then
> Deeps in him   C.116

SO THAT

These deeps Laforgue discovered in the Berlin aquarium, and they became for him 'the symbol of promised Nirvana', 'the silent deeps which know only eternity, for which Spring, Summer, Autumn and Winter do not exist',[1] the motif of nature in reverse, trees upside down which recall the many submarine sequences in *The Cantos* (the nymph transformed into coral in C.2, and others).[2]

Homage to Sextus Propertius (1917) is Pound's most successful longer shorter poem, naturally received at the time with contempt. It is also the real point of entry to *The Cantos*. Not only is it wholly a 'creative translation' in the sense usually applied to Pound, a 'mimetic homage'; not only does it adumbrate the underworld Persephone theme and let loose the notion of sex as a total, undivided pleasure, a generous, joyous, heedless thing—one of the recurring motifs in *The Cantos* (e.g. Cunizza who inspired Sordello, then loved a soldier, etc. and finally freed her slaves in the elder Cavalcanti's house); but the rhythms there exploited are the closest to that of *The Cantos*, although A. Alvarez calls them 'more or less regular elegiac pentameters . . . accommodated to the cadence of the English idiom'.[3] But let the student take even the first twenty lines or so and note no more than the number of polysyllabic endings (Italy, generalities, celebrities, circumstances, funeral, quality); as well as the other typically Poundian ending, the spondee:

> It is in your grove I wo'uld w'alk,
> I who come first from the cle'ar fo'nt . . .
> What foot beat out your ti'me-b'ar . . .
> Or of Hector spattering wh'eel-r'ims . . .

The spondee also occurs in mid-line: 'And there is no hi'gh ro'ad to the Muses'. Or in an Anglo-Saxon sounding (though wrong) alliteration:

[1] *Moralité légendaire Salome*, 1888.

[2] See Eva Hesse, *New Approaches to Ezra Pound*, ed. Hesse (London 1969), Introductory Essay.

[3] *Craft and Morals*, in Ezra Pound: Perspectives, *op. cit.* Admittedly he is referring only to the 'Persephone and Dis, Dis, have mercy upon her' passage which 'more or less' is, though even there I think it is misleading.

SO THAT

A new-fangled chariot follows the flower-hung horses

The last almost has a three beat ending, and this does in fact occur lower down:

> And who would have known the towers
> pulled down by a de′al-wo′od ho′rse

Which rhythm, fortunately for me, leads us straight into Canto 1 and its splendid opening:

> And then went down to the ship,
> Set keel to breakers, forth on the godly sea, and
> We set up mast and sail on that swart ship,
> Bore sheep aboard her, and our bodies also,
> Heavy with weeping, so winds from sternward
> Bore us out onward with bellying canvas,
> Circe's this craft, the trim-coifed goddess.

They arrive at 'the place / Aforesaid by Circe' and perform the rites:

> And drawing sword from my hip
> I dug the ell-square pitkin;
> Poured we libations unto each the dead,
> First mead and then sweet wine, water mixed with white flour.
> Then prayed I many a prayer to the sickly death's-heads;
> As set in Ithaca, sterile bulls of the best
> For sacrifice, heaping the pyre with goods,
> A sheep to Tiresias only, black and a bell-sheep.
> Dark blood flowed in the fosse,
> Souls out of Erebus . . .

The first three discarded Cantos were published in 1917, before *Propertius* (1919).[1] In *Quia Pauper Amavi* they are

[1] The first version of the first three Cantos appeared in 'Poetry' in 1917, and again in the American edition of *Lustra* (1917), as well as (shortened) in *Quia Pauper Amavi* (1919). The first version of Cantos IV–VII appeared in *Poems 1918–21* (New York 1921). The 'received' text appeared in 1924 (*A Draft of XVI Cantos for the Beginning of a Poem of Some Length*).

placed, not at the end as one might expect, since they were called the beginning of 'a poem of some length', but before *Propertius*. However, in the Collected Poems (*Personae*, 1926) and subsequent editions, the date 1917 is put in brackets under the title *Homage to Sextus Propertius*, and as we have seen with some of the early poems, Pound is very careful about such dates. This would mean that *Propertius* was composed immediately after and perhaps in part during, the discarded Cantos.

What is now Canto 1 came at the end of the discarded Cantos, and I don't think it is just hindsight that makes one feel the difference immediately. Now I am not going to drag these out for scrutiny. All I want to stress here is that working on *Propertius* must have released a tremendous force, latent since the earlier 'virile' poems such as *Cino, Sestina: Altaforte* etc., but too long pent-up or diverted in semi-scholarly efforts from Provençal and Cavalcanti to Fenollosa, in the launching of movements, in the finding of a language to think in and generally putting *le sue idee in ordine*.

For the original First Canto started with 'Hang it all, there can be but the one "Sordello" ' (weaker than the present opening of C.2), then ambled on, in tediously elegant iambics, addressing the ghost of Browning (though unnamed), saying what Pound's own poem is going to be about, reproaching Browning for his 'quirks and tweeks' which he himself would *not* use, but with a dreadful variation of the Elizabethan pun on stanza (room/verse-form): 'I stand before the booth (the speech) etc.'; and reminiscences of Venice (now in C.3 but without 'had my rolls for breakfast' and such). It looked as though the planned long poem was going to be very uncontemporary and uncommitted, reminiscent, genial and very self-indulgent.

Then suddenly towards the end, he tells us (still in iambics) how 'Justinopolitan, uncatalogued, / One Andreas Divus gave him in Latin / In Officina Wecheli. M.D. three X's eight, / Caught up his cadence, word and syllable':

SO THAT

'Down to the ships we went, set mast and sail,
Black keel and beasts for bloody sacrifice,
Weeping we went.'
I've strained my ear for -*ensa*, -*ombra* and -*ensa*
And cracked my wit on delicate canzoni,
                    Here's but rough meaning :
And then went down to the ship, set keel to breakers ...

And we're off. And that is the point I wished to make by con-
trasting the discarded parts with what we actually have. Canto 1
in fact is 'but rough meaning', compared to the rambling
cultured chattiness that precedes it. Yet how much more
precise.

Pound in fact salvaged quite a bit, but made some drastic as
well as some less drastic though judicious cuts: e.g. the 'lie quiet
Divus' is not cluttered with irrelevant detail ('plucked from a
Paris stall', plus the fact that Georgius Dartona Cretensis'
latin version of the *Second Homeric Hymn to Aphrodite* was
included in that edition, from which he quotes, etc. (see Dekker,
p. 153). More important, however, he had found what his poem
was going to do. He would be Odysseus, on a journey through
time and flux, he would raise the ghosts and make them speak
to us, he would set them in motion.

I am not suggesting that *Propertius* achieved *all* this. The
discarded Cantos and *Propertius* probably interacted on one
another. But the Persephone underworld theme, and the
mimetic homage, the right rhythm, elegiac but conversational
and above all flexible, epic, all these released for Pound the
right language that catches the old solemnity, the 'feel' of
antiquity when required, but otherwise speaks to us in our
modern idiom.

At first it seems that we are being given a magnificent
version of the Odyssey, goodness me, a modernized epic, with a
plot. This of course is impossible, we are not in the epic age.
And thanks be to the gods, Circe and Tiresias, we are not in
for that at all. Tiresias, for one thing, greets Odysseus curiously
thus : ' "A second time ? why ? man of ill-star, | "Facing the

sunless dead and this joyless region." '—the second visit
being of course Pound's. The fusion of Pound/Odysseus, which
is fundamental to *The Cantos*, is achieved from the start, and in a
subtly allusive manner. Then Tiresias, having drunk his fill :

> And he strong with the blood, said then : 'Odysseus
> 'Shalt return through spiteful Neptune, over dark seas,
> 'Lose all companions.' Then Anticlea came.
> Lie quiet Divus. I mean, that is Andreas Divus,
> In Officina Wecheli, 1538, out of Homer.
> And he sailed, by Sirens, and thence outward and away
> And unto Circe.
> > Venerandam,
> In the Cretan's phrase, with the golden crown, Aphrodite,
> Cypri munimenta sortita est, mirthful, oricalchi, with golden
> Girdles and breast bands, thou with dark eyelids
> Bearing the golden bough of Argicida. So that :

> > > C.2

> Hang it all, Robert Browning,
> there can be but the one 'Sordello.'
> But Sordello, and my Sordello?
> Lo Sordels si fo di Mantovana.

The ellipsis here achieved, compared to the discarded Cantos,
is masterly. Moreover, the transition carries the significance
of the whole Cantos. For Odysseus (as we have seen in the
passage quoted from C.47) came *from* Circe to the underworld,
in 'Circe's this craft' (C.1), at her command and guidance.
Thus we start (like all epics) *in medias res*. More than that, in
Homer Odysseus goes first back to Circe; then past the Sirens
(whose song he is able to hear, on Circe's advice, tied to the
mast, whereas his men put wax in their ears from fear of the
fatal lure); then he encounters Athene, of course, who guides
him throughout, merged, by Pound, as I have suggested, into
Aphrodite. Here Circe is placed in the middle (Sirens/Circe/
Aphrodite) because she represents Pound's middle way: the
Sirens are the destructive beauty exemplified by Helen and by

the scenes of violent passion (e.g. Nicolo d'Este in Cantos 8, 20, 24, who executed his wife Parisina and his son for incest, an incident specifically juxtaposed to the Agamemnon–Clytemnestra tragedy: 'For this tribe paid always, and the house / Called also Atreides'—C.8); or, in an opposite way, men giving in to the senses (the lotus-eaters) and 'abuleia' or drift, lethargy (Alessandro de Medici in C.7), and the general chaos of Western civilization in the first thirty Cantos: roughly, Pound's Inferno, though streaked with flashes of hope, the factive whole man in Malatesta (Cantos 8–11) or the still wisdom of Kung in C.13—both themes to be more profoundly developed later.

Circe, however, represents these same forces but as controlled and used by man: the crew who gave in to pure appetite and sexual desire were turned into swine; Elpenor in C.39 (also a pre-Tiresias scene) is drunk on Circe's roof with a fat panther and 'girls talked there of fucking, beasts talked there of eating', and he falls off the roof and dies (hence he is also one of the shades who meets Odysseus in C.1). Eurilochus, on the other hand, who is in a way a mirror of Odysseus's destructive aspect and represents a perversion of the intelligence, refuses to go in, refuses the experience of metamorphosis, refuses, in fact, the goddess, and is later destroyed by Poseidon.[1] As Pound says, he would have been better off as swine, at least he would have had the acorns:

> Eurilochus, Macer [lean], better there with good acorns
> Than with a crab for an eye, and 30 fathom of fishes
> Green swish in the socket . . .
>
> C.39

In this Canto Elpenor and his men hear Circe's song (KALON AOIDIAEI—[the beauty of her singing]) and say 'let us call

[1] C.39 is based on Book X of the Odyssey. Cp. Forrest Read, *A Man of No Fortune*, in *Motive and Method in the Cantos of Ezra Pound*, ed. Lewis Leary (Col. U.P. 1953). Elpenor (ἐλπίς *hope for*, and ἀνήρ *man*), the hopeful but passive man; Eurilochus (εὖρος *width* and λόχος *snare*) the man of widespreading snares. For the order Sirens/Circe/Aphrodite see D. S. Pearlman, *The Barb of Time* (O.U.P., New York, London 1969).

out to her quickly' (é theos ée guné . . . phtheggōmetha thasson). But Eurilochus is associated with an allusion to Dante's *Paradiso* (XXIII. 129, 'Che mai da me non si parte il diletto' . . .) where the redeemed form a crown of light around the Virgin and sing Regina Coeli—the pure disembodied love that Courtly Love eventually became, Aphrodite as unattainable beauty. Odysseus, however, sees the Virgins of Artemis singing and dancing 'to the beat of the measure', with a snatch from the fourteenth-century *Alysoun* (Betwene Merche and Aprile) and sap new in the bower.

For Odysseus is the only one who (admittedly with the help of Hermes) takes the middle way between passive surrender and ascetic refusal, and thus enters into a harmonious relationship with the goddess, accepting her not only as an alluring and above all co-operating lover, but, more important, as guide and mentor, who takes his pride down a peg and herself gives him the *moly* or herb that will release him from the passion:

> To the cave art thou called, Odysseus,
> By Molü hast thou respite for a little,
> By Molü art thou freed from the one bed
> that thou may'st return to another

C.47

though first he must go the road to hell (C.47) or [Pound's dots]:

> 'I think you must be Odysseus . . .   [Od. X/330]
>   feel better when you have eaten . . . [X/368]
> Always with your mind on the past . . .   [X/379]
> Ad Orcum autem quisquam?
>   nondum nave nigra pervenit . . . [X/502]
> Been to hell in a boat yet?'

C.39

And it is only after the hell and even during the purgatorio of the middle Cantos, and during the relived or truly lived hell of the *Pisan Cantos* (for there is no conventional chronology in the poem) that he will see the blinding glimpses of Aphrodite,

which occur whenever Pound recaptures, in the midst of
suffering, moments of exquisite beauty, before him, or in
memory, or even here, through accepting the experience of
metamorphosis and assimilating it : the 'Io! Io!' passage comes
just after the second version of the Circe episode in C.47. Or
again in *The Pisan Cantos* :

> La beauté, 'Beauty is difficult, Yeats,' said Aubrey Beardsley
> when Yeats asked why he drew horrors
> or at least not Burne-Jones
> and Beardsley knew he was dying and had to
> make his hit quickly.

hence no more B-J in his product.

> So very difficult, Yeats, beauty so difficult.

C.80

Aphrodite, right from the start, then, is introduced as 'bearing
the golden bough of Argicida', that is, the slayer of Argos, an
appellation of Hermes who summoned the souls of the dying
into the underworld, and who is also linked with the golden
bough which gave Aeneas access to Persephone's nether-
kingdom. Thus not only is Aeneas, who defended Troy, a sort
of double of Odysseus who helped to destroy it—both going on a
journey back to the origins of creation and destruction—but
Aphrodite herself is here goddess of death as well as of beauty,
merging with Persephone, as indeed the Mysteries of Eleusis,
concerned with ἄνοδος or the Rising of Persephone, were also
referred to as the birth of Aphrodite from the sea.[1]

For when Pound wrote the famous passage in his Cavalcanti
essay ('We appear to have lost the radiant world . . . of moving
energies . . .' see ch. 6, p. 80), he added of 'these realities
perceptible to the sense' that they were 'untouched by the two
maladies, the Hebrew disease, the Hindoo disease, fanaticisms
that produce Savanarola, asceticisms that produce fakirs, St
Clement of Alexandria with his prohibition of bathing by

[1] See Eva Hesse, *New Approaches to Ezra Pound* (London 1969, ed.
Hesse), Introduction, for Aphrodite and the bough of Argicida.

women. The envy of dullards who, not having *intelletto*, blame the lack of it on innocent muscles. For after asceticism, that is anti-flesh, we get asceticism that is anti-intelligence, that praises stupidity as "simplicity", the cult of naiveté.'

Pound is against all dualisms, and Circe represents his notion —which recurs in every form, political, economic, literary, sexual—that man must enter into a harmonious relationship with nature, must live according to its rhythms, everything in due season, action following thought, a time for silence and a time for speaking.[1] And nature must not be perverted. Usury which in his view is a perversion of nature (money breeding money ex nihilo, with no goods to back it), accelerates production beyond nature's capacity, accelerates the whole pace of life so that man no longer lives in harmony with the natural rhythms of nature. Crafts are destroyed, everything must be produced quickly ('Slowness is beauty', he quotes Binyon in C.87), mystery and ritual are destroyed, the gods within us are destroyed, everyone wants everything quickly including sex, which has become split into an intellectual obsession and a localized tickle—hence the general neurosis about it.

As important, however, as the Sirens/Circe/Aphrodite triptych announced, in that order, at the end of C.1, are the two facts that Odysseus has been raising the shades and is to go on a journey. A periplus through the flux of time and particular events, fables, anecdotes, periods of history, people—especially people—raised from the dead and all exemplifying in some way Pound's notion of order and disorder in the mind of man and his relation to an ultimate reality which he believes is a permanent basis underlying all change, a basis, moreover, which, however often it is lost, can be and is found again and put into action and made to work at quite different times and places, despite the loss and change and temporary acceleration. One of the chief

[1] *Tempus loquendi. Tempus tacendi*, the motto on the tomb of Malatesta's beloved Isotta in the Rimini Temple, which opens C.31, the Jefferson Canto. It comes from Ecclesiastes. The phrase 'I speak in season' in the final version of *Donna mi prega* in C.36 (which embodies all this through *intelletto d'amore* as a counterpart to C.39) is Pound's addition.

motifs emerging from the China Cantos (53–62, more forceful
and pithy than many critics have so far realized) is the demonstration, in action of course, and in particulars, that Con-
fucianism is not just an ancient outworn philosophy relevant
only to its own very distant time, but can and was put into
practice by some of the much later great Emperors such as
Kang Hi in the eighteenth century, of the Manchu (Ching)
dynasty which replaced the corrupt Ming, the same Kang Hi
who wanted 'la pureté du langage', and who, in another admirable transition: 'wuz emperor KANG HI 61 years / from 1662
and came after him [ideogram *yüeh* 4.5.: music, variant happi-
ness] (end of C.60):

C.61 [my cuts]

YONG TCHING

his fourth son, to honour his forebears
and spirits of fields
of earth
heaven
utility public
sought good of the people, active, absolute, loved
No death sentence save a man were thrice tried
and he putt out Xtianity
chinese found it so immoral
his mandarins found this sect so immoral . . .

Xtians being such sliders and liars.
. . . Xtians are disturbing good customs
seeking to uproot Kung's laws
seeking to break up Kung's teaching.
. . . 'You Christers wanna have foot on two boats
       and when them boats pulls apart
you will d/n well git a wettin' ' said a court mandarin
tellin' 'em.
. . . 'A man's happiness depends on himself,
         not on his Emperor
If you think that I think that I can make any man happy
    you have misunderstood the FU

SO THAT

福

(the Happiness ideogram) that I sent you.
Thus Tching whom Coupetai had brought up . . .[1]

And Yong Tching leads straight into the Adams Cantos—
John Adams having been born in 1735, year of Yong Tching's
death, and also, in a more American sense, founding a 'dynasty'
of men who devoted themselves to the public good beyond all
calls of the modern, over-emphasized, private ego. The
portrait of John Adams as a whole man, interested in all things,
possessing, like Jefferson, the Confucian/Dantean 'direction of
the will', had already been given in the Jefferson–Adams
correspondence of Cantos 31 and 32, where their insight is
contrasted with the ignorance of contemporary European statesmen, especially in economics and the science of government.

These, then, are the ghosts, and many others as we have
already partly seen, that Pound–Odysseus brings to life after his
first initiation through Hades. *So that*: it is very appropriate
that the first should be Robert Browning and his Sordello.
'But Sordello? And my Sordello?' And after Sordello, So-Shu
churning the sea again and whirling up a first glimpse of
Aphrodite in the shape of a seal ('Seal sports in the spray-
whited circles of cliff-wash, / Sleek head, daughter of Lir, /
eyes of Picasso . . . lithe daughter of Ocean'); and Eleanor,
merged at once with Helen via Aeschylus' destructive epithets;
and Homer blind but nevertheless with an ear for the sea-surge
and able to reproduce the tone and cadences of the old men of
Troy ('let her go back to the ships, / Back among Grecian
faces . . .'); and Acoetes and his vision on ship, the young god
Dionysus at his side whom the crew tried to sell for a slave in
Egypt ('I have seen what I have seen'). All this in Canto 2.

[1] The left component is 'light descending'; or as Pound explains in
his *Confucius*: 'light descending (from sun, moon and stars). To be
watched as component in ideograms indicating spirits, rites, ceremonies.'
Actually the radical shih (=omen). Right component is the phonetic
house: 豆 plus 田, field (grain in orderly rows).

SO THAT

They are, of course, Pound's Sordellos. The 'I' vanishes behind them, but they are his vision, his recreation, why not respect it? Of course his use of documents, of 'particulars' as we move forward into the Cantos, is eclectic, even unscholarly (i.e. one source only) and therefore biased: Mailla, for example, was obviously pro-Confucius and anti-Buddhist-and-Taoist (hence Pound's slightly vulgar or schoolboyish swipes at 'Taozers' and 'Buddfoes'). Similarly I am told that his undoubted examination of the Monte dei Paschi documents was a selective one—for his account, in Cantos 42–3, of the Bank of Siena, founded in 1624, which based credit 'on the abundance of nature / with the whole folk behind it' (C.52). Others say he has done the Bank of Siena justice. I don't happen to know nor do I think it matters. For as has already been mentioned, it is the very essence of Pound's ideogrammic method to bring things to life by using this double or treble or quadruple vision, seeing China through his own American eyes via the modern Italy he is in (itself visibly alive with the best of the Renaissance), via a Frenchman of the eighteenth-century Enlightenment. Or, by way of contrast, in *Thrones*, The Sacred Edict of K'ang Hsi via the Victorian Baller who, with a typical paternalism and arrogance, said of the Salt Commissioner's version that the student should learn these homely sayings, for the Chinese think in quotations, and one can add vivacity to one's style, though the 'mere morality' of these maxims was hollow and the people of China were still wrapped in darkness. Baller ends his introduction with a hymn, 'Thou bleeding Lamb . . . the best morality is love of Thee'. Here is Pound (when he at last gets around to the Commissioner of the Salt Works):

> Thought is built out of Sagetrieb,
> and our debt here is to Baller
> and to *volgar' eloquio*.
> Despite Mathews this Wang was a stylist.[1]

[1] In Mathews' dictionary the meaning of 'p'u' in Wang's name is given as 'simple, rough', hence without style.

171

SO THAT

Uen-li will not help you talk to them,
   Iong-ching republished the edict
But the salt-commissioner took it down to the people
   who, in Baller's view, speak in quotations;
     think in quotations:
  'Don't send someone else to pay it.'[1]
Delcroix was for repetition.[2]
   Baller thought one needed religion.
Without ²muan ¹bpo . . . but I anticipate.   C.98

Or again, Pound's re-creation, in Cantos 8–11, of Sigismundo Malatesta's 'factive personality' is typically biased. The Malatestas were a violent family, who came to prominence in the thirteenth century during the bitter Guelf/Ghibelline struggles which, in that area around Rimini, ended in 1295 with the victory of the Guelf Malatestas. The first great Malatesta of Verucchio, whom Dante calls 'the old Mastiff', began the family's lordship in Rimini in 1295, greatly helped by his cruel elder son Malatestino. He offered his forces to the Holy See in an act of submission and was a crafty statesman and soldier. But his other son Giancotto killed his own brother Paolo who had committed adultery with his wife Francesca da Polenta, an incident immortalized by Dante and which Pound does not fail to juxtapose with Nicolo d'Este (C.8, see p. 165, also ch. 11).

There were, of course, good, wise and astute Malatestas, such as the first two Pandolfos, Carlo of Rimini, son of Pandolfo III, and 'Novello', younger brother of Pound's Sigismundo Pandolfo Malatesta (a natural son, born in 1417). Sigismundo was the most famous of all the Malatestas and a fascinating

[1] Sacred Edict, ed. Baller, on prompt tax repayment: 'Don't commission someone else to take them, when he goes, or you will fall into the snares by which sharpers fleece people.'

[2] Carlo Delcroix, the Italian fascist deputy who in 1924 joined Dino Grandi in denouncing the killing of Matteoti. He turns up in Cantos 88, 92, 95, 97, 98, 101, in the Bridson interview, in *Jefferson and/or Mussolini* and in *Guide to Kulchur*, pp. 229 and 249.

mixture. At fourteen he took part in a revolt against his brother
Galeotto's government, at sixteen he became Lord of Rimini
and defeated his enemies in battle. At eighteen he was appointed
commander of the pontifical army in Romagna and the Marshes.
At twenty he fell in love with Isotta, an intelligent and cultured
girl, daughter of Francesa di Atto of the Atti, and continued to
love her throughout his life, but nevertheless married, first
Ginevra, daughter of Nicolo III, and after her death Polissena,
daughter of Count Francesco Sforza, both important lords. He
did not finally wed Isotta until 1456, after which she ruled the
state with skill during his frequent absences, even selling her
jewels to support him when he was in hiding in Rimini. He was
an astute soldier, and won battles against incredible odds, but
his chief enemy was Pius II, the 'monstrous, swollen, swelling
s.o.b.' of C.10, or Aeneas Silvius Piccolomini, historian and
later pope, who persecuted him with an almost pathological
hatred, excommunicated him and denounced him as an enemy of
peace and of the Church. Pio's successor Paul II, who had
awarded Sigismundo the golden rose as 'champion of christen-
dom' for the heroism he displayed in fighting the Turks for
three years in Greece, nevertheless also provoked him beyond
endurance by suggesting that he should exchange Rimini, his
family's town, for Spoleto and Foligno. Sigismundo, in a fit of
wrath, rode all the way to Rome but Paul had surrounded
himself with so many cardinals that Sigismundo could not get
at him and broke down and wept with sheer frustration. He
became ill, returned to Rimini but died quite soon at the age of
51, after months of physical and moral suffering.

Some of this appears here and there in the Malatesta Cantos—
indeed it is precisely the mixture of condottiere behaviour and
nobility which attracts Pound. But what he is really interested in
is the building of the Temple, Sigismundo's tribute to Isotta
and the manifestation of his wholeness as a man, as a patron of
the arts and a true representative of the Renaissance. The
Tempio Malatestiano in Rimini is an extraordinary monument.
Supposedly dedicated to St Francis, it is in fact partly a self-
glorification and mostly a paeon of praise to pagan gods. As

SO THAT

Pope Pius said in his long denunciation of Malatesta's life: 'Nevertheless, he built at Rimini a splendid church dedicated to St Francis, though he filled it so full of pagan works of art that it seemed less a Christian sanctuary than a temple of heathen devil-worshippers.'[1]

The simplicity is classic, bare, and at first it seems quite arid. Then it grows on you, and you begin to see, and see again, and are drawn into hour-long fascination with the proportions; and each of the side-chapels with their marvellous carvings (elephants, the zodiac, Diana, columns rising out of huge stone baskets of grapes), each artist allotted his particular task: Matteo de Pasti, Agostino di Duccio, Piero della Francesca, Simone Ferruci, Cristoforo Foschi, Matteo Nuti, even Giotto is supposed to have frescoed the apse. And the Malatesta Cantos (8–11) follow the very process of the building, the difficulties in getting marble, the setbacks, the misunderstandings, the correspondence about materials, all this despite and during battles, campaigns knee-deep in mud and frozen water. It is this act of creativity which is set against the Church's then sterile and repressive attitude, though Pope Pius' grudging admission that Malatesta had after all built the temple is crisply summarized as *templum aedificavit*, a phrase which re-echoes many times.

Thus Pound's Malatesta. For *The Cantos* are not history as we are taught at school. No Canute and the waves or Alfred and the cakes, not even 'let them eat cake'. No Caesar's conquests, Merovingians, Franks, Vikings, Holy Roman Empires. Even the culture-heroes are not Columbus or Magellan, nor are they Copernicus, Newton, Napier of the logarithms, Hargreaves of the spinning-jenny or Watt of the steam-engine who laid the foundations of our oh so efficient modern civilization and who, like the artists, are usually treated as admirable and obviously relevant phenomena but nevertheless existing parallel with and apart from the much more important linear

[1] The Commentaries of Pius II, as given in the explicatory series *The Analyst*, V, p. 14, ed. Robert Mayo, Northwestern University, Evanston, Ill.

progression of kings, diplomatic marriages, treaties, broken treaties, wars righteous and unrighteous according to the viewpoint taught. Not that Pound is uninterested in technological progress: to give one reference only, there is Jefferson's concern for the Erie canal in C.31, canals having been the first major breakthrough for the transport of goods during the Industrial Revolution, roads being then impassable for most of the year (roads came next, then the railway). Of course we can now say that the railway won, as roads are now winning over the railway. But they served for years. And what interests Pound is the fact that Jefferson the statesman is an all-round man with the *directio voluntatis* of the good leader; and the distinction, brought out in so many of the Cantos, between Confucius' mean man and master man, whose axis does not wobble: e.g. in the Mittel-Europa Canto (35)—itself juxtaposed between John Quincy Adams' all-round intelligence and keen insight into European affairs in Napoleonic times (C.34) and Cavalcanti's *Canzone d'amore* (C.36)—he sums up the European middle-class and its cultural chaos as 'sensitivity without direction' and 'the general indefinite wobble'. Earlier, in Cantos 31 and 32, we get the political acuteness of Jefferson and John Adams, the awareness that France is on the eve of a revolution and that the new American nation should stabilize its finance by getting a loan from Holland instead (successfully brought off in the later Adams Cantos). And of course, the later Bank wars, Jackson and Van Buren fighting the Second American Bank on behalf of the people: credit should belong to the people, not to the Banks, the Government *can* lend money, as was shown by Athens at the Battle of Salamis (a constantly recurring theme), should keep interest down and stop the Banks from coffering it. The people won. (Not for long, though).

I have perhaps exaggerated the unintegrated way that history is taught at school, in order to bring Pound's notion of history into sharp relief. I said 'linear progression' because that is the layman's view, a sequence of irreversible events in time, each with its cause and effect, infinitely extendable in one direction: past, present, future. Many modern historians and philosophers

175

of history agree that it cannot really be viewed in this way although for practical purposes it is still taught thus—or else in blocks (The Roman Empire, History of Russia, of Europe, of Sweden, etc.) with a faint hope that the reduplication will make the links clear to the poor student. There have been many theories of time in history, notably the Hegelian thesis/antithesis idea, with synthesis in the best periods, or the Spenglerian cyclical view of recurrence, and probably the latter is the closest to Pound's.[1] Indeed Kenner has defined *The Cantos* (in his chapter called *Plotless Epic*) as based on 'rhythms of recurrence', though this too has been criticized.[2]

In an essay I published in 1961, I compared Pound to Langland—not because of any supposed influence, for there is none, despite Pound's interest in Middle English—but for the similar way their minds work.[3] You don't have to go and look it up, and I only mention it because I there described the construction of both poems as a spiral. *The Visions of Piers Plowman* move structurally round a piece of land, the field full of folk, with Satan's Castle of Care on one side and the Tower of Truth on the other. As we go up the spiral on higher and higher levels we go through evil on one side and good on the other, and the Field of Folk recurs in different forms with enriched meanings : the muddled place of contrition where the Seven Deadly Sins confess; Piers Plowman's half-acre; various types of *activa vita*; the heart where grows the Tree of Patience, which is the land belonging to Piers Plowman; the place of the Crucifixion; the

---

[1] Pound may also have been directly or indirectly influenced by Vico's cyclical notion of history, which is so important in Joyce. (Giovanni Battista Vico, *Scienza Nuova*.)

[2] e.g. George P. Elliot, *Poet of Many Voices*, in *Ezra Pound: A Collection of Critical Essays*, ed. Walter Sutton (New Jersey 1963) p. 161 : 'If the recurrence and juxtapositions of the Cantos are there for their own sake, the poem is elaborately trivial. Kenner fails to make clear what structurally valuable end these recurrences serve.' Fails to make clear to G. P. Elliot.

[3] *Piers Plowman in the Modern Waste Land*, Rev. of Eng. Lit. II/2, April 1961, republished in revised form in *Ezra Pound: Perspectives*, ed. Noel Stock, Chicago 1965.

field where the Barn (the Church) is being built; the battle-ground of Anti-Christ.

So too the Cantos can be viewed as a spiral, whirling with events, which are reiterated at new levels, juxtaposed to new elements and made new. But it is a sort of conical spiral, which gets narrower and narrower at the top. That is, as you will have noticed during this chapter, the earlier Cantos and even groups of Cantos deal with 'whole' topics—though ideogrammic juxtapositions occur from the start. In other words a whole passage, a whole Canto or even a group of Cantos, can itself form an ideogrammic juxtaposition with another, whatever its juxtapositions within. And broadly speaking there is an Inferno, a Purgatorio and a Paradiso, though critics differ as to where the demarcation lines fall, for the simple reason that these are earthly hells, purgatories and paradises, within us and within our society, and each is streaked with the others, just as Langland's *Do-well*, *Do-Bet* and *Do-Best* constantly overlap.

But by the time we get to the later Cantos (*Rock-Drill*, *Thrones*), the juxtapositions are much closer together, often from line to line, which is why I started off by quoting from these, to get you right into his way of thinking, so that the rest would seem dead easy. Probably the spiral idea should not be pressed too far, but it seems to me more helpful in getting a grasp of the whole than the notion of, say, a fugue, which Pound himself put forward in its early stages.[1] But later he is pretty explicit:

'We do NOT know the past in chronological sequence. It may be convenient to lay it out anaesthetized on the table with dates pasted on here and there, but what we know we know by ripples and spirals eddying out from us and from our own time. . . .' *Guide to Kulchur* (1938) p. 60.

Moreover, the cyclical idea is close to Pound's notion of nature's rhythms.[2] For *The Cantos* are, as you will have

[1] *The Letters of Ezra Pound*, 1907–41, ed. D. D. Paige, New York 1950, pp. 210, 294. See also W. B. Yeats, *A Packet for Ezra Pound*, Dublin, Cuala 1929.

[2] See Daniel S. Pearlman, *The Barb of Time* (O.U.P. New York 1969), where the ideas expressed in this paragraph are worked out in detail.

gathered by now, achronological as regards history; but rooted to the notion of nature's time, the rituals of the seasons, the cycle of birth, death and rebirth, the migration of birds, the tides, the phases of the moon, the rising and setting of the sun, the stars by which man (Odysseus) navigates or calculates his time for ploughing, as Circe tells Odysseus, distinguishing woman's ignorance of these things (her role being different) and man's knowledge, the lines merging into the magnificent passage out of Hesiod in C.47:

> By Molü art thou freed from the one bed
>   that thou may'st return to another
> The stars are not in her counting,
>   To her they are but wandering holes.
> Begin thy plowing
> When the Pleiades go down to their rest,
> Begin thy plowing
> 40 days are they under seabord,
> Thus do in fields by seabord
> And in valleys winding down toward the sea.
> When the cranes fly high
>   think of plowing.
>
> C.47

Modern anthropologists like Lévi-Strauss and mythologists like Mircea Eliade have shown that primitive people have no sense of history as a linear progression of unrepeatable, irreversible events, but live in an ever-recurring present. This kind of freedom sharpens perceptions that are very different from ours, which have sharpened in other directions but have become, compared to theirs, very blunted with regard to the relation between cosmic and inner realities.[1]

Now Pound is not simply a regressivist or a put-the-clock-back idealist. I said in earlier chapters that from the masteries

[1] Claude Lévi-Strauss, *La pensée sauvage* (Paris 1962), *Anthropologie Structurale* (Paris 1958, transl. Basic Books, New York, 1963 London 1968). Mircea Eliade, *Les Cycles Cosmiques et l' Histoire* (in *Le Mythe de l' Eternel Retour—Archétypes et Répétition*, Paris 1949).

through which he trained himself Pound in effect took what he needed and no more; similarly, in his pedagogic aspect, he tells us what he thinks is the best. So it is with his didactic aspect— or, since that term is unpopular, his vision of what is wrong with modern civilization: he isn't telling us that we must become wholly and exactly like ancient China, or eighteenth-century America, or thirteenth-century and fifteenth-century Italy, or Greece of the Eleusinian mysteries, or Homeric Ionia. He is picking out the best from the flux, the whirling spiral, he is picking out the activating forces which he considers as true and permanent and workable at any time, in any conditions, in any society and in any one man. He may be wrong of course. So may the most brilliant and even workable scientific hypothesis turn out to be wrong as new data become available. But no one would deny that modern man is more and more out of touch with the inner core of his being, more and more rushed into more and more dissociated sensibilities. This may well be the way we must go, and personally I think it is, I have no hope for mankind at all. But I do not see why we should deny the validity of Pound's vision, as a vision, and whatever the errors of detail.

For surely it is time we stopped accusing Pound of being a lousy historian, economist, anthropologist, scientist, etc., whatever impression he may himself have given at various times— in his prose and in the more strident or more dully dogmatic parts of his poem—that he took himself seriously in these roles. Let us not fall into the intentional fallacy. Milton thought he was going to justify the ways of God to man and ended up justifying the ways of man to a rather horrid God. And why not, if the result is Book IX of *Paradise Lost*? But Noel Stock, for example,[1] complains that Pound, by his tone and method, forces us to treat his poetry not just as poetry but also as history, politics, economics, and that they are bad history etc., because his reading is highly selective, even cranky. Yet it never occurs to Mr Stock that 'orthodox' reading is precisely what has created the conditions Pound is against, and that any visionary is killed stone dead by the wholly orthodox. Stock is

[1] *Poet in Exile*, Manchester University Press, 1964.

clearly nagged by the idea that on many points, especially on usury, Pound may well be right, 'or if not right at least very close to being so.' It could be argued that it is the great poetry, orthodox or not, which survives, rather than the orthodox reading of the time, especially on matters so transient as political and economic systems. 'Literature is news that STAYS news.'[1]

Nor, however, do I want to fall into the two-truths fallacy (one truth for poetry and one for science or whatever). I shall get out of that one in the next chapter. For the moment I want to get back to Canto 1 and bring out the importance of that marvellous transition, from the brief prophecy of Odysseus' journey through the particulars as apprehended by the senses (Sirens/Circe/Aphrodite), into the next Canto.

For the *So that* not only leads us into immediate visions and raised ghosts; it not only announces the link between Odysseus' voyage and the WHOLE of the Cantos, as I have tried to show; it not only gives a forward leap (as Clark Emery has pointed out)—after the images of metamorphoses, of violence, of Malatesta's factive personality, after the hell, the peace of Kung, the war—to the temporary paradise of C.17 in Italy: 'So that the vines burst from my fingers. . . .' It is also a statement of method. Or, viewed in another way, it is a paradoxical challenge as to his alogical, achronological presentation. On the wrong side of the coin, it is also possible to look retrospectively on this *So that* as expressing, in unconscious tragic irony, the cussed, dogged kind of political linking which led Pound into such a cruel predicament. But here in Canto 1 its role is that of a gauntlet thrown down, as if to say: on the face of it, there is no logical link between Aphrodite bearing the golden bough and Browning's Sordello, or between Aphrodite and anything else in the poem; there is no cause and effect in time, but I will pretend that there is, in the time of my poem; and if you will accept this pretence, if you will submit to the metamorphosis, you will find that it is true. And:

'*Se non è vero è ben trovato.* No one has complained that this kind of joy is fallacious, that it leads to excess, that its enjoyers

[1] *ABC of Reading*, 1934, Paperback, 1961.

have need of detoxication. It has done no man any harm. I doubt
if it has even distracted men from useful social efforts.

'I shd. be inclined to give fairly heavy odds to the contrary.
An inner harmony seldom leads to active perturbing of public
affairs.'[1]

So Pound on the Neoplatonic visionaries, on Gemisto,
Porphyry, Psellos, Iamblicus. 'What remains, and remains
undeniable to and by the most hardened objectivist, is that a
great number of men have had certain kinds of emotion, and
magari, of ecstasy. They have left indelible records of ideas
born of, and conjoined with, this ecstasy.'

Born of, and conjoined with. For Pound is not dividing the
vision from the practical life. Pound never divides, he brings
together: in a whirling spiral perhaps, round a sometimes
marvellously still yet moving centre such as C.49 or C.51, and
sometimes not so still, an unwobbling pivot that wobbles
dangerously. And what he brings together are the moments,
the inklings of truth as he sees it, that have appeared here and
there in the great flux of events:

Ling[2]   [sensibility][2]

Our dynasty came in because of a great sensibility

All there by the time of Y Yin

All roots by the time of Y Yin.   (3)
Galileo index'd 1616.

[1] *Guide to Kulchur*, 1938, p. 225.

[2] Ling[2], Mathews 4071: the spirit of a being which acts upon others.
Couvreur: 'Intelligent, bon, âme d'un défunt.'

[3] Ideogram for I In, minister of T'ang to the young emperor T'ai kia
and successor of T'ang, first of Chang dynasty (1753–1720 B.C.). These
Cantos of *Rock-Drill* are based on Couvreur's edition of *Chou King*
(Shu-ching Book of History, a collection of ancient records about China
c. 2356 B.C. to 620).

SO THAT

Wellington's peace after Vaterloo

chih³ [1]

a gnomon,
Our science is from the watching of shadows . . .

C.85

[1] Mathew 939 : stop, desist.

CHAPTER TEN

'Timing the thunder'[1]

————————>>>>>§<<<<<————————

If you flick through *The Cantos* you will see that Pound loves visual effects on the page, ideograms, Egyptian hieroglyphs, a snatch of Provençal music in square notes at the head of C.91, the whole of C.75 consisting of two pages of music (Janequin's bird-song). But it would be wrong to think that these are decorative. Like his ideograms, all these have a functional purpose, the bird-song for instance emphasizing the unity, now lost, of poetry and music.[2]

Or again, Canto 88, which is based on Thomas Benton,[3] ends by hammering out the headlines of Benton's magnificent speech in the Senate in February 1831, against the renewal of the Bank Charter, together with the Senate's reactions, thus picking up the Van Buren Canto on the Bank War (C.37). But the end of the Canto seems (and is not) entirely visual:

> And as for the charter?
>   Seven violations,
>   15 abuses.'
> These Mr Clayton read to the house, not Polk,
>   Mr Clayton,

[1] From Canto 91.

[2] On Arnaut Daniel's bird-song and on the bird-chorus which Clement Janequin wrote three centuries later, cp. *ABC of Reading* (1934, Faber Paperback, London 1961) pp. 52–4: 'When Francesco da Milano reduced it for the lute, the birds were still in the music. And when Münch transcribed it for modern instruments the birds were still there. They ARE still there in the violin part.' Cp. also *Guide to Kulchur*, pp. 151–3, on Janequin, Vivaldi, Couperin, contrasted as 'two blessed categories', music of representative outlines and music of structure by Bach and Hindemith.

[3] Thomas H. Benton, *Thirty Years' View—Speeches to the Senate.*

from a narrow strip of paper, rolled round his finger
so that the writing shd not be seen,
    He not having had leisure to copy and amplify.

♥ And

♦ fifty

2

weeks

♣ in

4

♥ seasons

In the first edition of *Rock-Drill* the card suits were in red and black, instead of just black, which was not only prettier, but also emphasized the pairing of the seasons. The juxtaposition creates a marvellously active image. Time is not just years and dates, but weeks and seasons. Time is a pack of cards, to be shuffled by skill and chance, or gathered together in suits through complex games, built up or down black on red in endless sets of patience, or of solitaire, with care perhaps not to get the ace of spades (here printed upside down like a reflection of the ace of hearts and betokening ill-fortune) covered up so that you can't get him out, or a gambling game, no trumps, somebody winning and somebody losing, or else laid out in mysterious formulae from which some Madame Sesostris foretells the future, reads character, digs out the vital spots. The next Canto opens :

To know the histories

to know good from evil
(1)

And know whom to trust.

Ching Hao.
[Ch'êng Hao, 1032–1085,
Neoconfucian philosopher]

(1) The ideograms mean *Chou King* [Book of Conduct]. Ed. F. S. Couvreur S.J., from which Pound quotes extensively in *Rock-Drill*.

For Pound is not just writing history. 'An epic is a poem including history', he said in *Date Line*.[1] And he also said, when denying that one of his Money Pamphlets was a short economic history of the United States :

'For forty years I have schooled myself, not to write the Economic History of the U.S. or any other country, but to write an epic poem which begins "In the Dark Forest", crosses the Purgatory of human error, and ends in the light, "fra i maestri di color che sanno". For this reason I have to understand the NATURE of error. But I don't think it necessary to refer to each particular case of error.'[2]

Well of course in a way he does find it necessary, obsessively so. Just as some critics find it obsessively necessary to refer to Pound's each particular case of error. But that is not the point. We cannot expect an epic poem, or indeed any long poem, to be a scholarly economic history or any other kind of history in the usual sense of the word, and Pound rightly denies that this is what he has done. It is the work of a visionary and that is its value. Hence his disconcerting but essentially poetic use of innumerable sources, sometimes unorthodox, sometimes fabulous or partly legendary. Some of these sources, dismissed by experts as bad history, or bad economics, may turn out to be much nearer the basic truth than the experts had supposed.

One of these, Laȝamon's *Brut* (Early Middle English, end of twelfth century, itself based on Geoffrey of Monmouth's *Historia Regum Britanniae*) crops up in *Rock-Drill* (C.91). Donald Davie, who has written a brilliant chapter on this Canto,[3] calls these bits 'archaic English' and 'less archaic English', so that the implications, to my mind profound, of Pound's using Laȝamon at all, and the way he uses him, and the significance of Stonehenge, are overlooked.

I am going to analyze this passage in detail during this chapter, not only to bring out an important aspect of Pound's

[1] *Make It New*, 1934, *Literary Essays*, 1954.
[2] *Money Pamphlets by £*, No. 1 (first published in Italian, 1944), London 1950.
[3] *Poet as Sculptor*, London 1965, ch. XII, pp. 217 ff.

use of historical or (as here) semi-historical sources, but also to show that if one does take the trouble to compare Pound with his sources (a form of paradigmatic reading) the experience is a very special poetic experience, part scholarly and part irrational, apocalyptic, timeless. [1]

But first I should summarize Davie briefly, to set the passage in its context. He argues that the Reina whose eyes have been sunken for three hundred years (opening of the Canto) is the *forma*, which is lost and recaptured at various periods in human history, and which Pound was already talking about in *Guide to Kulchur*:

' "I made it out of a mouthful of air" wrote Bill Yeats in his heyday. The *forma*, the immortal *concetto*, the concept, the dynamic form which is like the rose pattern driven into the dead iron-filings by the magnet, not by material contact with the magnet itself, but separate from the magnet. Cut off by the layer of glass, the dust and filings rise and spring into order. Thus the *forma*, the concept rises from death . . .'[2]

In *The Cantos* as a whole this ideal is sometimes moral, spiritual, governmental, economic, aesthetic. Davie is here chiefly interested in it as artistic *forma*, not just a lost technique but tradition, glimpsed now and again, and intimately connected with Pound's theories of light and colour, of the artist drawing out of the material that which is inherent in it, rather than imposing on it a wealth of significance by an act of will: in literature, the distinction between metaphor and symbolism; in sculpture, the distinction between carving and moulding, the latter being like creating money out of nothing in excess of natural wealth.

I realize that you may be confused by this, since I have been insisting that Pound's material is made up of Pound's Sordellos, of what *he* does with his sources, imposing his view and above all

---

[1] Anyone not interested in the minute textual analysis which creates this experience can skip the rest of this chapter. For anyone further interested, it is abridged from my essay *Lay me by Aurelie*, in *New Approaches to Ezra Pound*, ed. Eva Hesse, Faber & Faber, 1969.

[2] *Guide to Kulchur*, 1938, p. 152.

his presence upon another's. But there is no real contradiction, (cp. p. 44) and as I have said before, one of the tensions which holds the poem together (and sometimes tears it apart) is precisely this paradox, as in all great art, of impersonality and the highly personal voice, the absence and the presence. Pound, however, utterly believes that what he sees is really there, whether it be a coral nymph in the sea or usury as the root of all evil. The sculptor, as Davie's book makes it quite clear, does not merely knock at a block of stone but brings out (as the male force brings out of the female) what is there.

Davie goes on to analyze the implications of these theories in C.91, linking the Reina with some of Pound's female archetypes that always accompany the *forma*, here with Elizabeth as Virgin Queen, with Diana, with Ra-Set, the invented Egyptian goddess made up of Set, the evil male deity, and the sun-god Ra, whose hieroglyph the 'bark of dawn'—which accompanied the dead on their journey—is given, and who with Diana reiterates the sun and moon together as total light process.

Elizabeth, incidentally, is metamorphosed here into a mirror of history by means of a remarkable image, for Drake sees the whole armada in the reflection of her eyes: 'Miss Tudor moved them with galleons / from deep eye, versus armada / from the green deep / he saw it, / in the green deep of an eye'; and a little later: 'That Drake saw the splendour and wreckage / in that clarity / Gods moving in crystal.'

But here is the passage I am going to analyze. I give it in full, let it slide over you for the moment:

'Ελέναυς That Drake saw the armada
                         & sea caves
Ra-Set over crystal

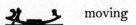   moving

in the Queen's eye the reflection
& sea-wrack—
                green deep of the sea-cave

ne quaesaris.
       He asked not
nor wavered, seeing, nor had fear of the wood-queen, Artemis
          that is Diana
nor had killed save by the hunting rite,
                      sanctus.
Thus sang it :
       Leafdi Diana, leove Diana
       Heye Diana, help me to neode
Witte me thurh crafte
      whuder ich maei lidhan
      to wonsom londe.
              Rome th'ilke tyme was noght.
So that he spread a deer-hide near the altar,
Now Lear in Janus' temple is laid

 timing the thunder

Nor Constance hath his hood again,
    Merlin's fader may no man know
    Merlin's moder is made a nun.
Lord, thaet scop the dayes lihte,
    all that she knew was a spirit bright,
A movement that moved in cloth of gold
    into her chamber.
'By the white dragon, under a stone
    Merlin's fader is known to none.'
Lay me by Aurelie, at the east end of Stonhenge
    where lie my kindred
Over harm
Over hate
       overflooding, light over light
And yilden he gon rere
           (Athelstan before a.D. 940)
the light flowing, whelming the stars.

In the barge of Ra-Set
On river of crystal
So hath Sibile a boken isette.   C.91

When discussing Pound's use of pronouns in ch. 8 I said I
would return with a more complex example and this is it.

'He asked not' refers grammatically back to Drake who 'saw
the armada', but the actual context ('nor wavered, seeing, nor
had fear of the wood-queen') could refer to Drake and Elizabeth
but is much more clearly applicable to Actaeon, one of Pound's
favourite metamorphoses.[1] By making two different predicates
depend on the one pronoun, Pound changes Drake into Actaeon,
Drake's vision into Actaeon's vision and the virgin-queen into
the virgin-goddess. The word 'Ελεναυς (destroyer of cities)
moreover recalls Helen of Troy and in the Diana-context
reminds us that a third identity may be involved, namely
Agamemnon, who was linked in C.89 with Judge Marshall
('Judge Marshall, Father of War / Agamemnon killed that
stag, against hunting rites') in an allusion to Agamemnon's
sacrifice of Iphigenia to the winds after his fleet had been wind-
bound because of Diana's anger at him for having killed one of
her stags. So Agamemnon, like Actaeon sinning against Diana,
was father of war.[2]

By a further juxtaposition, Pound changes Drake/Actaeon/
Agamemnon into Brutus, mythical founder of 'Brutaine' or the
British nation. For the next sentence, 'Thus sang it', which
appears to refer back to the same 'he', in fact introduces the
prayer to Diana sung by Brutus in Laȝamon's *Brut*.[3]

The story (I summarize) runs as follows: Brutus was the

[1] Cp. the fusion of Actaeon with Vidal, C.4, mentioned in ch. 8.
[2] Cp. also the early poem *The Coming of War: 'Actaeon'*, where
Actaeon is connected with the 'hosts of ancient people', possibly the dead
warriors of Stonehenge.
[3] Ed. Sir Frederick Madden, Soc. of Antiquaries, 3 vols., 1847. I shall
be quoting from this edition, which counts half-lines as lines, making it
seem even longer than it is, because it is the one Pound used and because
only one volume of the more modern edition by G. L. Brook & R. F.
Leslie (E.E.T.S. 1963) has so far appeared.

great grandson of Aeneas who had escaped from Troy and become king of Italy. A prophecy had foretold that he would slay his parents, which he did (his father by mistake, his mother in childbirth); then he went to Greece and helped free his Trojan kinsmen, left with the king's daughter and came to an island, empty except for wild deer. His men found a marble temple with the image of Diana and were frightened, but Brutus, unafraid, entered the temple alone, with a vessel of red gold, full of milk from a white hind he had shot, and wine separately. He made a fire, walked nine times round it, kissed the altar, poured milk on the fire and spoke these words (Pound's quotes in italics):

> *Leafdi Diana: leove Diana* : *heʒe Diana* . *help me to neode.*
> Wise me & *wit*ere : *þurh þine wihtful craft.*
> *Whuder ich maei liðan* : & ledan mine leoden.
> *to* ane *wnsome londe:* þer ich mihte wunien.[1]

He falls asleep and Diana tells him in a dream to go to Albion, where there is fish, fowl, wood, water and desert, a 'winsome land' inhabited by giants but empty of men. He is to build a new Troy there and have royal progeny. Which he does, landing at Totnes [Devon], like most British kings in the *Brut*.

Pound's next line, 'Rome th'ilke tyme was noght' is not from Laʒamon but from Robert of Brunne, a fourteenth-century adapter of these British histories and Pound has lifted it from a footnote by Madden. He has gone right back to the beginning of the *Brut*, when Aeneas lands in Italy and where Laʒamon is less vivid than Robert (I modernize): 'In Italy they came to land, where Rome now stands. Many years under the sun, Rome was not inhabited.'[2] Madden notes that Wace has 'Ni ert de Rome uncore nule chose', which Robert of Brunne renders 'Of Rome th^t ilke tyme was noght'.[3] Clearly Robert's way of putting it

---

[1] Lady Diana, dear Diana, high Diana, help me in my need. Teach me and counsel me through thy wise skill, where I might go, and lead my people to a winsome land where I might dwell (ð,þ =th; ʒ =gh).

[2] Madden 106 ff.: 'On Italiʒe heo comen to londe : þar Rome nou on stondeð. / fele ʒer under sunnan : nas ʒet Rome bi-wonnen.

[3] Pound has changed the small t (=that) into an apostrophe.

was more to Pound's purpose here, echoing his own marvellous ellipsis about Rome out of Paul the Deacon (see ch. 8, p. 146). Moreover, Pound is being what Donald Davie would call 'slightly less archaic' because he is evoking Laȝamon as narrator, that is, much later than the event told, and so chooses a narrator later than Laȝamon but earlier than Pound (our view of Rome being timeless).

In other words, he quotes directly from Laȝamon *only for the prayer itself* (oratio directa), to give it its oldest possible English flavour, but uses a later narrator for the comment on Rome, then slips back into his own modern English to effect the time-leap from Brutus ('So that he spread a deer-hide near the altar') to Lear (Leir in Laȝamon), many generations later, the film-like transition-shot being fused in the two temples, that of Diana for Brutus, that of Janus for Lear, Diana being the female counterpoint of double-headed Janus.[1]

In Laȝamon the Lear story ends somewhat differently from Shakespeare's version: Cordoille having married the king of the Franks, welcomes her penitent father and together with her husband helps him regain his kingdom, where she then joins him after her husband's death. Leir dies three years later and she buries him in Leir-chester (Leicester), 'inne Janies temple: al swa þe bac tellet' (as the book tells).

The ideogram chên[4] which follows, with Pound's extraordinary translation, 'timing the thunder', is composed of the radical yü[3], meaning rain (the pictograph shows the dripping roof of heaven—the same radical incidentally, as in the ling[2]

[1] See A. B. Cook, *Zeus* (1914–20, Vol. I, pp. 392–422) and G. R. Levy, *The Gate of Horn* (London 1948, p. 120). Janus ruled the double gates of birth and death, which is the earth. Cp. the importance of gates in C.47, 'by this gate art thou measured / Thy day is between a door and a door' (an image of life which also occurs in Bede's famous comparison of the soul as a bird flying in through one door and out of the other). In C.94: 'And that all gates are holy.' The concept of the gate is reflected in the trilithons of Stonehenge and other megalithic monuments, notably the lion-gate at Mycenae, related to the neolithic concept of cave as tomb and temple, womb of the Mother Goddess. Diana/Artemis was also a goddess of the underworld, as shown by her Ephesian image (many-breasted goddess suckling the new-born dead), hence Brutus' sacrificial milk.

ideogram for sensibility at the end of the last chapter), above the phonetic component ch'ên², which used by itself means a period of time or, in certain contexts, temporal, vegetative changes, plants transformed by the elements. Conventionally ch'ên⁴ means 'awe' or 'tremble' or 'quake', as at or in an earthquake,[1] but Pound is breaking it up etymologically with his gloss, which evokes (together with the sudden modern English), Shakespeare's storm-tossed Lear, himself a sort of Father Time or Janus figure, double-faced in his foolish past and the new year of his lesson learnt about the true meaning of love. But the whole significance of the ideogram (awe) is also there, recalling the other temple, Diana's, and the vision of Brutus, and the time passed, Leir being after all part of the royal progeny foretold to Brutus by the goddess.

After this leap forward from Brutus to Leir, itself firmly linked both back to Brutus and to Rome, and forward to Elizabethan England, Pound switches to what Davie calls 'less archaic English', and what I shall call 'synthetic Laʒamon' (i.e. by Pound), that is, Pound/Laʒamon narrative, earlier than Shakespeare but later than Leir or other matter told. For the line about Constance makes another huge leap to post-Roman Britain, to Constantin the Fair, brother of Aldroein of Britanny. The Britons are in trouble as usual, under Febus of Rome, and send to Aldroein for help. He sends Constantin who lands (of course) at Totnes and becomes king. Constantin has three sons: Constance, who becomes a monk at his father's wish; Aurelius, surnamed Ambrosius; and Uther.

We have reached the beginning of the Arthurian legend. When Constantin dies the people choose the boy Aurelius (Aurelie in Laʒamon), Uther being too small. But Vortiger, a crafty earl, half Welsh, visits the monastery and persuades Constance, a fool, to shed his hood and become king, with himself as steward. Constance accepts and is smuggled out in a knight's cloak while a swain is dressed in his habit ('the hood hanged down as if hiding his crown'). The abbot, who thought

[1] Hugh Gordon Porteus in a private letter.

192

the knights had come to bid Constance 'hold his hood', is furious and threatens to 'unhood' Constance. The people don't want a monk for king but Vortiger explains that Constance is now unhooded, the bishops are too afraid to protest, and 'Constance deserted God's hood and had sorrow'. For this is part of Vortiger's plan. Constance knows nothing of government, and lets Vortiger rule 'except in the one single thing that he be still called king.'[1] Vortiger laughs, makes an alliance with the Picts, who in his arranged absence seize the king, cut off his head and send for Vortiger, who weeps and pretends the Picts have betrayed him by killing the king. The Britons march against the Picts and slay them to a man.

Wise men then take the children Aurelie and Uther overseas to 'the less Britain' where Biduz the king brings them up. Vortiger becomes a very cruel king, invites Hengest and Horsa from Alemaine (the 'Angles' and 'Saxons') and is reproached by the people for befriending pagans. Vortiger's sons attack him, his son Vortimer becomes a good king, Hengest flees, Vortiger wanders for five years all over Britain. But he returns and sends for Hengest again and Hengest promises peace, in a plain near Ambresbury 'now hight Stonehenge', where the Britons give up their weapons in token of good will and are massacred.

Pound has here telescoped a whole era of lost kingship and good government into one sentence, which also fuses all Laȝamon's 'hood' phrases, where 'hood', in this context, means 'God's hood' or holy orders, or grace, as well as the crown, never really worn, and the head lost. Constance's foolishness is linked with Leir's (who was blind to love), just as Leir is linked, through the temple and deer-hide and religious ceremony, to Brutus and Diana and Troy and early Rome.

But Diana's prophecy about Brutus and his progeny is already rocked about. Hengest now rules and Vortiger flees again to Wales, where he tries to build a castle which keeps falling down,

[1] Cp. *King Lear*, Act I sc. 1 : Only we still retain / The name, and all th'additions to a king. The sway, / Revenue, execution of the rest, / Beloved sons, be yours . . .

until a wise man (Merlin's rival) tells him that the clay needs the blood of a man born of no father. Vortiger's men overhear a boy (Merlin) being taunted by children for having no father and a whore for a mother. The boy's mother is sent for, who had become a nun.[1] She explains that she was the daughter of king Conaan, and dwelt in a rich mansion, and how one night, at fifteen, 'when I was wrapped in bed, softly in my sleep . . . the fairest thing that ever was born came before me, like a great knight, *all clothed in gold* [basis for Pound's line]. . . . This thing *glided before me*, glittering in gold. Often it kissed me, often it embraced me, often it approached me, and came very close to me. When at length I looked at myself . . . my flesh was loathsome to me, my limbs unfamiliar. . . . Then I perceived at last that I was with child. . . . I do not know who on this earth his father was . . . nor whether it is an evil creature, or made on God's behalf.'[2]

Pound does not quote direct but takes what he wants (I am not commenting on 'Lord thaet scop the dayes lihte' for the moment). The three lines that come after the ideogram all refer to the same period, later than the previous but still remote enough in time and historical veracity for a suggestion of archaism to feel right. The two lines after the modern 'hood' line (Constance), about Merlin's 'fader' and 'moder', are in 'synthetic Laȝamon', which manages to echo the boys' taunts to Merlin as well as the comically crude story of the sailor in C.12 (' "I am not your fader but your moder" quod he'), and also, quite distinctly, the 'no-man' tag of Odysseus. And the moment we think of Odysseus in a context suggesting magic (Merlin), we can't help thinking of Circe, which takes us back to the beginning of the passage, when Brutus' men are frightened by the temple of Diana ('the devil loved her'), and one of whose names was after all Hecate. This in itself echoes the various

[1] Madden 15640: 'Nu wes Maerlinges moder: wundermere i-wurðen / in ane haȝe munstre: munchene ihaded' (literally: now was Merlin's mother wonderfully become, in a high monastery, a hooded nun).

[2] Madden 15706 ff. My translation. Brunne has no golden creature, just an abstract being (ywist).

Circe passages in the Cantos, Odysseus being at one with the goddess, but his men frightened of her. Clearly Pound made the connection too, for 'help me to neede' is repeated in C.106, in a Circean context, together with the thunder/vegetation allusion.[1]

The 'archaic' or true Laȝamon line which follows ('Lord, thaet scop the dayes lihte') does not in fact belong to the mother's story but is taken from Aurelie's prayer before battle (see below), i.e. once again a prayer, in *oratio directa*. Here it serves to introduce, in the English language nearest to the event, the account of Merlin's immaculate conception, the magic, the *forma*, but because both Merlin and the *forma* are timeless, the actual account is given neither in Laȝamon's words nor in 'synthetic Laȝamon', but in Pound's modern English, delicately cutting across the nun's own story.

Merlin duly explains (in Laȝamon) that two dragons, North and South, red and white, fight at midnight under a stone under the castle, which is why the castle keeps crumbling. And so it turns out. Vortiger asks the meaning and is told that Aurelie and Uther are landing the next day at Totnes. Aurelie will have the kingdom first, but will be poisoned, then Uther, who will also be poisoned, and there is to be much contest. Uther will have a son out of Cornwall, a wild boar, who will rule Rome (Arthur).[2] Pound telescopes all this into one phrase, in modern English, which mentions only 'the white dragon, under a stone' (Aurelie, who is to lie under Stonehenge) and then recalls (in 'synthetic Laȝamon', i.e. Pound/Laȝamon the

[1] . . . but Circe was like that / coming from the house of smoothe stone / 'not know which god' / nor could enter her eyes by probing . . . Circe / Zeus : Artemis out of Leto / Under wildwood / Help me to neede / By Circeo, the stone eyes looking seaward . . . The temple shook with Apollo . . . And in thy mind beauty, O Artemis . . . Whuder ich maei lidhan / help me to neede / the flowers are blessed against thunder bolt / helpe me to neede.

[2] The germ of this story is first found in Nennius (fl. 769) *Historia Britonum* (ed. Josephus Stevenson, London 1938, pp. 31 ff.), where Merlin is called Ambrosius. The two dragons fight and the white one is defeated. Ambrosius explains that the Saxons will be driven out by the Britons.

narrator, but still in the same quotation marks as what Merlin says, thus fusing the two with the magician) that 'Merlin's fader is known to none'. A strange fusion of Odysseus/Pound/Laȝamon/Merlin/Aurelie thus takes place.

Aurelie becomes king and fights Hengest. Before the battle he prays aloud : 'ȝif ich mot ibiden : þat ich aȝaen ride. / & hit wulle *drihte : þe scop þes daȝes lihte*. / þat ich mote mid ifunde : biȝite mine ikunde. / chirchen ich wulle araere : & god ich wulle haeren. / ich wulle alche cnihte : ȝeuen his irihte.'[1]

With the exception of the later reference to Athelstan and the final reference to the Sibyl, this phrase from Aurelie's prayer and that from Brutus' prayer to Diana are the only direct quotations from Laȝamon. The phrase is transferred to Merlin's mother, not just by attributing it to her but by Pound's telescoping method. The fact of the immaculate conception is given in modern English because it is timeless and the quaintness of direct quotation might lose the sobriety of the nun's account. But the mystery, and its possible divine origin—of which she herself has doubts—is hinted at in this direct quotation, more like an oath on her part as to the truth of her story, and left in 'archaic' English.[2] The phrase is transferred, moreover, from a prayer before a battle of ethnic significance (Britons versus Saxons) to a context of mystery important in Pound's theory of imaginative creation, and it thereby retains both connotations.

When Hengest is finally defeated and killed Aurelie goes to Ambresbury (Amesbury) and sends for Merlin, asking him where he can find men who can hew stone to build a lasting work in memory of the Britons massacred there by Hengest.[3]

[1] The prayer is in rhyme (unusual in alliterative verse) : If I might abide, that I should ride back, and if *the Lord will it who created the daylight*, that I might in safety obtain my right, I will build churches, and worship God, I will give each man his right.

[2] Pound amusingly casts doubt on the whole thing a page later : ' "A spirit in cloth of gold" / so Merlin's moder said, / or did not say.'

[3] He seems to have forgotten his promise to build a church. But see fuller discussion of this point in the original essay. To Geoffrey of Monmouth (Laȝamon's source) who 'invented' this story, the monument would be a church, like Battle Abbey built by William the Conqueror on the site of his victory.

Merlin tells him to go to Ireland and transfer the Giants' Ring stones from Mount Kilara to Britain. After fighting the king of Ireland they find the stones but can't move them. Merlin then uses some clever engines which shift the stones as if they were light as feathers, and on Whitsunday they hallow the new place called Stonehenge.

Aurelie duly dies, poisoned, and says: '*& leggeð me an aest aende : inne Stanhenge. | [ware lip mochel of mine cun]*.[1]'

When Uther eventually dies he does not say 'bury me by Aurelie', or indeed anything, but he is buried in Stonehenge: 'Then the people took the dead king . . . and carried him forth into Stonehenge, and buried him there, by his dear brother; side by side they both lie.' (Madden 19816 ff.). Once again Pound telescopes two different parts of Laȝamon: Aurelie *asks* to be buried in Stonehenge, where lie his kin; Uther *is* buried there, by Aurelie. Clearly he cannot make such a telescoping by quoting direct. Nor does he use 'synthetic Laȝamon', but modern English. The period is still remote and legendary, but this is a dying statement, as in a Will (from the reader's viewpoint, a tone of do-not-misunderstand-me), and on the other hand it also jerks us back to the present: not in the third person narrative we were given for Drake/Actaeon/Brutus, then Leir, Constance, and Merlin's mother; but in the first person, 'me', quite suddenly, as if it were the poet himself rather than or as well as Uther asking to be buried by Aurelie in Stonehenge. The whole passage began with a similar metamorphosis achieved by making a pronoun do more than double duty. Pound momentarily identifies with Uther, and since Uther's words were in fact spoken by Aurelie there is a double identification.

Aurelie/Uther/Pound is thus to lie with his kindred beneath the monument at Stonehenge, 'Over harm / Over hate', these thereby acquiring a double meaning: Hengest's massacre of the Britons and wars in general, together with a more personal connotation, Pound's own harm and hate, both by and towards

---

[1] Madden 17842. The interpolated half-line used by Pound is from the other MS., printed parallel. 'And lay me at the east end, in Stonehenge, where lie much of my kin.'

himself. The reference is all the more poignant if we remember that Diana's advice to Brutus to go to Albion and build a new Troy there (Trinovant, later called Ludinum, from a king Lud, according to Geoffrey's splendid eponymous etymologies), and her prophecy about his royal progeny, ultimately came to nothing. In Laȝamon, as in his source Geoffrey of Monmouth, the history of the British people ends with the sad story of Cadwalader as an exile in Britanny, hearing of Athelstan's success (Pound's mention of Athelstan's gilds effects a leap of several centuries). Cadwalader gathers his ships but dreams of Christ telling him to go to Rome instead, where he must be shriven and die, for neither he nor any other Britons are ever more to possess England, which Alemainish men shall have, until the time comes that was declared by Merlin, when Britons shall go to Rome and get Cadwalader's bones and carry them to Britain, and become bold, and prosper. His wise men consult the histories to see if the dream accords with the prophecies of Merlin and those of the Sibyl, and they find that it does. So Cadwalader calls his sons and explains, adding that Merlin said it in words 'and *Sibillie* þa wise : | *a bocken hit isette.*'[1]

It is interesting that Pound, quoting this line at the end of the passage (after the reference to Athelstan setting up gilds[2]), manages to link the Sibyl (herself linked to Merlin as her male counterpart) back to Ra-Set and the 'river of crystal', that is, the total light process ('the sun and the moon', see p. 95), part of which is Diana, and hence by implication back to Diana's prophecy to Brutus.

Cadwalader obeys, and his bones are still in Rome. Laȝamon ends his history with these moving words : 'And the English kings ruled these lands, and the Britons lost it . . . so that nevermore were they kings here. And this same day came not, be it

[1] Madden 32182–3. Sibyl the wise set it in a book.
[2] The phrase is also from Laȝamon : 'hu Aðelstan her com liðen . . . *& ȝilden he gon rere* (Madden 31989 ff.). I shall not discuss this here, see my essay. They are not guilds in the mediaeval sense but peace-gilds set up by the bishops and reeves of London for mutual protection against cattle-thieves (*Laws*, VI Athelstan), echoing Pound's idea of good government.

henceforth as it may; happen what happens, happen God's will. Amen.' (Madden 32232–41). For Pound too, in a sense, lost England, and lost America, or they lost him. Nevertheless the composite figure Pound/Uther/Aurelie lies under a great monument, 'over-flooding, light over light.' The idea is itself folded round the reference to Athelstan setting up gilds, also a kind of monument left by him, just as Aurelie is said to have left Stonehenge, and Pound is leaving *The Cantos*.

One of the reasons why I have gone into this passage in such detail— apart from the sheer fun of it—is to take up the question of a historian's 'truth' in relation to the story of Stonehenge and the 'legendary' history of Britain as given by Laȝamon's source, Geoffrey of Monmouth.[1]

Stonehenge was not, of course, built in the fifth century A.D., the supposed Arthurian times, and therefore not by 'Aurelius'. Ambrosius Aurelius is paralleled in Bede and in Gildas, and was probably a real person, who defended the Britons after the Roman withdrawal.[2] Geoffrey is one of the 'romancers', who had an immense influence on the vogue of 'Matter of Britain' stories which had already begun in the twelfth century, but who, like Pound himself, has been castigated by scholars as a bad historian. Certainly his predecessors and contemporaries do not present innumerable generations of pre-Roman British kings from 'Brutus' on (though Brutus occurs in Nennius), indeed they do not deal with pre-Roman times at all.[3] Even in the nineteenth century the editor of Gildas tells us in typical scornful terms: 'Geoffrey of Monmouth, upon whose veracity as a historian no reliance can be placed, speaks confidently of a book

[1] *Historia Regum Britanniae*, ed. Acton Griscom, London 1929.

[2] Arthur E. Hutson, *British Personal Names in the Historia Regum Britanniae* (Univ. of California Publications in English, vol. V, 1944); Lloyd, *History of Wales* (London, 1939, p. 100); Maynardier's discussion in *Anniversary Papers by Colleagues and Students of G. L. Kittredge* (1913, pp. 119–26).

[3] Gildas and Bede start with a chapter on the geography of Britain based on Pliny, Solicius and Orosius, then plunge in with Julius Caesar up to the Saxons. So William of Malmesbury in the twelfth century, bringing it up to his own times.

by Gildas, *De Victoria Aurelii Ambrosii*, a production which no one, it is believed, except himself, has had the good fortune to see.'[1] And at the end of his history Geoffrey adds a taunt to William of Malmesbury and Henry of Huntingdon, leaving them the Saxon kings but bidding them be silent as to the British kings, since they did not possess a 'most ancient book, written in the British tongue, which Walter archdeacon of Oxford brought out of Britain.'

The quarrel about Geoffrey and the ancient book has gone on for years. Acton Griscom, Geoffrey's editor, defended him as a historian of pre-Roman times and Arthurian times, not of course denying that he invented a great deal, but insisting that he had access to Welsh and Breton oral and possibly written traditions at a time when these were still familiar, before Saxon, Danish and Norman invaders destroyed written records. Griscom's views did not find favour at the time, and yet modern archaeology has proved Geoffrey right in some of his detail as well as in general, broad outline.

The story of the transport of the stones by miraculous engines from Ireland, for instance, was long regarded as a flight of fancy. Yet in 1923 (and inexplicably ignored by Griscom, though he uses other more local arguments from archaeology, about Vortiger and about a massacre of Roman legionaries—see my essay), it was discovered that the bluestones at Stonehenge, as opposed to the local sarsen stones, were in fact transported, and by water, from an almost equally distant place, namely Prescelly, a holy mountain in Wales. They came along the coastal trade-route which was also used for the transport of copper and later bronze from Ireland, and then up the Avon, and this in a period before the invention of the wheel (around 1700 B.C., stage II of Stonehenge), by methods amazing enough to have left a tradition of magical engineering that would easily give rise to Merlin's part in the story.[2]

[1] *De Excidio Britanniae*, ed. Josephus Stevenson, 1838. The reference is to *Historia Regum Britanniae*, IV/xx.

[2] Cp. R. J. C. Atkinson, *Stonehenge* (London 1956, Pelican Book 1960), and Stuart Piggot, Antiquity XV (1941, pp. 269–86, 305–19)

Secondly, it is quite clear from what we now know of the many waves of peoples or 'cultures' who came to England in prehistoric times that Geoffrey, though romanticizing, was not totally inventing. In my essay I link these waves to what Professor Atkinson has to say about the different stages of Stonehenge, and anyone interested in that kind of detail can read it there. But to make it brief, most of these waves of cultures came from the Mediterranean, via Spain, Western France and Britanny, or else from S.W. and Central Europe, via the Rhine. Stonehenge itself is distinctly linked, at one of its stages, with Minoan Crete and the Mycenean civilization (see Atkinson, who even suggests a visiting Minoan architect). None of these 'waves' was of course Celtic or 'British':

Before 2300 B.C. : indigenous, mesolithic, hunting/fishing/ gathering of wild fruit and natural raw materials.

Around 2300 B.C. : Windmill Hill Culture, Western Neolithic from East Mediterranean, via Iberia, France, Switzerland, Channel coasts. Agriculturers, stock-raisers. Long barrows and cattle-corrals.

Around 1900 B.C. : Megalith Builders, also Neolithic, bearers of potent religious doctrine, collective tombs, S.W. France, Bay of Biscay, Breton peninsula, Gloucestershire, Silbury Hill.

1900–1700 B.C. : Secondary Neolithic, nomadic, fishing, hunting, dealings in antlers, hides, vegetable ropes etc., exploited flint mines for axes to be traded over hundreds of miles; tribal; embanked enclosures (Woodhenge and early wooden stage of Stonehenge, now gone); probably a chthonic religion.

Around 1700 B.C. : Beaker Cultures (Bell Beaker from S.W. and C. Europe, Necked Beaker mingling with warrior invaders from Russian steppes via Rhine). Fabrication of objects for prestige trade-routes from Ireland (Stonehenge

who discusses Geoffrey's source and concludes that we cannot rule out the possibility that he had access to a written oral tradition. Atkinson observes that the correspondence between legend and fact is so striking that we cannot dismiss it as mere coincidence.

II and transport of bluestones). Probably a sky-orientated religion.

About 1500 B.C.: Wessex Culture, Early Bronze Age but mingling with previous. Rich graves, warrior chieftains, vast commerce with metal centres in S. Germany and Bohemia, amber from S.C. Europe instead of direct from Scandinavia, probable trade with Minoan Crete (dagger and double-axe motifs at Stonehenge link with both Mycenae and Britanny). Evidence of concentration of power in hands of single strong man, whose memorial Stonehenge may be (Stonehenge III, one prehistoric burial found).

It is clear even from this very rough summary that Geoffrey had access to some genuine traditions concerning the Mediterranean origins of what (being a Welshman) he calls the British people, their continual comings and goings and new landings (representing new waves perhaps), as well as their continuing links, friendly or hostile, with that area ('Rome', 'Troy'), with the Rhine, Southern Germany, Bohemia ('Alemaine'), with Britanny and the Bay of Biscay ('Less Britain', 'Armorica') and Ireland. Of course he (or the author of the 'most ancient book') formalized it with names of kings who no doubt never existed in the mediaeval sense that Geoffrey had in mind. He imposed his own concepts on ancient times just as, for that matter, Shakespeare did.

The historical aspect of Geoffrey and of Stonehenge deserves consideration in such detail because it brings out a similar aspect of Pound. Of course Pound isn't concerned with the historical truth of Laʒamon (and hence of Geoffrey) in this archaeological sense, at least not in this passage. But he is a visionary in much the same way that Geoffrey was, and like all visionaries he may (or at times may not) get hold of some essential truth by what can only be termed intuitive means, and through the 'tradition' or what he calls Sagetrieb. Put in the barest terms, Pound's interest in Stonehenge and the extraordinary telescoping of periods, the timing the thunder, which he achieves in this passage means this (I put the legendary material in italics):

Britain, the present home of the English language, was once a Mediterranean culture, *guided to these shores by the goddess of the hunt and of the moon of purity, of birth and death,* and throughout retained its links with that area. A monument remains testifying to this, *built by magic, Merlin's magic, to commemorate the fallen in a Saxon massacre of the Britons, by Aurelius, a temporary victor over the Saxons,* through early connections with both Ireland (the trade route) and holiness (the mountain of Prescelly, the chthonic religious doctrine of the Megalith builders from the Mediterranean via Britanny, the sky-orientated religion of the Beaker Cultures), as well as with pre-Hellenic Greece (Mycenae). In this link with Mycenae it represents the notion of perfect proportion so dear to Pound. *But the Britons lost this land,* these traditions, this *forma,* only to glimpse it now and again (one of the immediate examples being Athelstan's 'monument'), *and its representatives lie buried under the monument of Stonehenge, just as Leir lies buried in his temple.* 'The temple is holy because it is not for sale' is a line which occurs three times in C.97. This monument is as one temple (that of Diana, that of Janus, Stonehenge), as the body is the temple of the spirit, eyes looking out of the cave, where Brutus/Actaeon/Drake/Odysseus/Pound have their visions of the goddess, the temple where lies Aurelie/Uther/Merlin/Laʒamon/Geoffrey/Athelstan/Pound. And the monument remains, and the treatment of Laʒamon in C.91 is a perfect example of the carver's art, related, as always in Pound at his best, to the whole, e.g. the opening of C.90:

> 'From the colour the nature
> & by the nature the sign!'
> Beatific spirits welding together
> as in one ash-tree in Ygdrasail.
> Baucis, Philemon.
> Castalia is the name of that fount in the hill's fold.
> the sea below,
> narrow beach.

Templum aedificans, not yet marble,
              'Amphion!'
And from the San Ku

       to the room in Poitiers where one can stand
                   casting no shadow,
That is Sagetrieb,
                        that is tradition.
Builders had kept the proportion,
             did Jacques de Molay
                   know these proportions?
and was Erigena ours?
                   Moon's barge over milk-blue water
Kuthera δεινά
Kuthera sempiterna
                   Ubi amor, ibi oculus.

Colour is the active mode of the object as love is the active
mode of the soul, and we love the object or the soul through these
their manifestations. In mythical terms, although the roots of
things are in another realm, we worship by understanding
particular manifestations on earth. So with the tree of
'Ygdrasail', which already occurred in C.85: 'That you lean
'gainst the tree of heaven, / and know Ygdrasail'. Yggdrasil is
from Norse mythology, the world ash on which the structure of
the universe was based, but Pound is referring to Frobenius'
idea of all cultures unfolding 'as a single unity. . . . The whole
of it one huge tree, the tree of heaven, Ygdrasill.'[1]

Baucis and Philemon (in Ovid) were a poor old couple who
entertained the gods Zeus and Hermes. These had come to visit
mankind in disguise and had been repulsed by the rich. To

[1] Eva Hesse, *New Approaches to Ezra Pound* (London 1969, ed.
Hesse, Introduction); Frobenius, *Von Kulturreich des Festlandes*, 1923.

reward the couple they saved them from a deluge and granted them a wish. They asked to be made priest and priestess of the gods, and their house was changed into a temple. (Cp. the pines of Takasago—a Nō play on a legend of idyllic married love— merge with the pines of the Shinto shrines at Ise in C.4, immediately after the Actaeon passage.)

Castalia is the fountain in the rock at Delphi, where spoke the Sibyl of Apollo's oracle. *Templum aedificans* echoes the pope's grudging reference to Malatesta's Tempio, templum aedificavit. So Amphion (also in C.62) raised stones in his track with the music of his lyre (not yet marble but music). And the San Ku was a council of three ( = 3) established by Cheng Wang of the Chou dynasty, associated in Pound's mind (possibly through Couvreur's quasi-masonic terminology, 'le grand maître' etc.) with the idea of a secret tradition of people who kept the proportions, as exemplified here by de Molay and Erigena. The council's function was to 'étendre partout la réforme, s'appliquant avec respect à faire briller l'action du ciel et de la terre' (*Chou King*, ed. Couvreur, p. 333). This leads straight to the tower in Poitiers, built by the Knight Templar Jacques de Molay, where no shadow falls in a certain room at a certain time, and on to Erigena who was tried centuries after his death for saying that 'Authority comes from right reason, / never the other way on' (C.36) and whom Pound also has saying *omnia quae sunt lumina sunt*; and on to Aphrodite (Kuthera deina) and the quotation from Richard of St Victor, Ubi amor, ibi oculus. The tradition is slow to develop. Already in C.87 we had :

> Only sequoias are slow enough.
> BinBin 'is beauty'.
> 'Slowness is beauty'.
> from the

San

Ku

to Poictiers.
The tower wherein, at one point, is no shadow,
        and Jacques de Molay, is where?
and the 'Section', the proportions,
                              [Section d'or, see p. 219]
    lending, perhaps, not at interest, but resisting.
Then false fronts, barocco.
    'We have', said Mencius, 'but phenomena.'
monumenta. In nature are signatures
        needing no verbal tradition,
oak leaf never plane leaf. John Heydon.[1]   [cp. p. 139]

For Pound believes that the Neoplatonic and gnostic philosophies preserved these secret traditions from earliest times. The fact that the axis of Stonehenge is so important to the falling of the first light of sunrise on midsummer day may be linked to the unwobbling pivot of Confucius, to the tower in Poitiers, and also to the peculiar shape of the fortress-temple on the mountain-top at Montségur (like an elongated pentagon, built so that the sunrise should fall on the altar at a certain time), where the Cathars made their last stand in the Albigensian Crusade and were destroyed to a man (burnt alive) by Simon de Montfort. The Cathars were of course Gnostics, so that Pound links them with the much earlier 'heretic' Scotus Erigena, who put Greek tags in his verse (charmingly shown as putting them in while the queen stitches Charlemagne's 'shirts or whatever' in C.83), Erigena the Irishman who was dug up as a Manichaean: 'They probably murdered Erigena, / Athelstan gon yulden rere, after 925' (C.105). Or:

[1] Cp. Walter Baumann, *Secretary of Nature, J. Heydon*, in *New Approaches to Ezra Pound*, ed. Eva Hesse London, 1969. BinBin is the poet Laurence Binyon, from whom Pound quotes the phrase 'Slowness is beauty' in *Guide to Kulchur* (p. 129). Cp. also Pound's very funny and ambiguous essay on Binyon's translation of Dante (*Hell 1934*, in Lit. Essays, 1954).

TIMING THE THUNDER

Sunt lumina

that the drama is wholly subjective
stone knowing the form which the carver imparts it
the stone knows the form.

C.74

Sunt lumina

CHAPTER ELEVEN

'and they dug him up out of sepulture
soi disantly looking for Manichaeans'

——————⁓⁓⁓⁓⁓⁓——————

I n the last chapter I tried to show what Pound does with
different layers of language and aspects of history, and the
very particular pleasure which can be derived from *The Cantos*
if one enters into the associations of the creative process with him.

In this one I am going to link back to Chapter Nine—for
those who skipped Chapter Ten—as well as with the end of
Chapter Ten, and attempt to deal with Eros and economics
together : partly because I've been shying off the economics and
have little room left, and in any case know a good deal more
about Eros than about economics, but also because Pound
himself is continually linking them, not only explicitly as in
the two Usura Cantos (45 and 51), but implicitly as in his
treatment of Circe, or in the juxtapositions of the Church's
persecution of the Catharist 'heresy' (which many scholars
believe lies behind the doctrine of Courtly Love) with hard
economic facts or with the similar kind of intolerance, the
Protestant intolerance of the flesh which divides flesh and spirit,
and creates the hypocrisy that only the flesh is sin, thus pervert-
ing nature and diverting the energy so obtained into other more
radical perversions of nature through money, profiteering, power,
war, or in Freud's interestingly capitalist term, reinvesting it.

'sunt lumina', said the Oirishman to King Carolus,
                   'OMNIA,
all things that are are lights.'
and they dug him up out of sepulture
soi disantly looking for Manichaeans.

THEY DUG HIM UP OUT OF SEPULTURE

Les Albigeois, a problem of history,
and the fleet at Salamis made with money lent by the state to
the shipwrights
Tempus tacendi, tempus loquendi.
Never inside the country to raise the standard of living
but always abroad to increase the profits of usurers,
dixit Lenin,
and gun sales lead to more gun sales
   they do not clutter the market for gunnery
     there is no saturation
Pisa, in the 23rd year of the effort in sight of the tower
and Till was hung yesterday
for murder and rape with trimmings plus Cholkis
   plus mythology, thought he was Zeus ram or another one
     Hey Snag wots in the bibl'?
     wot are the books ov the bible?
     Name'em, don't bullshit ME.

莫   ΟΥ ΤΙΣ

a man on whom the sun has gone down
the ewe, he said had such a pretty look in her eyes . . .
C.74

Poor Till, co-prisoner of Pound in the U.S. Detention Camp at Pisa, whose culture is reduced to that of Quiz-shows, has at least been immortalized by Pound and placed, as it were, among the gods, the uncontrollable mystery on the bestial floor. The ideogram mo⁴ means 1/ NOT, DON'T, and 2/ (more current) NO-ONE, NOBODY (hence the gloss ΟΥ ΤΙΣ, no-man, the pun on his name Odysseus gives to Polyphemus). At the same time, Pound obviously saw the lower component as 'man', and indeed the Professor of Chinese in the University where I teach also said it was 'man', with the cross bar for 'strong man', until we looked up the seal style of the whole ideogram and saw that the lower component was a stylization of the upper component for plants (Ψ Ψ) which shows that Pound's 'mistakes' are not always barmy, and that one should not be too pedantic. And he therefore saw the middle component, sun, under plants, as 'going down' on a man. The ideogram does not mean and has

never meant sunset, but there is a similar ideogram, mu⁴

which does mean sunset, and which Pound may have caught sight of in Mathews. The point is that mo⁴ is made visually to illustrate three different meanings in the text, a brilliant use of one ideogram in juxtaposition.

Pound is here more concerned about Till and the intolerance shown towards him than about the intolerance towards himself. Already in the very early Cantos he was presenting the myths of self-centred violence, in which no one is able to break out of their own passion to comprehend the other, as in the Itys story (C.4), or the juxtaposition of Nicolo d'Este's murder of his wife and son with the murder of Paolo and Francesca, and the juxtaposition of the Malatesta family (his wife Parisina's) with the Atreides, Agamemnon and Clytemnestra :

> And Mastin[1] had come to Verucchio,
>   and the sword, Paolo il Bello's,
>   caught in the arras
> And, in Este's house, Parisina
> Paid
> For this tribe paid always, and the house
> Called also Atreides'.
>
> C.8

Canto 3 had already foreshadowed the Este theme by ending with the Este motto in the palace at Mantua, juxtaposing the murder of Ignez da Castro (whom her young husband Pedro set up as a dead body on a throne for all the lords of Lisbon to pay homage to, as told in C.30—an image of artificial arrest of time), that is, passing from Ignez of Portugal to Este's palace in Ferrara via a wall and silk tatters :

[1] Malatesta of Verucchio, see ch. 9.

Ignez da Castro murdered, and a wall
Here stripped, here made to stand.
Drear waste, the pigment flakes from the stone,
Or plaster flakes, Mantegna painted the wall.
Silk tatters. 'Nec Spec Nec Metu.'

[with neither hope nor fear]

The arras in C.8 is then sufficient to fuse Parisina and
Francesca as an echo during Nicolo's ravings in C.20, when stray
images of pride float before him : he calls on his son Borso (then
twelve years old, but Malatesta was already fighting at fourteen) to keep the peace, and Borso was later known as keep-the-
peace-Borso; then he fuses himself with Roland whose idiotic,
destructive pride in not sounding his horn for help was responsible for the massacre at Roncesvalles (cp. *The Spirit of
Romance*, pp. 74–8) :

And he said : 'Some bitch has sold us
          (that was Ganelon)
'They won't get another such ivory.'
And he lay there on the round hill under the cedar
A little to the left of the cut (Este speaking)
By the side of the summit, and he said :
     'I have broken th horn, bigod, I have
'Broke the best ivory, l'olofans.' And he said :
'Tan mare fustes!'

[Tant; so unfortunate you were, Roland 2034]

French romances were much in vogue in Ferrara under
Nicolo : in C.24 Parisina is shown, with tragic irony, ordering
the binding of 'un libro franxese che si chiama Tristano', and
the Estes claimed to be descended from the knights of Charlemagne, their enemies saying 'Ah yes, Ganelon'. There follows
a flash of sudden understanding for incestuous passion in a
memory of a Spanish incident on the walls of Toro (later used
in a play by Lope de Vega) when the king sees his sister Elvira
and not recognizing her has an erection :

211

'God, what a woman!
My God what a woman' said the King telo rigido. [with
'Sister!' says Ancures, ' 's your sister!'   rigid javelin]
                                                          C.20

Then Nicolo remembers his own crime: ' "Este, go' damn
you," between the walls, arras, / Painted to look like arras.'
In C.23 the arras returns, fusing the lovers again in an unspecified echo ('As we had lain there in the autumn / Under
the arras, or wall painted below like arras'), which is itself
juxtaposed with the story of Pierre de Maensac, troubadour,
who carried off Bernart Tierci's wife and went to the Dauphin
of Auvergne, the latter protecting the lovers from Tierci's
attack. Tierci then joined (a little late in the day) Simon de
Montfort's Albigensian Crusade, which destroyed a whole
civilization and its hard clear poetry of erotic love:

> And came to Auvergne with the army
> But never got Pierre nor the woman.
> And he went down past Chaise Dieu,
> And went after it all to Mount Segur,
>   after the end of all things,
> And they hadn't left even the stair,
> And Simone was dead by that time,
> And they called us the Manichaeans,
> Wotever the hellsarse that is.

                                                          C.23

The last line perfectly expresses the confusion of the time.
The term 'Manichaean' had become a general term for all
heresies which had spread over Northern Italy and Southern
France, the chief of which was that of the Cathars, who did in
fact derive their doctrine, in a remote and roundabout way, from
the earlier and supposedly stamped out religion of Mani, with
traces of Arianism as well. So much has been written about this
and about its influence on the sudden outburst of Courtly Love,
or, as it is sometimes called, Romantic Love, and there has been
so much disagreement, that I shall not attempt to summarize

it here.[1] What interests me is the way the general confusion and disagreement seem to be reflected in Pound's own highly contradictory attitudes, but then we must remember that *The Cantos* is a life's work, representing different phases as well as a desperate attempt at synthesis.

I will try therefore to express my own views, as simply as I can, and not get bogged down in scholarly complications. There are two completely contradictory aspects.

In one sense the love-poetry of the eleventh and twelfth centuries represented a sudden outburst of Eros, such as we are also witnessing today on every poster, in every film. Certainly morals were slack, not only in the castles (the lord away fighting, other lords and/or troubadours paying court to the lady), but everywhere, not least among the clergy. Life in the *midi* was gay and luxurious as well as cultivated, for the area had grown rich from the Crusades. Toulouse and Avignon were far more opulent than Paris, the langue d'oc was the literary language, there was continuous contact with the Arab world, the Jews were not debarred from public life or the universities. But it is also true, as Georges Bataille says, that society cannot really tolerate Eros: work means order, and all taboos are ultimately against the disorder of death, violence, excess. Yet the taboos themselves belong to the irrational, and create fascination, transgression, which is not a negation of the taboo but goes beyond it, confirming it.[2] For Eros is closely linked with death, as we all know since Freud.[3] Or, to get back

[1] The most popular treatments are: Denis de Rougemont, *L'Amour et l'Occident* (Paris 1939 and 1954); *Passion and Society* (London 1940); and *Comme Toi-même* (Paris 1961); *The Myths of Love* (London 1964); Zoe Oldenburg, *Le Bûcher de Montségur* (Paris 1959); *Massacre at Montsegur—A History of the Albigensian Crusade* (London and New York, 1961). For the complex theological background of mediaeval love-poetry, see Peter Dronke's scholarly *Medieval Latin and the Rise of European Love-Lyric* (O.U.P. London 1966).

[2] *L'Erotisme* (Paris 1957), chs. 2–5. See also Freud, *Civilised Sexual Morality and Nervous Illnesses of Modern Times* (1908, Compl. Wks. VII); Herbert Marcuse, *Eros and Civilization—A Contribution to Freud*, Boston 1955.

[3] *Beyond the Pleasure Principle* (1920).

to the twelfth century, and in simple terms, romantic love is the love of love, the desire to lose yourself totally. Hence the strong link with Eastern philosophies, via the Eleusinian mysteries and the Platonist and Neoplatonist stream that runs parallel with and often merges into, Christianity; in the Platonic ladder, you will remember, the lover first loves a particular person, but through that love goes up the ladder until the self is annihilated, he can fuse with the absolute and, as it were, kick away the ladder. Romantic love in fact disregards the person. Both persons.

It disregards the loved person in the sense that, for instance, Zoe Oldenburg can say, with some justification, that Courtly Love is coupled with an unbounded admiration of one's own personality. 'The adoration of the Lady, that marvellous and inaccessible Lover, is nothing else, surely, but the urge to proclaim a triumph of self-will? . . . These sighs and torments, these protracted vigils and metaphorical deaths seem at once passionately sincere and, somehow, a little unreal. What the poet seems to be admiring, all through these bouts of suffering, is his own exquisite soul.'[1]

In psychoanalytical terms, 'le désir de l'homme est le désir de l'Autre', constantly reinvested in other objects (l'autre).[2] Freud early recognized the force of a primary normal narcissism which, according to mechanisms of reinvestment he analyzes, lead to various and common neuroses.[3]

But these metaphorical deaths also represent the self-annihilation of the Platonic and Neoplatonic (hence Gnostic and Catharist) tradition, the idea of climbing up and up and fusing with perfection, the love that is like the Unmoved Mover, 'drawing all to his stillness', as Pound marvellously mistranslates Cavalcanti.[4] Cavalcanti is of course much more complex, for he

---

[1] *Op. cit.*, p. 26.
[2] Lacan, taking up Hegel's dialectic of Master and Slave: *Subversion du sujet et dialectique du désir dans l'inconscient freudien* (*Ecrits*, pp. 793 ff).
[3] *Introduction to Narcissism* (1914, Compl. Wks. X).
[4] Canzone d'Amore: *ne movagia pero ch'a lui si tiri* (love has so

does believe in the person as well as in *intelletto d'amore*, and the *Canzone d'amore* is a rejection of the Provençal view of love which by then had degenerated into a mere affection. Nevertheless for him love is in one phase a sort of perfect form, held in the memory, which in a second phase occurs in 'accidente' (which Pound, wrongly I think, translates as 'an affect', to avoid confusion with the normal modern meaning) when this form happens to be incarnated or be met with in a particular person.[1]

For the Christian idea of love as *Agape* rather than as *Eros* is of God (or love) coming *down* to meet the person who fulfils himself through it, finds and accepts himself—hence the command 'love thy neighbour as thyself' (i.e. first fully accept and love yourself and you will love others).

Now of course Christians don't achieve this, but that's irrelevant. If Eros and Agape have to be mutually exclusive (which I don't believe), I prefer the Christian idea, as an idea, to that of erotic love, which is destructive. And Denis de Rougemont has argued it out convincingly, if not always reliably. In *The Myths of Love*, he analyzes the Tristan myth (and the Don Juan myth as obverse of the same medal) in these terms: Tristan does not love Iseult but love; King Mark, representing society, cannot tolerate this kind of love and they run away to the forest; but they don't stay there, they don't really want each other (love once attained ceases to be the unattainable and dies) and so they go back to the society which kills them, and indeed all lovers who try to exclude society in a

benumbed the lover that he doesn't move when he is being shot at). Pound's text (*Lit. Essays*) has *E non si mova* (Ms ca. *Ne mova già*) *perch'a llui si tiri.*

[1] Cp. Dante, *La Vita Nuova*, xxv, transl. by Mark Musa, Indiana Un. Press, Bloomington 1962, p. 53: 'It may be that at this point some person, worthy of having every doubt cleared up, could be puzzled at my speaking of Love as if it were a thing in itself, as if it were not only an intellectual substance but also a bodily substance. This is in reality false, for Love does not exist in itself as a substance, but rather it is an accident in substance.'

secretive grand passion lose their love.[1] Eros alone is destructive. But in fact Eros and Agape need not be mutually exclusive, and Agape alone can mean sublimation and another kind of destructiveness, as Cavalcanti, in his own terms, saw.

Pound at his best treats them as inseparable, and his notion of religion as essentially theanthropic (allowing a constant interaction between man and god) shows that he is closer to the Christian tradition than to the purely Platonic, or rather, closer to the Neoplatonic and theanthropic elements in Christianity than he is to the extreme Platonic or extreme Old Testament traditions.[2]

On the other side of the argument, it is probably true that the Cathars were puritans and dualists.[3] They derived from Mani the idea of two opposing principles of Good and Evil, God being good but not omnipotent, Satan having created the world and the flesh, but, incapable of creating life, having asked God to breathe a soul into this clay body. These souls came from captive angels and were condemned to fearful torments within this body, and to a perpetual metempsychosis from body to body (the

[1] He also analyzes three modern novels which according to him retell the Tristan myth, but in terms of the only taboos left in a sexually permissive society; all three are also portraits of a society: Nabokov's *Lolita* (girl under-age; America); Musil's *A Man without Qualities* (incest; pre-war Vienna); Pasternak's *Dr Zhivago* (Lara removed for political reasons; revolutionary Russia).

[2] See Tadeusz Zielinski (one of Pound's unappreciated savants), *La Sybille* (Paris, 1925) and Eva Hesse, *New Approaches to Ezra Pound* (London 1969) Introduction, on the gods being within us: 'Zielinski made a fine distinction between theocratic religions, "in which an impassible abyss separates the divine from the human", and theanthropic religions "which allow a connection between the two natures in the shape of a god-man or even a man-god", and showed moreover that all theanthropic elements in Christianity derive from the Mediterranean mystery cults, while theocratic elements all go back to the monotheism of the Old Testament. Hence Pound's belief that the real Old Testament is to be found in Hesiod and Ovid, and that "Christ follows Dionysus" (*Mauberley* III).'

[3] What we know about them comes chiefly from the Church's propaganda against them, on their *errors*. The only two surviving documents about their ritual are exceedingly innocent of these 'errors' (see Oldenburg).

216

influence of Oriental doctrine). Hence to marry and procreate was a dreadful cruelty to mankind. Even Christ did not 'really' assume a body or 'really' die on the Cross in this body or 'really' resurrect, he just, as it were, pretended, he was a sort of phantom, part of a divine plan to deceive the devil, and the Church fell into the same trap of believing it all. The Cross itself became a symbol of this gross mistake, a materialistic thing, which was therefore reviled. The Cathars denied the flesh, and of course the Sacraments, and ate nothing that was a by-product of procreation, not even milk or eggs. The initiates were called *perfecti*. Like all reforming sects they declared themselves nearer to the original spirit of Christianity, nearer to the Apostolic succession, and the only ones to have kept the Holy Spirit as bestowed by Christ upon the early church.

Now the really peculiar thing about this fight-to-the-death between the Church and its rival (for it had become more than a sect, it was a rival church, with intentions to overthrow) is that apart from the most glaring 'errors' (e.g. the rejection of the Sacraments), both sides were much closer to each other than can have appeared at the time. Dualism in particular had affected, or infected, the Church from earliest times and was, as Zoe Oldenburg puts it, 'a natural development from belief in the Devil, who assumed vast importance for Christians throughout the Middle Ages.' The Church 'may not have actually claimed that matter was the work of the Devil, but it *behaved* exactly as though it thought it were. . . . Between a universe created by the Devil, which was merely tolerated by God, and a universe created by God, but wholly corrupted and perverted by the Devil, there might seem to be no great difference—not, at least, in practice.'[1]

Well, I'm not going to get entangled in the Problem of Evil at this stage, but these two basic contradictions—'pure' love for love versus love as fulfilment of total persons, and dualism versus integration or the sacramental view—do affect Pound very much. I have already shown how, with the first contradic-

[1] *Op. cit.*, pp. 39–40.

tion, he veers from one extreme to another: the pure pre-Raphaelite, world-abandoning vision of his early poetry, the very explicit condemnations of complete self-annihilation through the senses, including dope (the lotus-eaters, the recurring denial of Baudelaire's artificial paradise in *The Pisan Cantos*—'le paradis n'est pas artificiel'), through to the endorsement of de Gourmont's idea of love as an intellectual instigation, the *intelletto d'amore* of Cavalcanti; the superb treatment of the two extremes and the Circean middle way in Cantos 39 and 47, contradicting his view of woman as a chaos (see p. 134) formed by the male creative force ('He hath made god in my belly', C.39, or, implying some chaos of imperception, 'that . . . the phallos perceive its aim', C.99); and a strange reversal, at times, in the later Cantos, to an almost collective view of sex, especially in his emphasis on the rituals of Eleusis.

And yet it seems to me that the most pervasive view is that expressed in the Circe episode and the Cavalcanti essay. Already in *Troubadours—Their Sorts and Conditions* (1913) he was throwing scorn on 'the modern Provençal enthusiast in raptures at the idea of chivalric love (a term which he usually misunderstands)', though even here his primary interest is in the art of verse. And in the Cavalcanti essay he tries to define this particular mediaeval quality, this 'assertion of value' which 'has not been in poetry since':

'The Greek aesthetic would seem to consist wholly in plastic, or in plastic moving towards coitus, and limited by incest, which is the sole Greek taboo. This new thing in mediaeval work that concerns us has nothing to do with Christianity, which people both praise and blame for utterly irrelevant and unhistorical reasons. Erotic sentimentality we can find in Greek and Roman poets, and one may observe that the main trend of Provençal and Tuscan poets is not toward erotic sentimentality.'

Hence his treatment of Virgil's Dido in her boat, a treatment overlaid with Dowson and Verlaine, juxtaposed with Dante's *piccioletta barca* in C.7:

O voi che siete in piccioletta barca,
Dido choked up with sobs, for her Sichens
Lies heavy in my arms, dead weight
          Drowning with tears, new Eros[1]

                                        C.7

But, he continues in the Cavalcanti essay, '[the Provençal
and Tuscan poets] are not pagans, they are called pagans, and
the troubadours are also accused of being Manichaeans, obviously because of a muddle somewhere. They are opposed
to a form of stupidity not limited to Europe, that is, idiotic
asceticism and a belief that the body is evil. . . . The whole
break of Provence with this world, and indeed the central theme
of the troubadours, is the dogma that there is some proportion
between the fine thing held in the mind, and the inferior thing
ready for instant consumption.' And later, after his attack on the
two asceticisms, anti-flesh and anti-intellect, he says : 'Between
these two diseases, existed the Mediterranean sanity. The
"section d'or", if that is what it meant, that gave the churches
like St Hilaire, San Zeno, the Duomo di Modena, the clear
lines and proportions. Not the pagan worship of strength, nor
the Greek perception of visual non-animate plastic, or plastic
in which the being animate was not the main and principle
quality, but this "harmony in the sentience" or harmony *of* the
sentient, where the thought has its demarcation, the substance
its *virtu*, where stupid men have not reduced all "energy" to
unbounded undistinguished abstraction.'

Which leads me to the second contradiction, that of dualism.
Explicitly, in his prose, Pound is against all dualisms as we have
seen, and in his poetry he seems at least to be against that of
flesh and spirit :

Anselm : that some is incarnate awareness,
          thus trinitas ; some remains spiritus.
'The body inside'. Thus Plotinus,

[1] The Dante line is re-echoed much later, in *Rock-Drill*, C.93 : 'Oh
you, as Dante says / in the dinghy astern there'; and it ends *Thrones* :
'you in the dinghy (piccioletta) astern there' (C.109).

But Gemisto : 'Are Gods by hilaritas';
        and their speed in communication.   C.98

But even that is ambiguous. And abstract. Nevertheless his hell and purgatory and paradise are here on earth, made up of people and their actions. Which is why Eliot's attack on the 'Hell' Cantos (14–16), though a brilliant piece of work from his Anglican outlook, seems to me to miss the point.[1] Eliot, taking up Pound's own phrase 'without dignity, without tragedy', says it is a 'Hell without dignity', which *therefore* implies a Heaven without dignity (why?), and that Pound does not distinguish between 'essential Evil and social accidents', so that 'the Heaven (if any) implied will be equally trivial and accidental. Pound's hell, for all its horror, is a perfectly comfortable one for the modern mind to contemplate, and disturbing no one's complacency : it is a Hell *for other people*, the people we read about in the newspapers, not for oneself and one's friends.' And D. S. Carne-Ross approvingly agrees that 'Pound's evil, like his good, is never radical. Primarily monetary, issuing in usury and the corruptions of the will which usury produces, it gives no hint of the permanent essential Evil underlying this or that manifestation.'[2]

Clark Emery, commenting on this 'permanent essential Evil', asks wittily of Carne-Ross : 'is he a Manichaean?' He might have asked the same question of Eliot's 'essential Evil'. And both, as he points out, have taken 'the effect, usury, as the cause'.[3] It is true that Pound's Hell Cantos don't come off, except in vivid patches, but this is because the tone is wrong, too strident (overstressing the case always weakens it). But he does not, like Dante, put lovers in hell, not even in the top layer where Francesca and Paolo are made to suffer minor torments (lust being the least important sin to the Middle

[1] *After Strange Gods, a Primer of Modern Heresy* (London, New York, 1934) pp. 46–7.
[2] *An Examination of Ezra Pound—a collection of essays*, ed. Peter Russell (London, Norfolk, Conn. 1950) p. 151.
[3] *Ideas Into Action—A Study of Pound's Cantos*, University of Miami Press 1958, p. 21.

Ages, pride the worst, and Dante puts Cunniza in the *terzo cielo*).
The real point about Pound's usurers (also in Dante's hell,
which Eliot ought also to disapprove of, on his own argument),
perverters of language etc., is that despite the harm they do, the
hell they create is here on earth, which is why they are shown as
merely chasing each other around, eating each other in a sense-
less circle but almost unaware of it. They are not being *punished*.
And this seems to be what Eliot cannot accept. The hell is too
comfortable. But usurers, journalists etc. *are* comfortable. They
don't even suffer as lovers do.

The 'Christian' dualism displayed by Eliot and Carne-Ross,
this thinking in irreconcilable opposites, is alien to Pound, who
thinks in polar opposites or polarities, where there are gradations between terms—the words *gradations* and *degrees* are
constantly emphasized in his writings, and in C.84 brought
together with chung[1], balance: 'quand vos venetz al som de
l'escalina / ηθος gradations / These are distinctions in clarity /

ming 明 these are distinctions / John Adams, the Brothers

Adam / there is our norm of spirit / our 中 / whereto we may

pay our / homage' (cp. pp. 44 and 126). He is to that extent
'Chinese': things are not this or that but midway, heading this
or that way. Plotinus also did not believe in evil but in gradations of being.

A similar West European-Christian arrogance crops up in
Dekker when he calls the blood-rite by which Odysseus gains
knowledge from Tiresias barbaric: 'Homer's conception of the
"life after death" (about which Confucius said nothing—C.13)
is generally conceded to be primitive, much more so than
Virgil's where the idea of reward and punishment is well
developed. But as we have seen in connection with the "Hell
Cantos", Pound is quite incapable of the kind of thinking and
feeling that goes with a sophisticated religious vision. . . .
Homer's conception of Hades is, however, more amenable; and

the very fact that it is not so well mapped out makes it possible for Pound, in C.47, to associate Odysseus' voyage to Hades with the rape of Proserpine. How important that association is, of Eros and knowledge, I have already shown.'[1]

I am at a loss to understand all this, and in any case the last sentence alone would seem to justify Pound. The Christians have a blood-rite too, and drink the blood not of sheep but of a man-god murdered by man, and for the same essential reason of bringing to life a dead soul, or soul deadened to God. But of course by the time of Christ it was euphemized into a metaphor or sacrament (wine is blood), and the Protestants further euphemized it into a mere symbol. That makes it all right, 'civilized'. As for 'the idea of reward and punishment', when 'well developed', being more 'civilized' than Homer's Hades of true Jungian archetypes for the sufferings and deep emotions of man, it leaves me speechless, devoid, as it were, of blood. The Christian hell seems to me quite childish and primitive, indeed, on Christian terms I have always felt that if God's mercy really is perfect and infinite hell must be empty. And have not modern psychoanalysis, sociology and anthropology been obliged to turn wholly to these Greek myths in most of their nomenclature, in order to name the unnamable, like Wanjina, 'thereby making clutter, / the bane of men moving'? The Christian terminology has become pretty useless, even as the bane of men moving.

For Pound, hell and heaven are here on earth, within ourselves, and no one has a greater right to speak of hell, who has been through it, who has consciously exposed himself, for forty years, to occult experiences and passions and caring about the world, bringing himself, as Eva Hesse says, 'if not to madness, at least to the outermost borders of rational thinking.' Miss Hesse compares this aspect with Pound on Whitman in *Patria Mia*: 'a desire for largeness, a willingness to stand exposed:

> Camerado, this is no book;
> Who touches this touches a man.

[1] George Dekker, *Sailing after Knowledge*, London 1963, p. 36.

222

'The artist is ready to endure personally a strain which his craftsmanship could scarcely endure.'[1]

Not only is Pound's evil conceived as here on earth but it is also bound up with time ('Time is the evil' he says about Pedro's attempt to set up his murdered queen Ignez da Castro on her throne for the Portuguese nobility to honour). But this is time in the linear sense of Western and Christian civilization, or, as Kenner puts it, 'the attempt to educe a false stability out of flux', or, as I would put it, to ignore the seasons and their cyclic ritual, to pervert nature as some types of love pervert nature, as perverters of language set up 'counters', debased coinage with no real goods behind them, as usury perverts nature by accelerating rhythms and creating consumer societies and making gold breed *ex nihilo*.

'Money is a kind of poetry' said Wallace Stevens,[2] and so Pound has made it. C.97 opens with Abd-el-Melik (one of the Omayyad Caliphs, the first to have coinage), juxtaposed with Edward I. It is based on various sources, but chiefly on Del Mar, and indeed Pound at this point gives the specific reference: '(Systems p. 134)'.[3] Del Mar is always worth reading, as are most of Pound's sources. A mining engineer and director of the U.S. Treasury Bureau of Statistics, he discovered that gold and silver were produced, on the average, at a loss, and were circulating through the world at a value in services and commodities far below the current cost of their production. This led him to formulate various tenets on the true nature and function of money, the facts of which, he held, had been obscured, chiefly by the Coinage Act of 1866. So Pound, in a broadcast interview: 'Now as I see it, billions of money are being spent to hide about seventeen historic facts which the copyists in the Middle Ages or recently have been too stupid to cross out.'[4] Or earlier in the same interview:

---

[1] *New Approaches to Ezra Pound*, ed. Hesse, London 1969, Introduction. *Patria Mia* was written in 1912, published Chicago 1960.

[2] *Opus Posthumous*, ed. S. F. Morse, London 1959, p. 165.

[3] Alexander del Mar, *A History of Monetary Systems*, London 1895, New York 1903 (Pound using the latter). Also *A History of Money in Ancient Countries*, London 1885, *Money and Civilization*, London 1886.

[4] With D. G. Bridson, B.B.C. Third Programme, 11th July 1960.

'And the Usura Cantos would be more comprehensible if
people understood the meaning of the term "Usury". It is not
to be confused with the legitimate interest which is due, Del
Mar says, to the increase in domestic animals and plants. The
difference between a fixed charge and a share from a proportion
of the increase.'[1]

One of the by-products of Del Mar's activity was a most
interesting lecture on *Usury and the Jews*, delivered to the
Young Men's Hebrew Association in San Francisco in 1897,
which 'received great applause'. In this lecture Del Mar shows
how the mediaeval Church and monarchs, needing money for
their wars and luxurious courts, got around the long and
traditional condemnation of usura or high rates of return on
loans and investments (a condemnation going back not only to
the Old Testament but to Aristotle, which fact is noted by
Marx). They simply forced the Jews into being money-
lenders by closing all other trades and professions to them.
Clough and Cole support this, saying that by the eleventh
century a small class of money-lenders had arisen, mainly Jews,
who were excluded from land-holding and most mediaeval
pursuits, and who would be unaffected by the Christian prohibition (though this was based on Exodus 22–25 and Leviticus
25–36 as well as on Luke 6/35). However, these Jewish money-
lenders provided mainly consumption credit (financing needy
peasants as well as nobles, and demanding high rates of interest
and good securities such as jewels, rather like modern pawn-
brokers). The two basic mediaeval economic doctrines still

[1] At the end of C.45 in the New Directions edition (but not in the
Faber edition) there is printed this brief note, which is clearer than the
above, and clearer than anything Pound has said in his *ABC of Economics*
or in his *Money Pamphlets*: 'N.B. Usury: A charge for the use of
purchasing power, levied without regard to production; often without
regard to the possibilities of production.' Pound's many writings on
money have been collected in *Impact: Essays on Ignorance and the Decline
of American Civilization*, ed. Noel Stock (Regnery, New York 1961).
The best brief summary of his views is by Hugh Kenner, *Pound & Money*
(National Review 1961, reprinted in *Agenda*, Special Issue in honour of
Ezra Pound's eightieth birthday, London Oct.–Nov. 1965).

held, more or less: that of *just price* (upheld by Aquinas and dear to Pound), and the *prohibition of usury*—both appropriate to the limited economy of the early Middle Ages. Which is why the Jew became (most unfairly in the hypocritical circumstances) a hated figure. The earlier feeling had been that money was sterile, that if you lent a man a field, he could raise crops on it or build a house or feed a horse, whereas money could only be spent, money could not breed money. Aristotle had said so.

But by the end of the late Middle Ages, both these doctrines were more and more being flouted as the merchant banks arose. The Church, the governments as well as the merchants were ignoring the original ban and for the first time it became socially acceptable and even respectable for a man to make as much money as he could: the profit-motive of our modern capitalist society became the dominant motive in life.[1]

I have already tried to make clear Pound's moral objection to usura, as treated poetically and in relation to love and creativity in *The Cantos*. And I mean poetically, for some critics have objected even to this. A. Alvarez, for example, condemns the Usura Cantos (45 & 51, which I have not quoted as they are so well known and easy to understand) as static, repetitive, without development of the idea.[2] The idea is of course developed in the historical Cantos on usura. But in any case that is the point: the two Cantos reiterate ritualistically, like inverted litanies (and litanies are repetitive), the condemnation of Usura. They are like exorcisms. Pound is in effect trying to stop, to still the accelerated pace of usury which throws time out of joint, or, as Eva Hesse puts it, 'the cancerous growth of the cells gone mad and proliferating at the expense of the organism as a whole'.[3]

[1] See S. B. Clough and C. W. Cole, *Economic History of Europe* (Boston 1941, 3rd ed. 1952).

[2] *Craft and Morals*, in *Ezra Pound: Perspectives*, ed. Noel Stock, Chicago 1965.

[3] *New Approaches to Ezra Pound*, ed. Hesse, London 1969, Introduction. Eva Hesse has pointed out to me Marx's interesting footnote in *Das Kapital* (Frankfurt 1967 I/619, 7th Section) where Marx quotes Luther on the Usurer (*Wucherer*, the German word *Wucher* means both

But Pound goes much further than poetic exorcism, and for this too he has been reviled, not entirely without reason, as an anti-Semite (see next chapter) and as a man with a bee in his bonnet who has ruined his Cantos with a lot of cranky ideas. Certainly there is often a serious lapse of tone, perhaps inevitable in circumstances which must have produced a feeling that he was banging his head against a brick-wall, a world conspiracy.

Similarly his taking up of Douglas' Social Credit and Gesell's stamp-scrip (the latter idea causing Douglas to dissociate himself from Pound) may seem cranky to orthodox economists today, but they are only part of his insistence that credit belongs to the people and not to the banks, which seems to me perfectly reasonable socialist theory if not practice.

Douglas was a kind of non-Marxist Socialist, and his ideas were based on the fact that, in the economy of the twenties (and this still holds true today) wages never catch up on price increases, since payment of more wages puts up prices, so that the two lines move together but not at the same pace. Keynes' solution was for the Government to pour money into the economy in various ways, such as subsidies, during times of depression. Douglas wanted every man to have a dividend of the gross national product, but that this should not be passed onto the price; he also wanted a form of subsidy, but one which would have entailed such complex, constant and accurate statistics about the two lines as to create a bureaucrats' paradise. (This of course has occurred anyway, and in theory should not be beyond the computer age to solve.) However, he was never able to answer the question put to him: what do you do if a man runs short of money and sells his life's dividends to a richer man for an immediate loan? The only possible answer is severe restriction, inconceivable in a free society. In other words, like most reformers' schemes, his took no account of the human element and could only work in a small Utopian community.

usury and rank growth) as a monster, 'wie ein Beerwolffder alles wüstet, mehr den kein Cacus, Gerion oder Antus'. Geryon is also one of Pound's favourite names for the evil, as is canker.

Silvio Gesell's idea of *Schwundgeld* or perishable currency seems also to have succeeded only in the small Austrian town of Wörgl. Gesell had noted that allowances had to be made for the perishability of goods, just as in Argentina all transactions by cattle-ranchers made proper allowance for loss of cattle through disease etc. In order to establish equity between cattle-breeders/manufacturers/retailers on the one hand and the owners of capital on the other, he conceived the idea of perishable currency. The mayor of Wörgl (a small industrial town suffering, like the rest of the world in 1932, from the slump) happened to read Gesell's *Die natürliche Wirtschaftsordnung* and persuaded the local council to try an experiment. He had 'Arbeitscheine' (work certificates) printed and circulated as money. Any holder of this scrip money had to affix to it once a month a stamp representing 1 per cent of its value. This encouraged the holder to spend the scrip before having to affix a new stamp. Money was thus kept in rapid circulation—a ten Schilling note changing hands once a day meant a turnover in goods of 300 Schillinge a month. Business revived, employment increased, artisans found work, shopkeepers sold their goods, debts and taxes were paid off, the local council was able to start a programme of public works. The money was accepted everywhere locally as legal tender. Delegations arrived from abroad to witness the experiment, among others the French Prime Minister Daladier who recommended it in a public speech, and the U.S. economist Irwin Fischer who reported on it favourably in his book. The Austrian government ended the experiment after the intervention of the Austrian National Bank, the main argument being that it would endanger the interest rate if the experiment were allowed to spread to other areas. The depression returned.

Pound wrote in *Guide to Kulchur* (1938) : '. . . Gesell saw how to focus all or a reasonable part of them on the medium of exchange. The state serves in creating a MEASURE of exchange. A tax that can never fall on any man save one who has a hundred times the amount of the tax in his pocket AT THE MOMENT the tax falls due, is the least nocive of taxes.' Earlier in the same book he brackets Gesell and Douglas with the Canonist doctrine of economics 'wherein interest is treated under the general head of just price', and asks the reader to compare this with the actual practice and achievement in the corporate states of our time (*Kulchur*, p. 277, p. 173).

Or in C.74:

> a nice little town in the Tyrol in a wide flat-lying valley
> near Innsbruck and when a note of the
> small town of Wörgl went over
> a counter in Innsbruck
> and the banker saw it go over
> all the slobs in Europe were terrified
> 'no one' said the Frau Burgomeister
> 'in this village who cd/ write a newspaper article.
> Knew it was money but pretended it was not
> in order to be on the safe side of the law'.
> But in Russia they bungled and did not apparently
> grasp the idea of work-certificate
> and started the N.E.P. with disaster
> and the immolation of men to machinery
> and the canal work and gt/ mortality
> (which is as may be)
> and went in for dumping in order to trouble the waters
> in the usurers' hell-a-dice
> all of which leads to the death-cells
> each in the name of its god
> or longevity because as says Aristotle
> philosophy is not for young men . . .

Gesell's scheme sounds to me wildly unpractical on a large scale, but people who unquestionably understand these things better than I can ever hope to do spoke well of him. Keynes devoted several pages to him:

'In spite of the prophetic trappings with which his devotees have decorated him, Gesell's main book is written in cool, scientific language, though it is suffused throughout by a more passionate, a more emotional devotion to social justice than some think decent in a scientist. . . . The purpose of the book may be described as the establishment of an anti-Marxist Socialism, a reaction against *laissez-faire* built on theoretical foundations unlike those of Marx in being based on an unfettering of competition instead of its abolition. I believe that the future will learn more from the spirit of Gesell than from that of Marx. The preface to *The Natural Economic Order* will indicate to the reader the moral quality of Gesell. The answer to Marxism is, I think, to be found along the lines of this preface.'[1]

He then, however, describes the theory in detail and points out its defect:

'But, having given the reason why the money-rate of interest unlike most commodity rates of interest cannot be negative, he altogether overlooks the need of an explanation why the money-rate of interest is positive, and he fails to explain why the money-rate of interest is not governed (as the classical school maintains) by the standard set by the yield on productive capital. This is because the notion of liquidity-preference had escaped him. He has constructed only half a theory of the rate of interest.

'The incompleteness of his theory is doubtless the explanation of his work having suffered neglect at the hands of the academic world. Nevertheless he had carried his theory far enough to lead him to a practical recommendation, which may carry with it the essence of what is needed, though it is not feasible in the form in which he proposed it. He argues that the growth of real capital is held back by the money-rate of interest, and that if this brake were removed the growth of real capital would be, in the modern world, so rapid that a zero money-rate of interest would probably be justified, not indeed forthwith, but within a comparatively short period of time. Thus the prime necessity is to reduce the money-rate of interest, and this, he pointed out, can be effected by causing money to incur carrying-costs just like other stocks of barren goods. This led him to the famous prescription of "stamped" money, with which his name is chiefly associated and which has received the blessing of Professor Irving Fischer.' (*op. cit.*)

[1] J. M. Keynes, *General Theory of Employment, Interest and Money*, London 1936, p. 355.

Keynes then goes on to work out a different rate of stamp, as Gesell's was too high for existing conditions, and ends :

'The idea behind stamped money is sound. It is, indeed, possible that means might be found to apply it in practice on a modest scale. But there are many difficulties which Gesell did not face. In particular, he was unaware that money was not unique in having a liquidity-premium attached to it, but differed only in degree from many other articles, deriving its importance from having a *greater* liquidity-premium than any other article. Thus if currency notes were to be deprived of their liquidity-premium by the stamping system, a long series of substitutes would step into their shoes—bank-money, debts at call, foreign money, jewellery and the precious metals generally, and so forth. As I have mentioned above, there have been times when it was probably the craving for the ownership of land, independently of its yield, which served to keep up the rate of interest; though under Gesell's system this possibility would have been eliminated by land nationalisation.' (*op. cit.*)

Hugh Gaitskell too, devoted a whole essay to Gesell :

'His aim was to reform the individualist system not by restricting or controlling the economic activities of individuals but by abolishing, in what to him seemed a simple way, two things—the existence of unearned income whether in the form of rent or interest, and the industrial fluctuations generally known as the Trade Cycle. The first of these objects, which, in his opinion, would also involve the second, shows that he had something in common with the Socialists. But the point of agreement is to be found only in this—that Gesell also wished to abolish what Marx called "Surplus Value". The method by which it was to be done was substantially different. Gesell was emphatically hostile to State Socialism. . . . For Gesell there was a better way out—the introduction of "Free Land" and "Free Money".'[1]

[1] H. T. H. Gaitskell, *Four Monetary Heretics* [Douglas, Soddy, Gesell, Eisler], in *What Everybody Wants to Know about Money*, ed. G. D. H. Cole (London 1933). The 'Free Land' theory was derived from Henry George, and according to Keynes was 'altogether of secondary interest'.

Gaitskell then describes the theory and goes on :

'Theory would anticipate and practice has shown that given certain conditions the adoption of Free Money must improve a bad trade situation. But Gesell does not merely or even mainly claim this as its merit. He claims that it will reduce the rate of interest to zero and combined with budgetary and banking policy eliminate all industrial fluctuations. It is these claims and the arguments on which they are based which we must first examine.' (*op. cit.*)

This Gaitskell proceeds to do and concludes :

'When therefore we realise the relative unimportance of currency compared with bank-money, the possibility of variation in velocity even with a depreciating currency, the uncertainty that this attempt to stabilise velocity, even if it should succeed, could really master the forces behind the depression, we must remain more sceptical than its originator about the virtues of Free Money. Nevertheless as a policy for a depression, especially in countries where notes are used very freely, it is theoretically sound, and as the quotation set out below shows [*Week*, 17/5/33, on Wörgl] appears to have been successful enough in practice. Moreover it is one of the few attempts which have been made to deal with what is undoubtedly *one* of the intractable elements in industrial fluctuation. The prolongation of the depression in face of vigorous expansionist monetary policy can only be ascribed to the further fall in velocity. Any method for dealing with this must merit attention. From this account of his views and the quotations from his work it will be seen that Silvio Gesell was an amateur with a very ingenious albeit illogical mind, who unlike many of his fellows expressed himself not only vigorously but also clearly.'

I quote from contemporary economists rather than modern ones, partly because inevitably Gesell has vanished from the latters' view, but also to show that if orthodox economists of the time took him seriously enough to discuss him in their books, a layman like Pound cannot be regarded as all that batty. The depression was a traumatic experience for everyone, and Pound was surely courageous in tackling it at all.

Considering that Pound is generally regarded as (*a*) a crank and (*b*) a fascist, it is astonishing, despite his passionate endorsement of Gesell, how often he seems to echo not only some orthodox socialist thinking but also Marx. The terminology is similar : the personification of Geryon for example and Marx's 'strange God who perched himself on the altar cheek by jowl with the old Gods of Europe and one fine day with a shove and a kick chucked them all of a heap' and 'proclaimed surplus-value making as the sole end and aim of humanity'.[1] But there is also the whole attack on the system of public credit which began in Genoa, Venice and Florence, i.e. the National Debt or the alienation of the state (any state, whether despotic, constitutional or republican). The German word for alienation (Veräusserung) also means 'selling out'. For it keeps the people in perpetual debt while the Nation's creditors coffer in 'to the last shilling'. And since the National Debt found its support in the public revenue, it gave rise to the modern system of taxation as 'the necessary complement to national loans'. And with the National Debt arose an international credit system, which is often one of the sources of accumulation by this or that country, creating panics, possible (and in the thirties actual) collapses of the whole system, and even, Pound would say, wars. Public credit, Marx says, is the Credo of Capitalism, and to betray it is the real 'blasphemy against the Holy Ghost, which may not be forgiven'.[2]

One wonders sometimes if that is not Pound's real treason, which the Western world cannot forgive. And Marx goes on to trace the modern system as we have it back to the foundation of the Bank of England (1694), just as Pound does : its first director, William Paterson, a Scot, having said, in Pound's rendering, Hath benefit of interest on all / the moneys which it, the bank, creates out of nothing (C.46). Marx compares the modern financiers to the Alchemists (but cleverer), creating

[1] *Capital*, I, Part VIII, Ch. XXXI, Genesis of the Industrial Capitalist (transl. from the 3rd German ed. by Samuel Moore and Edward Aveling, Chicago 1915).

[2] *Ibid.*

gold out of nothing, and he goes back to Aristotle's division between Chrematistics and Economics, the distinction between money and wealth which Pound is always on about, the one being for immediate barter, the other for circulation.[1]

It may be worth quoting Ernest Barker, translator of Aristotle's *Politics* on the present 'separate' treatment of economics. The *Politics*, he says, 'dealt partly with household management (the literal meaning of *oikonomia*) and partly with public economy or state finance . . . the famous and profoundly influential theory of exchange and of interest in the first book which affected so deeply the Canonists of the Middle Ages. Such economic theory, which in turn is subordinated to (or, perhaps one should rather say, is the crown of) ethics, admits of no isolation of the economic motive, and of no abstraction of economic facts as a separate branch of enquiry. It is a theory of the ways in which households and cities can properly use the means at their disposal for the better living of a good life. Wealth, on this basis, is a means to a moral end . . . it is necessarily limited by the end, and it must not be greater—as equally it must not be less—than what the end requires. This is not socialism, but it is a line of thought inimical to capitalism.'[2]

So Pound is always quoting the phrase *Metathemenon te ton krumenon* from Aristotle (*'if those who use a currency give it up in favour of another* that currency is worthless, and useless for any of the necessary purposes of life'), i.e. its value is revealed as fictitious—Cantos 53, 74, 76; and in C.78 with just the one word: 'the root stench being usura and METATHEMENON'. Or, more comically in C.77:

> ## METATHEMENON
> we are not yet out of *that* chapter
> Le Paradis n'est pas artificiel.

I realize that my linking Pound with Marx is incompatible with the outdated image which many people, even some Poundians, have of him. But I do so in order to show how irrele-

---

[1] Aristotle, *De Rep.* I.c. 8 & 9.
[2] *The Politics of Aristotle*, translated by Ernest Barker, Oxford 1946.

vant so many labels like Fascist and Communist are or have become. Communist governments pay only lip-service to Marx while Capitalist governments have in effect had to become more and more socialistically orientated, even when socialist governments are not actually in power. The Fascist governments began under the guise of socialism but were actually subservient to the military-industrial complex. Pound himself says : 'I suppose that real appreciation, that is, the real attempt to weigh Marx's veritable merit began with Gesell and with Gesell's statement that Marx never questioned money. He just accepted it as he found it.'[1] And on Communism :

'Communism as revolt against the hoggers of harvest was an admirable tendency. As revolutionary I refuse a pretended revolution that tries to stand still or move backward.

'Communism as theory is not only against the best human instincts, it is not even practised by the higher mammals. . . .

'A movement, against capital, that cannot distinguish between capital and property is a blind movement. Capital is a claim against others which is not of necessity extinguished even by continual payment at 5% or at 50%.

'The plough is NOT the same kind of thing or "instrument" as a mortgage. Homo even half sapiens ought to perceive a distinction.

'There is a borderline between public and private things. Sanity bids us observe it.

'A system which becomes in practice merely another hidden and irresponsible tyranny is no better than any other gang of instigators to theft and oppression.'[2]

I understand very little about economics, and no expert has taken the trouble to deal with Pound.[3] But like many others, especially poets, I respond to Pound's brave attempt to engage

[1] *Guide to Kulchur*, p. 265.

[2] *Ibid.* p. 191.

[3] Since this was written Earle Davis has published *Vision Fugitive: Ezra Pound and Economics* (Univ. of Kansas Press 1969). Mr Davis does not claim to be an economist either but his book is a very useful guide to some of the more intractable political and economic allusions in *The Cantos*, as well as a clear summary of Pound's views.

himself in his own time and its evils, and this whatever his errors of detail. Herbert Read has said : 'From Orage we had both acquired similar ideas about politics and economics, and though these were to lead us to very different conclusions, we always agreed on two points—the evil wrought in post-mediaeval society by the Church's admission of the principle of usury, and the dependence of any social revolution on its ability to deal with the monetary problem.'[1]

Tom Scott, the poet, has said that one can't ignore 'what the obscurantists like to call "his monetary theories" ', for Pound 'has done no more than tell the simple obvious truth that the Western world is the victim of the most colossal fraud by private financiers that has been perpetrated in all human history. It is for telling this truth, of course, that he has barely escaped with his life. I disagree with much of his detail in his vision of finance-capitalist society, but not with his general view, and I applaud his caring about such things. Whatever "side" one is on in the present show-down, Pound has made it possible for poets to write about history and the things that really matter socially, and impossible to confine themselves ever again to moonshine and mountain daisies. Morality is a matter of economic behaviour, and the poet's concern with human values begins with money and worth, though it may end in New Jerusalem.'[2]

This is very well put. Personally I feel there is a timeless, apocalyptic quality in Pound's poetry which even his adverse critics seem to find disturbing, but which most poets respond to, even if they don't understand; there is a sense in which, despite many errors of detail, Pound may nevertheless be right. He seems to have been groping, if blindly, towards the same kind of synthesis between money and language as corruptible exchange, which is now occupying so many modern critics, notably, in a much more learned manner than Pound's, the

[1] *Ezra Pound*, in *Ezra Pound: Perspectives*, ed. Noel Stock, Chicago 1965.
[2] *An Appreciation*, in *Ezra Pound: Perspectives*, ed. Noel Stock, Chicago 1965.

young Marxist critics and semiologists of the French *Tel Quel* group.[1] Pound was proceeding by poetic intuition, and who knows, his may be the only comprehensible poetry to the twenty-first century, when a new economic order, unimaginable to us now, may have emerged from the present apparently irreconcilable dogmas; it may be, for that matter, a post-McLuhan age, an age of mixed media and ideogrammic thinking in quick cuts, when we may all be speaking Chinese, with nothing of our civlization left but the fragments he has 'shelved (shored)' against our ruin (C.8, a reference to Eliot's *The Waste Land*).

And since I seem (somehow) to have journeyed from Eros to Karl Marx in the course of this chapter, let me return to Cavalcanti, and show how Pound actually ends his translation of the *Canzone d'amore* in C.36, juxtaposing love already then with Erigena and the Manichaeans, with Aquinas turning Aristotle's *Metaphysics* upside down (i.e. turning a merely meta-Physics, the book which came after the Physics, into metaphysics), with the sacredness of coitus, with Sordello being offered five castles near Thetis in Italy and turning down this valuable property ('the land incult'), preferring his 'rich thought'; this folded round a short passage quoting the document as well as the pope's letter to Charles the Mangy of Anjou, thirteenth-century King of Naples and Sicily, in whose army Sordello served and who with the consent of Pope Clement IV attacked and defeated Manfred King of Naples and got his throne, giving Sordello the castles as a precondition:

'Called thrones, balascio or topaze'
Erigena was not understood in his time
'which explains, perhaps, the delay in condemning him'
And they went looking for Manichaeans
And found, so far as I can make out, no Manichaeans
So they dug for, and damned Scotus Erigena

[1] Philippe Sollers, Julia Kristeva and others in most numbers of *Tel Quel*. Collected in *Théorie d'ensemble* (Seuil, Paris 1968).

THEY DUG HIM UP OUT OF SEPULTURE

'Authority comes from right reason,
  never the other way on'
Hence the delay in condemning him
Aquinas head down in a vacuum,
  Aristotle which way in a vacuum?
  not quite a vacuum.
Sacrum, sacrum, inluminatio coitu.
Lo Sordels si fo di Mantovana
  of a castle named Goito.
'Five castles!
'Five castles!'
  (king giv' him five castles)
'And what the hell do I know about dye-works?!'
His Holiness has written a letter:
  'CHARLES the Mangy of Anjou . . .
. . . way you treat your men is a scandal . . .'
Dilectis miles familiaris . . . castra Montis Odorisii
Montis Sancti Silvestri pallete et pile . . .
In partibus Thetis . . . vineland
        land tilled
        the land incult
        pratis nemoribus pascuis
        with legal jurisdiction
his heirs of both sexes,
. . . sold the damn lot six weeks later,
Sordellus de Godio.
  Quan ben m'albir e mon ric pensamen.

            C.36

CHAPTER TWELVE

'There is no substitute for a lifetime'[1]

———————◆————————

I have left out a lot, naturally, in this brief ZBC for students. I have not dealt with Pound's versions of the Nō plays, of the Confucian *Odes* or of *Trachiniae*; nor with *Cathay*, or even properly with *Propertius* and *Mauberley* and I have only touched on some—I hope fundamental—aspects of *The Cantos*. Pound's work is not only large, it is inexhaustibly rich, one goes on discovering new facets, lines and passages that glow with sudden, previously unperceived significance in the light of others, which is why, once bitten, Poundian critics never seem to drop him but go on producing more books, more essays, thus contributing to the Pound Industry and, alas, in some ways debasing the currency, since all criticism necessarily reduces poetry to prose, and the moving image or 'intellectual and emotional complex in an instant of time' to explication.

I cannot, however (I suppose) leave out the sad and mucky political aspect which led to Pound being arraigned for treason, imprisoned at the age of 60 in an open-air cage barely fit for animals, taken to Washington, declared unfit to plead and incarcerated for twelve years in a hospital for the criminally insane. And when I say sad and mucky, the muck was not all on Pound's side, indeed, when one studies all the documents one can't help coming to the conclusion that most of it was on the side of whatever mixed human elements make up a government and its army, in this case that of the United States.

I shall not go into all the legal and other details, which are

[1] C. 98.

THERE IS NO SUBSTITUTE FOR A LIFETIME

available in two books.[1] I just want to bring out one or two points.

There is no doubt that Pound's determination, after leaving England and starting his life's work on *The Cantos*, finally to abandon the ivory tower, as it were, for *engagement*, led him into fields of study for which, with all his genius and insights, he was untrained; and that this, together with the superhuman creative effort, over so many years, of inventing a language to think in, a new poetics to which every modern English and American poet of any interest has declared himself indebted, brought him to the borders of irrational thought. Already in *Guide to Kulchur* (1938) the strident tone, despite the extraordinary quality and originality of the book, shows signs of a mind under intolerable strain. But he was not mad.

I have had occasion to mention Pound's errors of detail. I may not have sufficiently emphasized how often he was right, and not just in a long-term visionary sense, nor only on purely literary matters. His stress on Jefferson's and Adams' distrust of Alexander Hamilton, for instance, first U.S. Secretary to the Treasury, has, it seems, turned out to be well-founded. Hamilton's financial policy was to found a Bank of the U.S. on the model of the Bank of England, and so to involve the U.S. in international finance. He said to the Federal Convention: 'All communities divide themselves into the few and the many. The first are the rich and well born; the other the mass of the people, turbulent and changing, they seldom judge or determine right. Give therefore to the first class a distinct, permanent share in the Government.' He thought that the Constitution gave too many powers to the States and that old families, merchant ship-owners, public creditors and financiers must be made a loyal governing class by a direct policy of favouring their interests. He is generally supposed to have established a fiscal system and to have put national credit on a sound basis. In fact he put every obstacle in the way of Adams' attempts to keep

[1] Charles Norman, *The Case of Ezra Pound*, New York 1968; Julien Cornell, *The Trial of Ezra Pound—A documented account of the treason case by the Defendant's Lawyer*, London 1966.

239

the peace. He attacked two popular ideas, among others, first that republics are necessarily pacific, and second that 'the spirit of commerce has a tendency to soften the manners of men' (*The Federalist*, No. 6). But Hamilton was a complex character and also pointed out that any necessity which enhances the importance of the soldier 'proportionately degrades the condition of the citizen. The military state becomes elevated above the civil.' (*The Federalist*, No. 8.) It was partly to forestall the threat of a military dictatorship that George Washington took the lead in the drafting and ratification of the Constitution.[1] So Pound in *Money Pamphlets by £*, No. 6, *America, Roosevelt and the Causes of the Present War* (1950, first published in Italian, 1944); and in C.37 (Van Buren) :

> 'on precedent that Mr Hamilton has
> never hesitated to jeopard the general
> for advance of particular interests.'

and in C.62 :

> retirement
> (Washington's) removed all check upon
> parties
> Mr Jefferson, Mr Hamilton
> the latter not enjoying the confidence of the people at large
> to oppose Ham to Jeff wd/ be futile
> wherepon Ham set to undercut Adams

Canto 63 :

> and General Pinckney, a man of honour
> declined to participate
> or even to give suspicion of having colluded
> deficiency in early moral foundations (Mr Hamilton's)

and in Cantos 66, 69, 70 (John Adams says: 'Hamilton no command, / too much intrigue' and 'Hamilton's total ignorance (or whatever) / of practice and usage of nations') and elsewhere. I have only quoted passages where Hamilton is actually

[1] Ch. A. Beard, *The Republic*, New York 1943, pp. 212 ff.

named, which illustrate Adams' distrust, but all these Cantos are about, among other things, the beginning and development of colonial prosperity, England's efforts to impose its monetary monopoly, the struggle between Hamilton as conservatist agent of finance and Adams' administration, the Bank wars, the contraction of debts to New York bankers, especially by the South, leading to the War of Secession and the triumph of finance.

It has recently been established that Hamilton was engaged in shady negotiation with a British secret agent, Major Beckwith. He was known to the British, oddly enough, as Number 7.[1]

But that is only a non-error of detail. Much more important was Pound's whole attitude to America's involvement in war. Jefferson himself had wanted the new state to remain a small and free agricultural country, but this was not to be.[2] With this idealistic background, Pound was on the side of those who condemned F. D. R. Roosevelt's allegedly unconstitutional behaviour in preparing for war without asking Congress (the Destroyer Deal, the 'manœuvering' of Pearl Harbour). Only Congress can declare war (Constitution I/8, Clause 11) but by then, according to these views, it had no choice. As Charles A. Beard puts it in his book on Roosevelt and the war: 'Since the drafting of the Constitution, American statesmen of the first

[1] Julian P. Boyd, *Number 7. Alexander Hamilton's Secret Attempts to Control American Foreign Policy* (Princeton, London 1965). See also *The Times Literary Supplement* 22/5/1965; and the entry under Hamilton in *Encyclopaedia of the American Revolution*, Mark M. Boatner III, New York 1966.

[2] Thomas Jefferson: 'An equilibrium of agriculture, manufactures and commerce is certainly become essential to our independence. Manufactures, sufficient for our own consumption, of what we raise the raw material (and no more). Commerce sufficient to carry the surplus produce of agriculture, beyond our own consumption, to a market for exchanging it for articles we cannot raise (and no more). These are the true limits of manufactures and commerce. To go beyond them is to increase our dependence on foreign nations, and our liability to war.' (To Gov. James Jay, April 7 1809, *The Writings of Thomas Jefferson*, Washington 1903, Vol. XII, p. 271.) 'But for us to attempt, by war, to reform all Europe, and bring them back to principles of morality and a respect for the equal rights of nations, would show us to be only maniacs of another character.' (To William Wirt, May 30 1811, *ibid*. Vol. XIV, p. 50.)

order have accepted the axiom that militarism and the exercise of arbitrary power over foreign affairs by the Executive are inveterate foes of republican institutions. . . . But it is contended by some contemporary publicists, whose assurance is often more impressive than their knowledge of human government, that offense is the best defense, that unlimited striking power in the Executive is necessary to survival in an age of "power politics" and "atom bombs". Few of them, it is true, venture to say openly that the Constitution is obsolete, and that such a centralization of authority should be, in fact substituted for the system of limited government fortified by checks and balances. Yet the implication of their arguments is inexorable : constitutional and democratic government in the United States is at the end of its career.'[1]

The whole problem is enormously complex, and for the purpose of this book I am quoting on Pound's side rather than on the other. For Pound, whose criticisms of America stem from a deep love, saw all this coming already in 1941 and '42. He was immensely distressed by what he saw as Roosevelt's flagrant breach of the Constitution. And although it is true to say that he was out of touch with the genuine swing of public opinion from isolationism to war, the fact remains that Roosevelt had committed himself unreservedly to the antiwar covenants of the Democratic Party during his election campaign of 1940, and that by the end of 1941 the country was at war. However grateful much of Europe no doubt was at the time, I can see that from Pound's and in a way from any American viewpoint, as well as from today's much sadder standpoint, Roosevelt's change-over could be regarded not only as a further major step in a fatal series of errors, but as the final betrayal of Jefferson's ideal. This view is held by Charles Beard (*op. cit.*). The key document is a diary entry of the Secretary of War Henry L. Stimson at a meeting of the President and his War Cabinet on November 25, 1941 :

[1] Ch. A. Beard, *President Roosevelt and the Coming of the War, 1941— A Study in Appearances and Realities* (Yale U.P. 1948), last chapter on 'Interpretations Tested by Consequences'.

THERE IS NO SUBSTITUTE FOR A LIFETIME

'. . . At the meeting were Hull, Knox, Marshall, Stark and myself. There the President brought up the relations with the Japanese. The question was how we should maneuver them into the position of firing the first shot without allowing too much danger to ourselves.'

Twelve days later, on December 7, the Japanese obliged by bombing Pearl Harbour. General Marshall had great difficulty in extricating himself from Senator Ferguson's questions on that sentence at a Congressional Committee hearing on April 9, 1946.[1]

Pound, living in Rapallo, had been in touch with Radio Rome on cultural matters, notably the rediscovery and revival of Vivaldi's music, in which he had taken an energetic part. He was invited to broadcast on anything he liked, and did so, chiefly on literature, but also on economics and politics. After Pearl Harbour he was not heard on the radio for several weeks, but in January 1942 he 'chose to continue broadcasting'.[2]

This is the crux of the matter. Whatever the undeniable lapses of taste in the broadcasts (he railed against Krupp and others but tended to identify financiers with Jews and referred to the activities of everyone around Roosevelt, and for that matter Stalin, as 'kikery'), Pound was not, as he said himself, sending axis propaganda but his own views, which fact the announcer each time made clear. Pound said nothing that could be considered treasonable had it been said (and it was said, by others) on American soil, where the principle of free speech holds:

---

[1] *Congressional Joint Committee Report*, Part 11, pp. 5187 ff., quoted in Beard, Ch. XVII: *Maneuvering the Japanese into Firing the First Shot.*

[2] *Congressional Record*, April 1958, Appendix, A3896. (For brevity and clarity I shall not give each speaker's name when I quote from the *Congressional Record*, which can easily be looked up.) A footnote adds that several writers had suggested that Pound tried to return to the U.S. in 1941 and was refused permission. This is then denied, though 'the documents in the State Department files do not preclude the possibility of the development of a misunderstanding between Mr. Pound and a consular official which might have unintentionally aborted Mr. Pound's "attempt" to leave Italy.' Further evidence to that effect is given in A 3900.

Oh my England
that free speech without free radio speech is as zero
C.74

Nor was he warned, as P. G. Wodehouse (who broadcast for the Germans) was warned, and stopped.[1] When Pound heard, in 1943, that he had been indicted for treason, he wrote via the Swiss Legation in Rome to the Attorney General, Francis Biddle, protesting against the indictment:

'I have not spoken with regard to the war, but in protest against a system which creates one war after another, in series and on system. I have not spoken to the troops, and have not suggested that the troops should mutiny or revolt. . . .

'At any rate, a man's duties increase with his knowledge. A war between the United States and Italy is monstrous and should not have occurred. And a peace without justice is not peace but merely a prelude to future wars. Someone must take count of these things. And having taken count must act on his knowledge, admitting that his knowledge is partial and his judgment subject to error.

Very truly yours,

Ezra Pound.'[2]

Julien Cornell, later his lawyer, who listened to the broadcasts at the end of the war, says:

'The broadcasts did not sound treasonable to me. The crime of treason is defined in the Constitution as the levying of war against the United States or adhering to their enemies, giving them aid and comfort. There was no criticism of the allied war

[1] Pound's colleagues were not put on trial. Of the British: Olivia Rossetti Agresti (daughter of William Michael Rossetti) may have had dual nationality; Lt. Col. Rocke (cp. C.104 & *G. Kulchur* for his support of Abyssinian War) and Major J. S. Barnes (author of *Fascism*, Home University Library 1931) were never put on trial. The head of the department of the Fascist Ministry of Popular Culture, responsible for foreign-language broadcasts, was George Nelson Page, an American, arrested by the U.S. army but released after a few months because he had taken Italian nationality in 1935.

[2] Quoted in the *Congressional Record*, April 1958, A8896, Appendix.

effort in the broadcasts; nothing was said to discourage or disturb American soldiers or their families. Pound's main concern was with usury and other economic sins which he conceived were being committed by an international conspiracy of Jewish bankers who were the powers behind the throne in England and had succeeded in duping the government of the United States. The broadcasts were in essence lectures in history and political and economic theory, highly critical of the course of American government beginning with Alexander Hamilton, who Pound believed started the country down the road to financial ruin. . . . I never knew of anyone who heard these broadcasts over the radio, although they were received and monitored in the United States. As a radio figure, Pound did not command the interest of Lord Haw Haw, Axis Sally or Tokyo Rose. He was not an entertainer and apparently did not care whether anyone listened to him or not. It seems most unlikely that those who did hear him could have lost any affection for the United States or its war effort. It is also unlikely that any jury would reach the conclusion that the broadcasts gave "aid and comfort to the enemy" or that Pound was doing anything but exercising the good old American prerogative of criticizing his government including even President Roosevelt.'[1]

It is interesting to note that the Cramer case was quoted in Congress at the time (*Congressional Record, op. cit.*) : 'The crime of treason consists of two elements, both of which must be present in order to sustain a conviction : (1) adherence to the enemy, and (2) rendering him aid and comfort.'

The definition continues : 'The terms aid and comfort as used in the provision of the Federal Constitution defining treason as giving aid and comfort to the enemy contemplate some kind of affirmative action, deed, or physical activily tending to strengthen the enemy or weaken the power to resist him, and is not satisfied by a mere mental operation.'

And Thomas Jefferson is also quoted (letter April 24, 1792, when he was Secretary of State) : 'Treason . . . when real,

[1] *The Trial of Ezra Pound, op. cit.*, pp. 1–2.

merits the highest punishment. But most codes extend their definitions of treason to acts not really against one's country. They do not distinguish between acts against the government and acts against the oppressions of the government: the latter are virtues; yet they have furnished more victims to the executioners than the former, because real treasons are rare, oppressions frequent.'[1]

Or as Pound, who acted against his government for waging war, was to put it at the end of C.78:

> In the spring and autumn
> In 'The Spring and Autumn'
> there
> are
> no
> righteous
> wars

A nicely ambiguous quotation from Mencius, who said that no righteous wars are mentioned in Confucius' *The Spring and Autumn,* but went on to define a righteous war as one between a large state and a small one (which is swallowed up) and an unrighteous war as one between two big states which almost destroys them both. In his essay on Mencius, Pound glosses: 'In the *Spring and Autumn* there are no righteous wars, some are better than others.' In C.82, however, he is more explicit:

> there are no righteous wars in 'The Spring and Autumn'
> that is, perfectly right on one side or the other
> total right on either side of the battle line

In any case, Pound is stressing the absence of righteous wars in Confucius at the end of C.78, rather than remembering Mencius.

The broadcasts, incidentally, are very inaccurately and (if the case were not so sad) hilariously transcribed. Hugh Kenner's

---

[1] *Eight Writings of Thomas Jefferson,* Library Edition, Washington 1913, p. 332. Quoted in the *Congressional Record,* April 1958, Appendix, A3898.

246

comment in *Poetry Magazine*, Chicago, July 1957, is quoted in the *Congressional Record* of April 1958 (A3944) :

'It does not appear that he said anything that would have constituted treason had he said it in the United States Senate; what he did say it is difficult to discover, the indictment being publicly supported by transcripts of grotesque unreliability. On Feb. 12, 1942, for instance, he is alleged to have alluded to "Max Bearbon", "Helen of Troy", and the classical authors "Askulus" and "Propursious", and to have read, with a commentary, Canto 46, which according to the transcription of the broadcast in the Library of Congress, opens as follows :

' "And if you'll say that this day teaches a less, all that the Reverend Eliot (Haston) more natural language, you who think you'll get through hell in a hurry, huh, ah, that day how those cloud over his (horizon) and for 3 days snow clouds over the sea, banked like a line of mountains."[1]

'There is even, in an earlier broadcast, a reference to the "confusion system", the transcriber having evidently not been able to bring Confucius immediately to mind. . . .'

In 1944, as the Allies entered Rome, Pound hitch-hiked all the way to Gais, a village in the Italian Tyrol, near the Austrian border, where his daughter lived.[2] He arrived exhausted, his feet blistered and bleeding. He stayed a week then went to Rapallo. On May 2 the following year 'he surrendered near Genoa. He was sent to the MTOUSA Disciplinary Training Center at Pisa where he was incarcerated for over half a year. When Pound was first brought to Pisa, he was put in a specially-

---

[1] C.46 reads : And if you will say that this tale teaches . . . / a lesson, or that the Reverend Eliot / has found a more natural language . . . you who think you will / get through hell in a hurry . . . / That day there was cloud over Zoagli / And for three days snow cloud over the sea / Banked like a line of mountains.

[2] Mary de Rachewiltz in conversation. The village of Gais is where 'Herr Bacher's father made madonnas still in the tradition / carved wood as you might have found in any cathedral / and another Bacher still cut intaglios / such as Salustio's in the time of Ixotta, / where the masks come from, in the Tirol, / in the winter season / searching every house to drive out the demons' (C.74).

constructed grilled security-cage. He was kept in this cage for several weeks, after which he was transferred to a pyramidal tent.'[1]

There he really did break down :

'Not only was Pound deprived of rest by reason of the intense heat and glare, but he had no recreation or relaxation whatever. He was not allowed to leave his cage for meals and exercise like the other prisoners, but was at all times kept in solitary confinement. . . . He had no reading matter except two volumes of the Chinese text of Confucius which he had been translating into English.

'After a week or so of the mental and physical torment of confinement in the cage, Pound's mind gave way. He says that he can now recall only the sensation that the top of his head was empty; also that his eyebrows were constantly caught in a raised position, due to the heat and glare. As a result of the hardships of his imprisonment he was stricken with violent terror and hysteria, and also affected with amnesia. As a result of Pound's condition he was removed from the cage and placed in the shelter of a tent. He was also given a cot to lie upon[2] and given medical treatment [footbaths!][3] Gradually he recovered his health, but his mind apparently remained affected. . . . He says that one thing which helped to save his sanity during this

[1] Reported in the *Congressional Record*, April 1958, A3896, Appendix. See also A3943 for more detailed evidence from former guards : 'The first of these cages was torn down . . . and a new enclosure of heavy grillwork was built in its place . . . because of an alleged fear the Italian Fascists would attempt to rescue the accused traitor. . . . Pound did not remain longer than a few weeks in his gorilla cage because of his increasingly poor health.' 'The weeks in the cage were hard on Pound. As shelter, a piece of tar paper was thrown over the top. . . . Because the dust and harsh sun in the cage inflamed his eyes he was transferred to a tent within the Medical Compound.'

[2] In the cage he had only blankets. A photograph of the type of DTC Cages used at Pisa is published in *Ezra Pound*, Cahiers de l'Herne, Vol. 2, Paris 1965.

[3] Mary de Rachewiltz in conversation. Pound suffered his mental collapse after one week in the cage, but was left there for another two weeks, in a state of amnesia, hysteria and claustrophobia.

period was the discovery of an anthology of poetry in the privy; also the kindness shown to him by a colored soldier who brought him his meals. The latter was the only person who was able to speak to him, and although he was confined to remarks about the food, he managed to convey sufficient sympathy by voice and glance to give much comfort to his fellow prisoner.'[1]

Pound was imprisoned for thirteen years, as Cornell points out, 'because of an alleged crime which was never proved'. And the two most distressing aspects, to me, are : first, the reports of the psychiatrists before the treason trial that never took place (reports which astonished Cornell who assumed that there would be a trial and that Pound would be acquitted), and their evidence at the unfitness trial; there they ambled on incoherently about delusional systems, paranoia, daementia praecox, hypochondria (!) and above all about Pound's incoherence, one of them even admitting to having seen 'one of the Cantos' and answering the question 'And not being able to follow argument, do you think that is a good reason for not being able to stand trial?' with 'That is one reason'. Secondly, the contortions they all got into twelve years later when the whole thing had become a national embarrassment, in order to be able to say that on the one hand he was too mad to stand trial but on the other he was not mad enough to be incarcerated and ought to be let out.[2] During these thirteen years he was so mentally unfit that he wrote most of his best work: *The Pisan Cantos*, *Rock-Drill*, *Thrones*, the Confucian translations (*The Unwobbling Pivot*, *The Analects*, *The Odes*) and the magnificent translation of Sophocles' *Trachiniae* (*The Women of Trachis*).

They meant well no doubt. I am not up in American criminal law. But the fact remains that Pound, who never admitted to having committed any crime, who denied ever having been a Fascist, was never allowed to prove this and was incarcerated, at first into the snake-pit part of St Elizabeth's Hospital at

[1] Julien Cornell in a letter to Dr Wendell Muncie, Dec. 6 1945, printed in *The Trial of Ezra Pound*, op. cit., pp. 30–1.

[2] See Cornell, op. cit., Ch. IV, Medical Examination, App. IV Transcript of Trial.

Washington, together with the worst criminal lunatics, though later he was given a cubicle and allowed to write and see people.

Moreover, he eventually got out—and this thanks to the constant efforts of poets and other generous individuals from all over the world—but on the wrong terms, with the indictment withdrawn but never quashed, released as a harmlessly insane man with few legal rights, in the custody of his family. After the first euphoria had passed, he lapsed into a schizophrenic depression from which he will probably not recover, the primary cause of which very likely went back twenty years to the shock of Pisa : just as many German soldiers, in the terrible conditions of the Russian labour camps, felt fine as long as the outside pressure of hostile surroundings continued, but would collapse years later in perfectly normal circumstances; so with many of the surviving victims of German concentration camps. Medically the case is classical.

Pound did not know about the concentration camps, he was totally out of touch in Italy. This does not excuse him as a public preacher who should be informed. His anti-Semitism is (or was) nasty, an aberration, even if in intention focused on the financial question. But, if I may say so, for I was brought up in the thirties and heard the way grown-ups talked, it was part of the general hysterical, ill-informed atmosphere of propaganda and counter-propaganda of the time. Dear old ladies in Kent villages would talk about the Jews in a similar vein, if in more genteel terms. All this has fortunately passed, but at a terrible cost in human suffering.[1] And the colour-prejudice which now replaces it will also pass and one day seem as irrelevant as the religious wars of the sixteenth and seventeenth centuries, though possibly after another terrible blood-letting. This does not exonerate Pound, but he has paid, and heavily, and for many who got off scot-free.

As for his endorsement of Mussolini, it was for the same foolish and even innocent reason that so many people at first

[1] At least I hope it has passed : in the French university where I teach at the moment I have seen some pretty ugly posters and writings-on-the-wall, from both sides (and of course irrelevant—since both sides are semitic) with regard to the Israel conflict.

support dictators on the grounds of good government (they build splendid roads, thereby reducing unemployment, etc.). This is the perennial choice between a strong leadership that gets things done but tramples on precious freedoms, and the slow muddle of democracy which preserves these freedoms. It is not an insoluble problem but it is a difficult and delicate one. At the end of *Jefferson and/or Mussolini* (written in 1933, published 1935), Pound wrote:
'Towards which I assert again my own firm belief that the Duce will stand not with despots and the lovers of power but with the lovers of

ORDER
to kalón'

This equation of order with beauty had been clearly qualified in the pamphlet as not meaning regimentation: 'Kung taught that organization is not forced on to things or on to a nation from the outside inward, but that the centre holds by attraction' (pp. 112–13). And earlier (p. 45) he had taken up Jefferson's dictum 'The best government is that which governs least' and said: 'Mussolini has been presumably right in putting the first emphasis on having a government strong enough to get the said justice. That is to say taking first the "government" in our text and proceeding at reasonable pace toward the "which governs least".'

The notion of 'proceeding at a reasonable pace' towards less force is the usual mistake made by people who admire strong government. But it is an understandable one, and historically it is important to distinguish Mussolini from Hitler; indeed, Mussolini is now being defended and some argue that Pound was more or less right about him. Mistake or not, it was to have tragic consequences. But after all these years I can only agree with the poet Tom Scott who says: 'Pound is unhappy to wake up and find himself on the side that made Belsen; but I am unhappy to have been on the side that made Dresden and Hiroshima and Nagasaki. Let us forgive the past and get on with the job.'[1]

Meanwhile Pound is a broken man. And many even now are

[1] *An Appreciation*, in *Perspectives*, ed. Stock, Chicago 1965.

not willing to forgive the past.[1] This is why I have tried to describe this sordid story from Pound's viewpoint, although I feel certain that to the best and most serious part of the younger generation whom I address, and some of whom I teach, these issues are as dead as the religious wars : do we bother much now whether Agrippa d'Aubigné, the baroque religious poet, was on the Protestant or the Catholic side, except for points of exegesis? Yet people murdered each other for these issues. Does it matter to us today that Dryden was twice a turncoat? That Blake was tried for high treason or that Dante pleaded with the German Emperor, Henry VII, to destroy his native city of Florence?

Nevertheless many critics, and not merely the journalists, after writing a sensitive and perceptive book, still feel obliged to end with a huge hindsight qualification on Pound's 'failure'—rather like the perpetually qualified replies of the psychiatrists at the trial—perhaps to show how objective they are, and on the 'right side', thus leaving the reader with a nasty taste. Dekker's isn't too bad, though he is at other points (which I forbear to mention) quite rude. At least his qualification sticks to the work, but it is characteristically ambiguous :

'It may be objected . . . that the result (with a few notable exceptions) is a work which is neither scholarly nor poetic. This certainly seems to be true of a major portion of the poem. Yet, though I am not ready to prefer Pound's failure (so far as he has failed) to the general failure of contemporary poetry to be as great in scope as it is splendid in detail, I believe that it is important to recognize that *The Cantos* represent the only major twentieth century claim for the civilizing force of poetry. It may again be objected, and with truth, that Pound himself was not fully civilized, and that the claim might have been made more fortunately by somebody else. But it was not made by somebody else.'[2]

[1] E.g. Philip Toynbee, in a review of the Pound/Joyce letters (1969) which were written between 1913 and 1920 and were irrelevant to this, showing Pound at his generous best, drags the whole thing in again, saying that Pound was a Fascist and it was right to imprison him for thirteen years.
[2] George Dekker, *Sailing after Knowledge* (London 1963) p. 135.

THERE IS NO SUBSTITUTE FOR A LIFETIME

Much more seriously damaging is Donald Davie's insistence that 'Pound has made it impossible for any one any longer to exalt the poet into a seer. This is what Pound has done to the concept of the poetic vocation; and, challenged with it, all he can say is, "I'll split his face with my fists".'[1]

Davie quotes from a 'long and bitter comment' by William Carlos Williams, who said of Pound that 'he really lived the poet as few of us had the nerve to live that exalted reality in our time', but who never forgave him the wrong-headed war-time callousness of his letters (and who at that time was not at least a little callous on one side or the other?). Davie also reminds us of Pound 'mischievously consorting with rabble-rousers, and refusing to withdraw any of his rabble-rousing opinions' at St Elizabeth's. But the rabble-rousers were the only people who came to see him regularly (others came but more rarely, no doubt driven away by the rabble-rousers), and Pound was still in a fighting mood, in a confused and profoundly hurt, shocked condition. Davie goes on :

'When, in February 1949, the first Bollingen prize for poetry was awarded to *The Pisan Cantos*, and the award was upheld through the storm of protests that followed on the floor of Congress and elsewhere, this was enormously to the credit of American society, but it did nothing to vindicate the exalted reality of living the poet's life. For what it meant in effect was that American society accepted and recognized an absolute discontinuity between the life of the poet and the life of the man. Ever since, in British and American society alike, this absolute distinction has been sustained, and upheld indeed as the basic assumption on which society must proceed in dealing with the artists who live in its midst. Undoubtedly, at the present moment of history it is the most humane, and to that degree the most civilized arrangement possible. Still, the privilege that it extends to the artist is the privilege of the pariah; and

[1] Donald Davie, *Poet as Sculptor* (London 1965) p. 243. The reference is to an Italian newspaper report quoted in Charles Norman's *Ezra Pound* (New York 1960), a somewhat unscholarly biography. Revised edition, Macdonald (London 1969).

it is not at all such a solid or exalted platform as some people thought when from that vantage point they fulminated righteously at Russia over the case of Pasternak's Nobel prize. In Russia the artist was found fit to plead, whereas in Britain and America he is found unfit: which conception of the artist is more exalted? In the event, of course, the Russians, though with a bad grace, decided to agree with the Americans that the artist is, or is likely to be, a political imbecile; whereupon Western observers forgave them for having entertained more exalted ideas of a poet's wisdom and responsibility.

'And for much of this Pound is to blame.'

Why?—Because of what was done to him? Because of society's sick behaviour? That is really turning the argument on its head. And this quite apart from the naïve notion that in Russia the artist has at any time been found fit to plead; his trial is a legal farce, deriving, it is true, from the writer's power, or what Conor Cruise O'Brien has called a relation of *compression* between the writer and the power structure (the writer feels pressure from the state but so does the state feel pressure from the writer), as opposed to the relation of *diffusion* in the West (the writer feels no pressure but exercises none).[1]

Nevertheless I think that the Pound/Pasternak analogy is misleading. Pasternak had committed no technical crime, he had merely written a novel about the Revolution, published it in the West and dared to accept the Nobel Prize, which he was not allowed to receive—a sufficient example of compression. No one, it seems, listened to the Pound broadcasts, yet the State did considerably more than thank itself for the existence of free speech. Moreover the whole difficult and complex situation in both parts of the world has arisen over a long period and for a

[1] *Homer Watt Lecture* (New York, Spring 1966): 'The Western power structure is not unmindful of the importance of writers. Nor is it entirely inaccessible to criticisms and protests of writers and intellectuals. Such criticisms reach it, but seem to have to traverse great reaches of space and time and to arrive attenuated and distorted. In the East, a writer whispers and the giant squirms and heaves. In the West, many writers shout in chorus and the giant, after a long time, thanks itself for the existence of freedom of speech.'

large number of causes. I think that Davie goes a bit far when he says that 'for much of it Pound is to blame'. He adds, magnanimously: 'To be sure, he was out of his mind. But American society has refused to see him as therefore a special case. Nor is this unjust, for madness is one of the risks that the poet runs.

Pound had forestalled that one already in the *ABC of Reading* (1934), under PERCEPTION:

'Artists are the antennae of the race'.

Can you be interested in the writings of a man whose general perceptions are below the average?

I am afraid that even here the answer is not a straight 'No'. There is a much more delicate question:

Can you be interested in the work of a man who is blind to 80 per cent of the spectrum? to 30 per cent of the spectrum?

Here the answer is, curiously enough, yes IF . . . if his perceptions are hypernormal in any part of the spectrum he can be of very great use as a writer—

though perhaps not of very great 'weight'. This is where the so-called crackbrained genius comes in. The concept of genius as akin to madness has been carefully fostered by the inferiority complex of the public.

Here it may be worth quoting a letter in the *American Journal of Psychotherapy*, 1949 (cited in evidence in the *Congressional Record*, April 1958, Appendix, A3942):

Dr. Frederic Wertham:

'The Counsel for the defense used the expression "insanity common to genius". Ezra Pound himself answered long ago:

It has been your habit for long to do away
  with good writers,
You either drive them mad, or else you
  blink at their suicides,
Or else you condone their drugs, and talk
  of insanity and genius,
But I will not go mad to please you . . .

Surely the psychiatrists know the difference between a political conviction and a delusion. . . . Ezra Pound has no delusions in any strictly pathological sense.'[1]

Well of course Pound did, in a tragic way, 'go mad to please them'. Perhaps that is what Donald Davie means. He did not, however, do it on purpose, as anyone reading *The Pisan Cantos* can surely see, where all the images of his life and reading come crowding in to jostle the present suffering :

<blockquote>

Frobenius der Geheimrat
der im Baluba das Gewitter gemacht hat
      and Monsieur Jean[2] wrote a play now and then or the
                                Possum
      pouvrette et ancienne oncques lettre ne lus[3]
I don't know how humanity stands it
      with a painted paradise at the end of it
      without a painted paradise at the end of it   C.74

dry friable earth going from dust to more dust
    grass worn from its root-hold
    is it blacker ? was it blacker ? Νύξ animae ?
    is there a blacker or was it merely San Juan with a belly ache
                   writing ad posteros
    in short shall we look for a deeper or is this the bottom ?
    Ugolino, the tower there on the tree line
Berlin   dysentery   phosphorus
               la vieille de Candide
(Hullo Corporal Casey) double X or bureaucracy ?
                   Le Paradis n'est pas artificiel
  but spezzato apparently   C.74
Le Paradis n'est pas artificiel
    States of mind are inexplicable to us.
  δακρύων   δακρύων   δακρύων[4]

</blockquote>

[1] The poem is 'Salutation the Third', *Blast*, 1914, *Collected Shorter Poems*, 1962. The line-division is incorrect.

[2] Jean Cocteau.

[3] From *Aucassin et Nicolette* (thirteenth-century prose tale).

[4] Weeping, genitive plural of tears. L.P. may stand for Le Paradis.

L.   P.   gli onesti
                        J'ai eu pitié des autres
probablement pas assez, and at moments that suited my own
                                                    convenience
                    Le paradis n'est pas artificiel,
                        l'enfer non plus.
Came Eurus as comforter
and at sunset la pastorella dei suini
        driving the pigs home, benecomata dea[1]

                                                    C.76

And, after the passage about the book of poetry found in the
privy, which I quoted on p. 145 :

            repos donnez à cils
                senza termine funge   Immaculata Regina
                Les larmes que j'ai créées m'inondent
                Tard, très tard je t'ai connue, la Tristesse,
                I have been hard as youth sixty years

                                                    C.80

I think that Pound's personal tragedy has fascinated many
people who then work on him without sufficient sensibility. It
has also focused the attention of even good critics on his
supposed madness, producing a false syllogism : he became mad
therefore the later Cantos are a chaos. One wonders whether
some of these critics, if he hadn't made that fatal error which led
to his predicament, would not take the same sort of trouble
with his later Cantos as they do with the earlier Cantos and the
early poetry. But it is a fruitless question, for he would then
never have written The Pisan Cantos, or Rock-Drill or Thrones
in the form in which we have them. Which are great. Which are
chaos. So the argument runs in circles.

Of course there are essential contradictions in Pound, as well
as moments of chaos, without which he would not be a great
poet. The Cantos arise out of these tensions. The very synthesis
attempted, between East and West, Greece and mediaeval

            [1] Recalling Circe, 'trim-coifed goddess' in C.1.

Christianity, literature and politics, Chêng ming and money, almost tear the poem apart at times. But only almost, and only at times. Of course Pound can be a bore, and below par. So could Milton, so, dare I say it, could Shakespeare, and even Homer nods. Actually Pound rarely nods, he yells or cuts himself off. Of course it is rather tiresome in *Thrones* for instance, to find that he has vanished into a fourteenth-century Codex of the Edict of Leo the Wise (Leo VI, 886–912), the 'Eparch's Book', edited in Greek and Latin by the Genevese professor Jules Nicole.[1] He even breaks into sudden prose, about the curiosity that reaches into greater detail (see p. 147). And he certainly has fun with the greater detail of the text: 'δέκα νομισμάτων (Nicole: purpureas vestas) τὰ βλαττιά / but the ἀναιδῶς is rather nice, Dr. Nicole'; 'κατὰ τὴν ἐξώνεσιν νομίσματος ἑνὸς / that's how Nicole slanted it, grave on the omicron, / meaning one aureus, bankers / to profit one keration 2 miliarisia'; '& that Nicephoras / kolobozed the tetarteron / need not have applied to the aureus / or caused Nicole to understand token coinage'; 'have codified πολιτικῶν σωματείων / (To Professor Nicole's annoyance) Leo 886–911' [actually 912] (C.96).

But as he said in C.85, in the middle of a lot of Chinese characters from the *Chou King*: 'Awareness restful & fake is fatiguing' (*Chou King* XX. 18). Nevertheless: 'We flop if we cannot maintain the awareness' (*Chou King* XVI. 4).

'You can't have literature without CURIOSITY', he insisted to D. G. Bridson in the B.B.C. interview (*op. cit.* 11/7/1960), and if he exaggerates at times, no one can deny that *The Cantos* are literature. And as he said in another context:

'I hope the reader has *not* "understood it all straight off". I should like to invent some kind of typographical dodge which would force every reader to stop and reflect for five minutes (or five hours), to go back to the facts mentioned and think over their significance for himself.'[2]

[1] *Le livre du Préfet*, Geneva 1893.
[2] *Money Pamphlets by £*, No. 6 (in Italian, Venice 1944, in English, London 1950).

THERE IS NO SUBSTITUTE FOR A LIFETIME

Well, he invented it all right. But the cost has been enormous. Of Bartok's Fifth Quartet he said : 'It has the defects and disadvantages of my Cantos. . . . Or perhaps I shd qualify that : the defects inherent in a record of struggle.'[1] Or on the Tempio : 'The Tempio Malatestiano is both an apex and in verbal sense a monumental failure. It is perhaps the apex of what one man has embodied in the last 1000 years of the occident. A cultural "high" is marked.'[2] And in *Polite Essays* : 'Art very possibly *ought* to be the supreme achievement, the "accomplished"; but there is the other satisfactory effect, that of a man hurling himself at an indomitable chaos and yanking and hauling as much of it as possible into some sort of order (or beauty), aware of it both as chaos and as potential.'[3]

Pound has never regarded *The Cantos* as telling the absolute dogmatic truth about anything, but rather, like the syllogism to the Stoics, as 'merely useful for hypothesis and discussion. Didn't PROVE anything.' Of course he believes that everything he sees is really there, and that 'the gods exist'. Of course he wants us to see it too, but above all he wants us to 'go back over the facts mentioned and think over their significance' for ourselves. And if some of the facts seem to contradict others, well, maybe they don't when we think about them. For his contradictions are not irreconcilable, they are part of a dialectic, like the paradoxical element which Cleanth Brooks held was inherent to lyric,[4] only on a much larger scale. And some of them are part of the poet himself, of the poem which is a record of struggle. For Pound's life, from the beginning, was a series of reactions against himself. Even his DON'TS in 1914, as de Nagy was the first to point out, were really addressed to what he himself DID. So in the late Fragments (all written in 1958–9, though one is dated 1960), he echoes that marvellous line of Herakles in *The Women of Trachis*—'What splendour, it all coheres'—but poignantly :

(1) *Guide to Kulchur*, 1938, p. 135.   (2) *Ibid.*, p. 159.
(3) *Polite Essays*, 1937, p. 77.
(4) *The Language of Paradox*, in *The Well Wrought Urn* (New York 1947, ch. I).

I have brought the great ball of crystal;
　　　　　who can lift it?
Can you enter the great acorn of light?
　　　　　But the beauty is not the madness
Tho' my errors and wrecks lie about me.
And I am not a demigod,
I cannot make it cohere.
If love be not in the house there is nothing.
The voice of famine unheard.
How came beauty against this blackness . . .

　　　　　　　　　　　　　　　　　C.116

And a little later:

　　　but about that terzo
　　　　　　third heaven,
　　　　　　　　that Venere,
　　again is all 'paradiso'
　　a nice quiet paradise
　　　　　　　over the shambles,
　　and some climbing
　　　　　　before the take-off,
　　to 'see again,'
　　the verb is 'see', not 'walk on',
　　i.e. it coheres all right
　　　　　　even if my notes do not cohere.
　　Many errors,
　　　　a little rightness,
　　to excuse his hell
　　　　　and my paradiso.

　　　　　　　　　　　　　　　　　C.116

But even in this sad 'nice quiet paradise' he does not forget old
loyalties, or lose his interest, his 'curiosity':

 chih³   [stop, cp. p. 182]

and there is no *chih* and no root.

Bunting and Upward neglected,
  all the resisters blacked out,
From time's wreckage shored,
  these fragments shored against ruin,

and the   jih[4-5] [sun]

  new with the day.   C.110

Or echoing C.34 :

Enlarged his empire
  diminished his forces,
Ten years a blessing,
  five a nuisance,
that was Napoleon
with constitutional guarantees
  April 2nd.
'Very few interested'
  N. to Talleyrand, 'in civilization.'
So that Alexander asked Talleyrand what to do about
      France.
And 'to change the meaning of words themselves from one
     conference to another'.
    Oct. 31st, Wien
And 600 more dead at Quemoy—
  they call it political.
A nice quiet paradise,
   Orage held the basic was pity
    compassione,
   Amor

          C.111

Even old Plotinus is there, and Yeats, who in C.83 had been
gently mocked for admiring a symbol on Notre Dame and
missing Notre Dame ('and Uncle William dawdling around
Notre Dame / in search of whatever / paused to admire the
symbol / with Notre Dame standing inside it') :

That the body is inside the soul
the lifting and folding brightness
the darkness shattered,
the fragment.
That Yeats noted the symbol over that portico
(Paris) C.113

But Pound casts a sad look over his shoulder 'before the take-off':

The scientists are in terror
and the European mind stops
Wyndham Lewis chose blindness
rather than have his mind stop.
Night under wind mid garofani
the petals are almost still
Mozart, Linnaeus, Sulmona,
When one's friends hate each other
how can there be peace in the world?
Their asperities diverted me in my green time.
A blown husk that is finished
but the light sings eternal
a pale flare over marshes
where the salt hay whispers to tide's change
Time, space,
neither life nor death is the answer.
And of man seeking good,
doing evil.
In meiner Heimat
where the dead walked
and the living were made of cardboard. C.115

Oh yes, it coheres all right. Or rather, it would if Pound could finish *The Cantos*. But he has destroyed himself and been destroyed by society and therefore will not finish them:

M'amour, amour
what do I love and
where are you?

That I lost my center
    fighting the world.
The dreams clash
    and are shattered—
and that I tried to make a paradiso
      terrestre.
          Addendum to C.100

Well, he did, and a hell: ' "A man's paradise is his good nature" / sd / Kati.' (C.93) :

Lux in diafana,
    Creatrix,
       oro.
Ursula benedetta,
    oro
By the hours of passion,
      per dilettevole ore,
      guide your successor,
Ysolt, Ydone,
    have compassion,
Picarda,
    compassion
By the wing'd head,
    by the caduceus,
      compassion;
By the horns of Isis-Luna,
      compassion.
The black panther lies under his rose-tree.
J'ai eu pitié des autres.
    Pas assez! Pas assez!
For me nothing. But that the child
    walk in peace in her basilica,
The light there almost solid.
          C.93

For even throughout his hell there is the light of humour, and love for the people he respected, as in the splendid portrait of Henry James in C.7 :

And the great domed head, *con gli occhi onesti e tardi*
Moves before me, phantom with weighted motion,
Grave incessu, drinking the tone of things,
And the old voice lifts itself
               weaving an endless sentence.

   And the affectionate portrait of Yeats at Stone Cottage after composing *The Peacock*:

             and that day I wrote no further

There is fatigue deep as the grave.
The Kakemono grows in flat land out of mist
    sun rises lop-sided over the mountain
        so that I recalled the noise in the chimney
as it were the wind in the chimney
        but was in reality Uncle William
downstairs composing
that had made a great Peeeeacock
    in the proide ov his oiye
      had made a great peeeeeeecock in the . . .
made a great peacock
    in the proide of his oyyee

proide ov his oy-ee
as indeed he had, and perdurable

a great peacock *aere perennius*
    or as in the advice to the young man to
breed and get married (or not)
    as you choose to regard it

at Stone Cottage in Sussex by the waste moor
(or whatever) and the holly bush
    who would not eat ham for dinner
because peasants eat ham for dinner
      despite the excellent quality
and the pleasure of having it hot

well those days are gone for ever
    and the travelling rug with the coon-skin tabs
and his hearing nearly all Wordsworth
    for the sake of his conscience but
preferring Ennemosor on Witches

did we ever get to the end of Doughty :
    The Dawn in Britain ?

                      perhaps not   C.83

Or that of Professor Levy at Freiburg, asked about *noigandres*,
a crux in the Provençal poetry of Arnaut Daniel :

And he said : 'now is there anything I can tell you ?'
And I said : 'I dunno, sir,' or
'Yes, Doctor, what do they mean by *noigandres* ?
And he said : 'Noigandres ! NOIgandres !
'You know for seex mon's of my life
'Effery night when I go to bett, I say to myself :
'Noigandres, eh, *noig*andres,
'Now what the DEFFIL can that mean !'   C.20

Similarly Pound's paradise, flooded with light and with
Anselm's 'incarnate awareness' (C.98) is also shot through with
characteristically sharp asides : 'Ike driven to the edge, almost,
of a thought' (C.97); 'and as for those who deform thought
with iambics' (C.98); 'And as for what happened after the king
lost exclusivity / even Del Mar gasps with astonishment'
(C.104).

Not to mention, full circle, the Commissioner of the Salt
Works, the first passage I quoted on p. 2, and which, if you go
back to it, you will by now surely understand 'straight off'. Or
the second occurrence (partly quoted on p. 171) with which I
end, for the sake of the last line (C.98) :

A soul, said Plotinus, the body inside it.
'By Hilaritas', said Gemisto, 'by hilaritas : gods ;
    and by speed in communication.
Anselm cut some of the cackle, and relapsed for the sake of
                           tranquillity.

Thus the gods appointed john barleycorn Je tzu,
And Byzance lasted longer than Manchu
       because of an (%) interest-rate.
Thought is built out of Sagetrieb,
       and our debt here is to Baller
and to *volgar' eloquio.*
       Despite Mathews this Wang was a stylist.
Uen-li will not help you talk to them,
       Iong-ching republished the edict
But the salt-commissioner took it down to the people
       who, in Baller's view, speak in quotations;
       think in quotations :
'Don't send someone else to pay it.'
Delcroix was for repetition.
       Baller thought one needed religion.
Without ²muan ¹bpo . . . but I anticipate.
       There is no substitute for a lifetime.

CHRONOLOGY

(Life and Works : main events)⁽¹⁾

1885	Ezra Pound born at Haily, Idaho, 30th October, son of Homer Loomis Pound and Isabel Weston Pound. Family moves to Pennsylvania 18 months later.
1887–1901	Childhood in Wyncote, suburb of Philadelphia. Schools: Cheltenham Military Academy and Cheltenham High School.
1898	Travels to Europe with great-aunt, Gibraltar, Tunis, Venice.
1901	Travels to London with father.
1903–1905	Studies at Hamilton College, Clinton, New York. Ph.B. 1905.
1906	M.A. University of Pennsylvania, Fellow in Romanics.
1906–1907	Travels and studies in Spain, Provence, Italy.
1907	Instructor in Romance Languages at Wabash College, Crawfordsville, Indiana, resignation requested after four months for 'bohemian' behaviour.
1907–1908	Travels in Italy.
1908	*A Lume Spento* (Venice). Autumn, settles in London. *A Quinzaine for this Yule* (London).
1909	*Personae. Exultations* (both London). Meets Yeats. Friendship with Ford Madox Hueffer

---

⁽¹⁾ The emphasis here is biographical, a tableau of Pound's development and interests, hence only first editions are given, and the place. For other publication details see Bibliography.

(Ford Madox Ford). Lectures at London Poly-
technic on Romance Literature.

1910   *The Spirit of Romance* (London). *Provença*
(London). Works on Cavalcanti (the essay
published in 1934 is dated 1910–31).

1911   *Canzoni* (London).

1912   *The Sonnets and Ballate of Guido Cavalcanti*
(London). *Ripostes* (London). Writes *Patria Mia*
(pub. 1950). Literary association with H.D.,
Richard Aldington, Wyndham Lewis, James Joyce,
Yeats and others. 'Imagiste Manifesto'. Writes
for 'The New Freewoman', later called 'The
Egoist', and for 'The Little Review'. Foreign
editor of 'Poetry : A Magazine of Verse' (Chicago).

1913–1914   Works on Fenollosa papers. Important criticism :
Robert Frost (Freewoman 1913, Poetry 1914), *A
Few Don'ts* (Poetry 1913), *The Serious Artist*
(Egoist 1913), *Troubadours, their Sorts and Con-
ditions* (Qu. Rev. 1913), *The Later Yeats* (Poetry
1913), *Dubliners and Mr. James Joyce* (Egoist
1914), *The Renaissance* (Poetry 1914), *The Prose
Tradition in Verse* (Poetry 1914), all reprinted in
'The Literary Essays', 1954.

1914   Marries Dorothy Shakespear. Edits anthology
Des Imagistes. Meets T. S. Eliot, 24th Sept. Chief
contributor to 'Blast', 1914–15.

1915   *Cathay* (London). Edits *Catholic Anthology*. Preface to Poetical Works of *Lionel Johnson* [reprinted
in 'Lit. Essays' 1954].

1916   *Lustra* (London). *Gaudier-Brzeska: A Memoir*
(London, New York). *Certain Noble Plays of
Japan*, sel. Pound, introd. Yeats (Ireland). *'Noh'
or Accomplishment*, Fenollosa and Pound (London).

1917   First three *Cantos* published in 'Poetry', later withdrawn. Works on *Propertius* (pub. 1919, date
given as 1917). *Dialogues of Fontenelle*, transl.
Pound (London). Main criticism : *Notes on*

Elizabethan Classicists (Egoist 1917–18). *Irony, Laforgue and Some Satire* (Poetry 1917). *T. S. Eliot* (review of Prufrock, Poetry 1917). [All reprinted in 'Lit. Essays' 1954].

1918   *Pavannes and Divisions* (New York), including two essays on Dolmetsch & *A Retrospect*. Other criticism: *The Hard and Soft in French Poetry* (Poetry 1918), *Swinburne versus his Biographers* (Poetry 1918), *Henry James* (The Little Review 1918), *Joyce* (The Future 1918), *Early Translators of Greek* (Egoist 1918–19). [All reprinted in 'Lit. Essays' 1954].

1919   *Quia Pauper Amavi* (London, contains '*Three Cantos*' and '*Homage to Sextus Propertius*').
The Fourth Canto (London).

1920   *Hugh Selwyn Mauberley* (London). *Umbra* [early poems reprinted and translations Cavalcanti, Daniel] (London).
Instigations [incl. essays on *Remy de Gourmont, Arnaut Daniel, Wyndham Lewis*, reprint of *Early Translators of Greek*] together with *The Chinese Written Character as a Medium for Poetry*, by Ernest Fenollosa, ed. Pound (New York).

1921   Moves to Paris. Essay on *Brancusi* (Little Review).

1922   *The Natural Philosophy of Love*, by Remy de Gourmont, transl. and introd. Pound. Correspondence with Eliot and 'editing' of *The Waste Land*. Essay on *Ulysses* (Dial) [reprinted in 'Lit. Essays' 1954].

1923   *Indiscretions: or Une Revue de deux mondes* (Paris).
The Call of the Road, by Edouard Estaunie, transl. Pound (New York).

1924   Settles Rapallo. *Antheil and the Treatise on Harmony* (Paris).

1925   *A Draft of XVI Cantos for the Beginning of a Poem of Some Length* (Paris).

1926   *Personae: Collected Poems* (New York).

1928   *A Draft of the Cantos XVII–XXVII* (London). *Ta Hio, The Great Learning* (Seattle). *Selected Poems*, introd. T. S. Eliot (London). Essays: *Dr Williams' Position* (Dial), *How to Read* (New York Herald) [both reprinted in 'Lit. Essays' 1954].

1930   *A Draft of XXX Cantos* (Paris). *Imaginary Letters* (Paris).

1931   *How to Read* (London).

1933   *A Draft of XXX Cantos* (New York, London). *ABC of Economics* (London). Edits *Active Anthology*.

1934   *Eleven New Cantos, XXXI–XLI* (New York). *ABC of Reading* (London). *Make It New* (London) including Cavalcanti essay and *Date Line* [both reprinted in 'Lit. Essays' 1954].

1935   *Social Credit: An Impact* (London). *Alfred Venison's Poems: Social Credit Themes by the Poet of Tichfield Street* [E.P.] (London). *Jefferson and/or Mussolini* (London).

1937   *The Fifth Decad of The Cantos* [XLII–LI] (London). *Polite Essays* (London). *Confucius, Digest of the Analects* (Milano) [later included in *Guide to Kulchur*].

1938   *Guide to Kulchur* (London; Norfolk, Conn.).

1939   Visits U.S., Honorary degree from Hamilton College.
        What is Money for? (London) [No. 3 of 'Money Pamphlets by £', ed. Russell 1951].

1940   *Cantos LII–LXXI* (London; Norfolk, Conn.). *A Selection of Poems* (London).

1940–44 Broadcasts from Rome Radio.

1941   *Italy's Policy of Social Economics 1939–1940*, by Odon Por, transl. Pound (Istituto It. d'Arti Grafiche, Bergamo, Milano, Roma).

1942   *Carta da Visita di Ezra Pound* (Rome) [No. 4 of 'Money Pamphlets by £', ed. Russell].

1944   *L'America, Roosevelt e le cause della guerra presente* (Venezia) [No. 6 of 'Money Pamphlets by £', ed. Russell].
Oro e lavoro (Rapallo) [No. 2 of 'Money Pamphlets by £', ed. Russell].
Introduzione alla natura economica degli S.U.A. (Venezia) [No. 1 of 'Money Pamphlets by £', ed. Russell].

1945   *Ciung Iung. L'asse che non vacilla* (Venezia).
Imprisonment at Pisa (summer). Writes *Pisan Cantos*. Flown to Washington for trial on charge of treason (Nov.). Declared insane and unfit to plead, sent to St Elizabeth's hospital for the Criminally Insane, Washington, D.C.

1947   *Confucius—The Unwobbling Pivot and The Great Digest* (Norfolk, Conn.).

1948   *The Pisan Cantos* [LXXIV–LXXXIV] (New York). *The Cantos* (I–LXXXIV) New York.
If This be Treason (Siena).

1949   Bollingen Prize for *The Pisan Cantos*.
Selected Poems (New York).

1954   *The Classical Anthology Defined by Confucius*, translated Pound (Cambridge, Mass.).

1955   *Section: Rock Drill, 85–95 de los cantares* (Milano).

1956   *Sophokles: Women of Trachis, a version by Ezra Pound* (London).

1958   Released from confinement, April, returns to Italy.

1959   *Thrones: 96–109 de los cantares* (Milano).

1959–60   Works on later 'Fragments', 110–116.

1962   *Love Poems of Ancient Egypt*, translated by Pound and Noel Stock from Italian version by Boris de Rachewiltz (Norfolk, Conn.).

1964   *The Cantos of Ezra Pound* (1 to 109) (London).

1969   *The Fragments* [110–117] (Norfolk, Conn.).

271

BIBLIOGRAPHY

For full Bibliography including articles etc. see
Donald Gallup, *A Bibliography of Ezra Pound*
(Rupert Hart-Davis, London 1963, 1966)

———————⟡———————

WORKS BY POUND (in order of first publication)

I. POETRY

A Lume Spento (A. Antonini, Venice 1908). Repub. (New
Directions, New York; Faber & Faber, London 1965).

A Quinzaine for this Yule (Pollock & Co., London 1908; Elkin
Mathews, London 1908).

Personae (Elkin Mathews, London 1909). Contains some poems
from *A Lume Spento*. See *Exultations*. See also *Personae*
(1926).

Exultations (Elkin Mathews, London 1909). Contains some
poems from *A Lume Spento*. Republished with *Personae*
(Elkin Mathews, London 1909).

Provença (Small, Maynard & Co., Boston 1910). Poems from
Personae, Exultations; and *Canzonieri*.

Canzoni (Elkin Mathews, London 1911). Republished with
Ripostes (Elkin Mathews, London 1913).

Ripostes (Swift & Co. Ltd., London 1912). Republished (Small,
Maynard & Co., Boston 1913, Elkin Mathews, London
1915). Repub. with *Canzoni* (Elkin Mathews, London 1913).

Cathay (Elkin Mathews, London 1915).

Lustra (Elkin Mathews, London 1916). Another edition with
other poems incl. 'Three Cantos' (Alfred Knopf, New York
1917).

The Fourth Canto (The Ovid Press, London 1919).

BIBLIOGRAPHY

Quia Pauper Amavi (The Egoist Ltd., London 1919). Contains 'Three Cantos' and 'Homage to Sextus Propertius'. The latter republished (Faber & Faber, London 1934), and republished with *Hugh Selwyn Mauberley* as *Diptych Rome–London* (New Directions 1958, see infra).

Hugh Selwyn Mauberley (The Ovid Press, London 1920). Reprinted in *Poems 1918–1921* (Boni & Liveright, New York 1921), in *Personae* (1926) and in later collections. See also under *Quia Pauper Amavi* supra.

Umbra (Elkin Mathews, London 1920). Contains what Pound then wished to preserve from *Personae* (1909), *Exultations*, *Ripostes*, and translations of Cavalcanti and Arnaut Daniel, also the five poems of T. E. Hulme.

Poems 1918–1921 (Boni & Liveright, New York 1921). See under *Hugh Selwyn Mauberley* supra.

A Draft of XVI Cantos (Three Mountains Press, Paris 1925).

Personae: The Collected Poems of Ezra Pound (Boni & Liveright, New York 1926). Offset edition (New Directions, New York 1949, Faber & Faber, London 1952). Second edition as *Ezra Pound—The Collected Shorter Poems* enlarged edition with some additional material, chiefly from *The Classical Anthology Defined by Confucius* (Faber & Faber, London 1968).

Selected Poems, selected and introduced T. S. Eliot (Faber & Gwyer, London 1928).

A Draft of XXX Cantos (Hours Press, Paris 1930). Republished (Farrar & Rinehart, New York 1933; Faber & Faber, London 1933).

Eleven New Cantos XXXI–XLI (Farrar & Rinehart Inc., New York 1934). Republished (New Directions, Norfolk, Conn. 1940).

Homage to Sextus Propertius, first published in *Quia Pauper Amavi* 1919, republished (Faber & Faber, London 1934).

Alfred Venison's Poems: Social Credit Themes by the Poet of Tichfield Street [E.P.] (Stanley Nott, London 1935). Included in *Personae* (New Directions 1949; Faber & Faber, 1952).

The Fifth Decad of the Cantos XLII–LI (Faber & Faber, London

1937; Farrar & Rinehart, New York & Toronto 1937; New Directions, Norfolk, Conn. 1940).

Cantos LII–LXXI (Faber & Faber, London 1940; New Directions, Norfolk, Conn. 1940).

A Selection of Poems (Faber & Faber, London 1940).

The Pisan Cantos [LXXIV–LXXXIV]. (New Directions, New York 1948; Faber & Faber, London 1949).

The Cantos [I–LXXXIV] (New Directions, New York 1948; Faber & Faber, London 1954).

Selected Poems (New Directions, New York 1949, 1957).

The Translations of Ezra Pound, introd. Hugh Kenner (Faber & Faber, London 1953, 1963; New Directions, New York, 1953, 1963; Faber Paperback, 1971).

The Classic Anthology Defined by Confucius, translated by Ezra Pound (Harvard University Press, Cambridge, Mass., 1954; Faber & Faber, London 1955). Republished as *The Confucian Odes: The Classic Anthology Defined by Confucius. Ezra Pound* (New Directions, New York 1959).

Section: Rock-Drill, 85–95 de los cantares (All' Insegna del Pesce d'Oro, Milano 1955; Offset edition, New Directions, New York 1956, Faber & Faber, London 1957).

Sophokles: Women of Trachis, a version by Ezra Pound (Neville Spearman, London 1956; Offset edition, New Directions, New York 1957).

Diptych Rome–London: Homage to Sextus Propertius and *Hugh Selwyn Mauberley* (New Directions, New York 1958).

Versi prosaici (Salvatore Sciascia Editore, Caltanisetta, Roma, 1959) Fragments not in Cantos.

Thrones: 96–109 de los cantares (All' Insegna del Pesce d'Oro, Milano 1959; Offset edition, New Directions, New York 1959, Faber & Faber, London 1960).

Love Poems of Ancient Egypt, translated Ezra Pound and Noel Stock, from Italian versions by Boris de Rachewiltz (New Directions, Norfolk, Conn., 1962).

The Cantos of Ezra Pound I–CIX (Faber & Faber, London 1964; New Directions, New York 1965).

Canto CX (Sextant Press, Cambridge, Mass., 80 copies, 1965).

BIBLIOGRAPHY

The Fragments Cantos CX–CXVIII (New Directions, New York 1969; Faber & Faber, London 1970).

II. PROSE

The Spirit of Romance (Dent & Son, London 1910; E. P. Dutton & Co., New York prob. 1910). New edition with revisions, Peter Owen, London 1959, New Directions, Norfolk, Conn. 1959).

Gaudier-Brzeska: *A Memoir* (Bodley Head, London & John Lane Co. New York 1916). Reprinted by Laidlaw & Laidlaw, London 1939. New edition with additional material, The Marvell Press, Hessle, Yorks, England 1960; New Directions, New York 1961).

Certain Noble Plays of Japan: from the manuscripts of Ernest Fenollosa, sel. and worked over by Pound, introd. Yeats (The Cuala Press, Churchtown, Dundrum, Ireland, 1916). Reprinted without Introduction in *'Noh' or Accomplishment*, see infra.

'Noh' or Accomplishment, by Ernest Fenollosa and Pound (see supra) (Macmillan & Co., London 1916 [1917]; Alfred Knopf, New York 1917). Reprinted without App. IV in *The Translations of Ezra Pound* 1953. Republished as *The Classic Noh Theatre of Japan* (New Directions, New York 1959).

Dialogues of Fontenelle, transl. Pound (The Egoist Press, London 1917, Laidlaw & Laidlaw, London 1939). Reprinted in *Pavannes and Divisions* (1918) and *Pavannes and Divagations* (1958) see infra.

Pavannes and Divisions (Alfred Knopf, New York 1918).

Instigations, together with *The Chinese Written Character as a Medium for Poetry* (Fenollosa, ed. Pound) (Boni & Liveright, New York 1920, Faber & Faber, London 1967).

The Natural Philosophy of Love by Remy de Gourmont, transl. & introd. Pound (Boni & Liveright, New York 1922; The Casanova Society, London 1926; Neville Spearman, London 1957).

BIBLIOGRAPHY

Indiscretions; or, Une revue de deux mondes (Three Mountains Press, Paris 1923).

The Call of the Road, by Edouard Estaunie, transl. Hiram Janus = E.P. (Boni & Liveright, New York 1923).

Antheil and The Treatise on Harmony (Three Mountains Press, Paris 1924; Pascal Covici, Chicago 1927). Republished with *Patria Mia* as *Patria Mia and The Treatise on Harmony* (Peter Owen, London 1962).

Ta Hio, The Great Learning, an American version by E.P. (University of Washington, Book Store, Seattle 1928; Stanley Nott, London 1936 as 'Ideogramic Series' ed. Pound).

Imaginary Letters (The Black Sun Press, Paris 1930). Reprinted in *Pavannes and Divagations* (1958).

How to Read (Desmond Harmsworth, London 1931). Reprinted in *Polite Essays* (1937) and *Literary Essays* (1954), see infra.

ABC of Economics (Faber & Faber, London 1933; New Directions, Norfolk, Conn. 1940; Peter Russell, The Pound Press, Tunbridge Wells 1953).

ABC of Reading (Routledge & Sons, London 1934; Yale University Press, New Haven, Conn. 1934). Faber Paperback, London 1951.

Make It New (Faber & Faber, London 1934; Offset edition Yale University Press, New Haven, Conn. 1935).

Social Credit: An Impact (Stanley Nott, London 1935). Reprinted as No. 5 of 'Money Pamphlets by £' (ed. Peter Russell, London 1951) and in *Impact*, ed. Stock 1960, see infra.

Jefferson and/or Mussolini (Stanley Nott, London 1935; Liveright Publishing Corp., New York 1936).

Polite Essays (Faber & Faber, London 1937; New Directions, Norfolk, Conn. 1940).

Confucius. Digest of the Analects (Giovanni Scheiwiller, Milano 1937). Reprinted in *Guide to Kulchur* 1938.

Guide to Kulchur (Faber & Faber, London 1938). As *Culture* (New Directions, Norfolk, Conn., 1938; new edition with 'Addenda 1952', New Directions, Norfolk, Conn. and Peter Owen, London 1952).

BIBLIOGRAPHY

What is Money For? (Greater Britain Publications, London 1939). Reprinted with *Introductory Text Book* as No. 3 of 'Money Pamphlets by £' (ed. Peter Russell, London 1951) and in *Impact* (1960) see infra.

Italy's Policy of Social Economics 1939/40 by Odon Por, transl. Pound (Istituto Italiano d'Arti Grafiche, Bergamo, Milano, Roma 1941).

Carta da Visita di Ezra Pound (Edizioni di Lettere d'Oggi, Roma 1942). Transl. by John Drummond as *A Visiting Card*, No. 4 of 'Money Pamphlets by £' (Peter Russell, London 1952), revised and reprinted in *Impact* (1960) see infra.

L'America, Roosevelt e le cause della guerra presente (Casa Editrice delle Edizioni Popolari, Venezia 1944). Transl. John Drummond as *America, Roosevelt and the Causes of the Present War*, No. 6 of 'Money Pamphlets by £' (Peter Russell, London 1951). Reprinted as *America and the Second World War* in *Impact* (1960, see infra).

Oro e lavoro (Tip. Moderna, Rapallo 1944). Transl. John Drummond as *Gold and Labour*, later *Gold and Work*, No. 2 of 'Money Pamphlets by £' (Peter Russell, London 1951). Reprinted as *The Enemy is Ignorance* in *Impact* (1960, see infra).

Introduzione alla natura economica degli S.U.A. (Casa Editrice delle Edizioni Popolari, Venezia 1944). Transl. Carmine Amore as *Introduction to the Economic Nature of the United States*, No. 1 of 'Money Pamphlets by £' (Peter Russell, London 1950).

Confucius. The Unwobbling Pivot & The Great Digest, a version by Ezra Pound (Pharos, No. 4, New Directions, Norfolk, Conn., Winter 1947). See also infra.

If This Be Treason (printed for Olga Rudge by Tip. Nuova, Siena 1948).

Patria Mia (Ralph Fletcher Seymour, Chicago 1950). Written c.1912. Reprinted with *The Treatise on Harmony* (Peter Owen, London 1962).

The Letters of Ezra Pound 1907–1941, ed. D. D. Paige (Harcourt Brace & Co., New York 1950, Faber & Faber, London 1951).

277

BIBLIOGRAPHY

Confucian Analects, a version by Ezra Pound. (Square Dollar Series, New York 1951, Peter Owen, London 1956). See also infra.

Literary Essays of Ezra Pound, sel. and introd. T. S. Eliot (Faber & Faber, London 1954; New Directions, Norfolk, Conn. 1954, Faber Paperback, London 1960).

Pavannes and Divagations (New Directions, Norfolk, Conn. 1958; Offset ed. Peter Owen, London 1960). Prose and Poems, mostly from earlier work.

Impact: Essays on Ignorance and the Decline of American Civilization, by Ezra Pound, sel. and introd. Noel Stock, (Henry Regnery, Chicago 1960). Includes all Money Pamphlets mentioned supra.

EP to LU: Nine Letters Written to Louis Untermeyer by Ezra Pound, ed. J. A. Robbins (Indiana University Press, Bloomington 1963).

Confucius to Cummings: An Anthology of Poetry ed. Ezra Pound and Marcella Spann (New Directions, New York 1964).

Confucius: The Great Digest, The Unwobbling Pivot, The Analects (New Directions, New York 1969).

Pound/Joyce—The Letters of Ezra Pound to James Joyce, ed. Forrest Read (Faber & Faber, London 1968; New York 1968).

WORKS ON POUND (in alphabetical order)

This is a selected bibliography and includes only works in volume form. Particular essays referred to in this book can be found from footnotes and via the Index under the author's name. The same applies to Pound's numerous sources.

Baumann, Walter, *The Rose in the Steel Dust: An Examination of the Cantos of Ezra Pound* (Francke Verlag, Bern 1967).

Cornell, Julien, *The Trial of Ezra Pound: A Documented Account of the Treason Case by the Defendant's Lawyer* (The John Day Co., New York 1966).

Davie, Donald, *Ezra Pound, Poet as Sculptor* (Oxford Univ. Press, New York 1964; Routledge, London 1965).

BIBLIOGRAPHY

Davis, Earle, *Vision fugitive: Ezra Pound and Economics* (Univ. of Kansas Press, 1969).

Dekker, George, *Sailing after Knowledge, The Cantos of Ezra Pound, A Critical Appraisal* (Routledge, London 1963; Barnes & Noble, New York 1963).

Dembo, Lawrence Sanford, *The Confucian Odes of Ezra Pound, A Critical Appraisal* (Faber & Faber, London 1963; Univ. of California Press, Berkeley 1963).

Edwards, John Hamilton, and Vasse, William V., *The Annotated Index to the Cantos* I–LXXXIV, University of California Press, Berkeley and Los Angeles 1957).

Emery, Clark, *Ideas into Action, A Study of Pound's Cantos* (University of Miami Press, Coral Gables, Florida 1958).

Espey, John J., *Ezra Pound's Mauberley: A Study in Composition* (University of California Press, Berkely and Los Angeles 1955; Faber & Faber, London 1955).

Fraser, G. S., *Ezra Pound* (Oliver & Boyd, Edinburgh and London 1960; Grove Press, New York 1961).

Goodwin, K. L., *The Influence of Ezra Pound* (Oxford Univ. Press, London 1966).

Hesse, Eva (Ed.), *New Approaches to Ezra Pound* (Faber & Faber, London 1969; California Univ. Press, Berkeley 1969).

Hutchins, Patricia, *Ezra Pound's Kensington, An Exploration 1885–1913* (Faber & Faber, London 1965).

Jackson, Thomas H., *The Early Poetry of Ezra Pound* (H.U.P., Cambridge, Mass., O.U.P., London 1969).

Kenner, *The Poetry of Ezra Pound* (Faber & Faber, London 1951; New Directions, New York 1951).

Leary, Lewis (Ed.) *Motive and Method in the Cantos of Ezra Pound* (Columbia Univ. Press, New York 1954).

Mullins, Eustace Clarence, *This Difficult Individual, Ezra Pound* (Fleet Publishing Corp., New York 1961).

de Nagy, N. Christoph, *The Poetry of Ezra Pound: the Pre-Imagist Stage* (Francke Verlag, Bern 1960); *Ezra Pound's Poetics and Literary Tradition: The Critical Decade* (Francke Verlag, Bern 1966).

Norman, Charles, *The Case of Ezra Pound* (Macmillan, New

York 1960); *Ezra Pound, A Biography* (revised version of earlier edition, Macdonald, London 1969).

O'Connor, William Van, and Stone, Edward, *A Casebook on Ezra Pound* (Crowell, New York 1959).

Pearlman, Daniel S., *The Barb of Time* (O.U.P., New York & London 1969).

Rosenthal, M. L., *A Primer of Ezra Pound* (Macmillan, New York 1960).

de Roux, Dominique (Ed.), *Ezra Pound* (Les Cahiers de l'Herne, in two vols., Paris 1965, 1966).

Russell, Peter, *Ezra Pound: A Collection of Essays to be Presented to Ezra Pound on his 65th Birthday* (Peter Nevill, London 1950; and under title *An Examination of Ezra Pound: A Collection of Essays*, New Directions, New York 1950).

Ruthven, K. K., *A Guide to Ezra Pound's "Personae" (1926)*, (Univ. of Calif. Press, 1968).

Schneidau, Herbert N., *Ezra Pound: The Image and the Real* (Louisiana State Univ. Press, Baton Rouge 1969).

Stock, Noel, *Poet in Exile: Ezra Pound* (Manchester Univ. Press, Manchester 1964; Barnes & Noble, New York 1964); (Ed.) *Ezra Pound: Perspectives* (Henry Regnery, Chicago 1965); *Reading the Cantos: A Study of Meaning in Ezra Pound* (Routledge, London 1967); *The Life of Ezra Pound* (Routledge & Kegan Paul, London 1970).

Sullivan, J. P., *Ezra Pound and Sextus Propertius, A Study in Creative Translation* (University of Texas Press, Austin 1964; Faber & Faber, London 1964).

Sutton, Walter (Ed.), *Ezra Pound: A Collection of Critical Essays* (Prentice-Hall, Eaglewood Cliffs, New Jersey 1963).

Watts, Harold H., *Ezra Pound and the Cantos* (Henry Regnery, Chicago 1952).

Yeats, W. B., *A Packet for Ezra Pound* (The Cuala Press, Dublin 1929).

GENERAL INDEX

Page numbers in italics refer to occurrences in Pound quotations only

281

GENERAL INDEX

GENERAL INDEX

283

GENERAL INDEX

Greece 179, 190, 257

Greek 22n, 29, 30, 37, 40, 92, 147, *148*, *206*, 258
  aesthetic 218, 219
  poets, poetry (See also Homer, Aeschylus etc) 19, 24, 29, 70, 79n, 218

Gregory of Tours 40n

Grettirsaga 19

Griffith, Arthur 39

Griscom, Acton 199n, 200

Grosseteste, Robert *117*

Guide to Kulchur (EP) 6n, 7–8, 9–10, 12, 15n, 17, 18, 34, 35, 42n, 69, 72, 74, 115, 120, 125, 133, 134, 153, 177, 181, 186n, 227–8, *239*

Guido invites you thus (EP) 80n

Guido vorrei (Dante) 80n

Guillaume de Lorris Belated (EP) 61

Hades 139, 170, 222

Hagoromo (Noh) 99

Hamilton, Alexander 239–41

Hanno 16

Hard and Soft in French Poetry, The 70, 80n

Hegel(ian), G. W. 129, 176, 214n

Heine, Heinrich 19, 27

Heisenberg, Werner 123

Helen of Troy *23*, 24, 128, 148n, *155*, 164, 170, 189

Helios *155*

Hell (EP) 83, 87n

Hell Cantos 220, 221

Hengest 193, 196

Henry II of England 24

Henry of Huntingdon 200

Hera 139, 151

Heraclitus 35

Herder, Johann Gottfried 6n

Hermes *151*, 153, 167, 204

Herodotus 7

Herrick, Robert 19, 20

Hesiod 19, 178, 216n

Hesperus *153*

Hesse, Eva 24, *222*, 225

Heydon, John 139, *140*, 146n, *206*

Hia (dynasty) *118*

Hilaire, St (Church) *83*, *219*

Hilary, St *40*, *145*

Hindemith, Paul 183n

Hiroshima 251

Historia Regum Britanniae (Geoffrey of Monmouth) 185

Hitler, Adolf 251

Holland 175

Homage to Sextus Propertius (EP) 75, 83, 84n, 156, 157, 158, 160, 161, 162, 163

Homer 10, 18n, 19, 20, 21, 23, 24, 38n, 43, 114, 142, 147, 148n, 164, 170, 179, 221, 258

Horace 19, 79, 80n, 137

Hound of Heaven, The (Thomson) 53, 54, 79

House of Splendour, The (EP) 53n

Housman, A. E. 20, 130

How to Read (EP) 1n, 4, 18, 19n, 26, 27, 31, 127n, 129

Hugh of St Victor 33n

Hugh Selwyn Mauberley 75, 98, 134, 147n, *156*, 157, 158–9

Huguenots 40n

Hulme, T. E. 75, 76, 77, 93, 96

Humboldt, A. von 112

Husserl, Edmund 123, 124

Hutson, Arthur E. 199n

Iamblicus 181

Ignez da Castro 210, *211*, 223

Iliad 147

Imaginary Letters (EP) 119

Imagisme 9, 75–7, 92, 93–6

Imagiste Manifesto 75

Immorality, An (EP) 78

In a Station of the Metro (EP) 97, 100

India 16

In Durance (EP) 54, 58, 59, 79, 136

Instigations (EP) 8n, 24, 31, 86, 123n

In Tempore Senectutis (EP) 79

Iong Ching (Yong Tcheng) 4, 169, 170, *172*

Iphigenia 189

Ireland 197, 200, 201, 202, 203

Irony, Laforgue and some Satire (EP) 80n

Iseult 215

Isis 143, *263*

Italian 12, 27, 28, 32, 55, 65, 66, 81, 82, 134

GENERAL INDEX

287

GENERAL INDEX

GENERAL INDEX

290

GENERAL INDEX

GENERAL INDEX

INDEX OF THEMES

Cross-references to "Index" mean General Index. Page numbers in italics
mean that the reference occurs in quotation only

INDEX OF THEMES

INDEX OF CANTOS

INDEX OF CANTOS